This Day in *California* History

This Day in
California
History

CARL PALM

NB

NORTHCROSS BOOKS
AUSTIN

FIRST EDITION

Published by Northcross Books, P. O. Box 66772, Austin, Texas
78766.

Publisher's Cataloguing-in-Publication
(***Provided by Quality Books, Inc.***)

Palm, Carl.
   This Day in California History / Carl Palm. –
1st ed.
p. cm.
Includes bibliographical note and index.
ISBN-13: 978-0-9754832-2-0
ISBN-10: 0-9754832-2-6

   1. California—History. 2. California—Social
life and customs. 3. Popular culture—California—
History.
I. Title.

F861.P356 2008   979.4
                        QBI07-600192

Printed in the United States of America

For my wife, Suzette

CONTENTS

INTRODUCTION

THERE ARE MANY DIFFERENT WAYS to look at the history of a place. You can look at it chronologically. This happened at the beginning. This happened in "the middle". This happened recently.

You can look at it thematically, which is what I did in my first book, *The Great California Story: Real-Life Roots of an American Legend* (Austin: Northcross, 2004), where instead of looking at people, places and events in the order of their appearance *over time*, I looked at the central *themes* that have historically given California its identity, the things that capture its essence and therefore set it apart from other places.

Or, you can look at a place in what might at first appear a more haphazard way, the way the calendar organizes time: on this day, such and such a person was born; on this day, such and such a person died or did something memorable; on this day, such and such an event occurred or place became noteworthy.

Approaching things in this third way gives you an altogether different take on what a place is all about. There is chronology, yes, one thing after another, and themes to ponder, too, even if they emerge largely at the *edge* of the reader's consciousness, rather than being explicitly spelled out on each page.

INTRODUCTION

But the principal value in organizing the detail of history the way it's done here lies in a different direction altogether.

Doing things this way allows much that might not find its way into a more traditionally written history to be brought into the sweep of the story, gives the reader a broader sense than they might otherwise have of just what history *is*, and lets both reader and writer reflect upon a wealth of information that's simply interesting in and of itself. It is for these reasons that this approach is taken here.

ACKNOWLEDGMENTS

I WANT TO THANK MY FRIENDS Gene Bier of San Diego and Kerri Galvin, Howard Gentry and Diane Henderson of Austin for their careful reading of an earlier version of this manuscript. Their comments have challenged me to clarify my writing throughout and saved me from errors, too.

As I did in my first book, *The Great California Story*, I also want to thank all of those who have written so much and so well about California before me. Without all of their fine work, a book like this would be impossible to write.

This Day in *California* History

This Day

in

January

JANUARY 1

1890

The Rose Bowl—& "Tournament of Roses"

ON THIS DAY IN CALIFORNIA HISTORY the first Rose Bowl game was played in Pasadena.

The "Tournament of Roses," as it was called, did not initially include a football game, however. Originally, the purpose of the event (first staged in 1890) was simply to showcase Southern California's splendid winter climate, a place where orange trees held their green and gold, and roses bloomed, all year long.

The first parade consisted of a simple stream of flower-covered carriages, and after the parade, athletic exhibitions—footraces, polo matches, and tugs-of-war. In time, marching bands, motorized floats, and even races between exotic animals were added. As the crowds grew larger, bleachers were built along the parade route and newspapers reported on the parade for the benefit of their ice-bound readers in the East.

In 1902 a football game was added to the festivities and the first teams to play each other here were Stanford and the University of Michigan. But Michigan's victory was so lopsided, 49-0, that the football game was replaced with Roman-style chariot races in 1903. In 1916, however, football returned to the Rose Bowl and has remained the main athletic attraction of the event ever since.

On January 1, 1923, the stadium in which the game is played to this day was completed. Through the years the stadium's seating capacity has repeatedly been expanded—to 76,000 in 1928, 83,677 in 1932, 100,807 in 1949, and to 104,696 in 1972. On January 1, 1973, a record crowd of 106, 869 was seated here.

The first transcontinental radio broadcast of a sporting event was made from here (in 1927, on NBC), the first national telecast of a college game occurred here (in 1952, on NBC), and the first coast-to-coast color telecast of a college football game occurred here too (in 1962, also on NBC).

3

JANUARY 2

1910

Nation's First Junior High School *System* Opens

ON THIS DAY IN CALIFORNIA HISTORY America's first junior high school system opened in Berkeley. The system included just two schools, McKinley High and Washington High, both designated as "introductory high schools" and each including 7th-, 8th-, and 9th-grade classes. Both schools opened on January 2, 1910.

Junior high schools would, of course, go on to become a common feature of the American public school system. Through the years, literally millions of kids would find themselves moving through these "developmental links" between elementary and "high" school, and going through junior high school would become a familiar American rite of passage.

This was neither the first, nor last, time that California would find itself on the cutting edge of American education, either.

The first free public kindergartens in the nation were established here in 1878 and experimental elementary and secondary schools here have repeatedly provided "models" for elementary and secondary schools around the country.

California's "Master Plan for Higher Education," introduced in 1960, served as a blueprint not only for its own system of higher education, but for that of other states and other nations as well. During the '60s the state's universities encouraged new methods of undergraduate teaching, new attitudes toward academic freedom, and ultimately, a new management structure for the nation's state university systems.

During the 1970s the University of California became the first public university in the nation to incorporate "affirmative action" criteria into its college admissions process, and late in the century, the first to abandon those criteria, too. The first "junior high school system" grew out of this same now long-standing openness to educational reform.

4

January 3

1977

Apple Computer Incorporates

ON THIS DAY IN CALIFORNIA HISTORY Steve Jobs, Steve Wozniak, and a man named "Mike" Markkula incorporated the Apple Computer Company.

Jobs and Wozniak had found it difficult to find the money they needed to get their company off the ground, because most people thought that selling a computer to the average person was a crazy idea. Except for Steve Jobs, that is, who, with the help of two partners, quickly showed everyone just how smart an idea it was.

Jobs had it right, of course. The Apple II, released in 1977, is widely credited with having created the home computer market in America and, having done that, the home computer market worldwide. In fact, when the company went public in 1980, it raised more money than any new offering since the Ford Motor Company went public in 1956.

In 1976, the year he founded Apple, Jobs approached a nearby computer shop ("The Byte Shop" in Mountain View) to interest them in selling his new machine. They said they would, but only if it arrived fully assembled. The store's owner even said he'd order fifty of them and pay $500 for each one on delivery.

That was all Jobs needed to hear. He got the parts he needed to build those first machines from a firm called Cramer Electronics and told them that if they would give him the parts on credit, he would pay them just as soon as he could deliver completed machines.

These first Apple computers used a TV display screen (uncommon at the time) and, at the insistence of The Byte Shop's owner, included a cassette that played a key role in loading and saving computer programs. The machine was not complicated, using far fewer parts than any other machine of its type, and that, in large part, was its genius. The revolution it set in motion has yet to come to rest.

5

JANUARY 4

1965

Leo Fender Sells his Instrument Company

ON THIS DAY IN CALIFORNIA HISTORY Leo Fender spent his last day on the job at his Fullerton plant. He had just sold his electric instrument company to CBS Records.

Fender had been born on a ranch that straddled the then-still-heavily-agricultural Anaheim/Fullerton area in 1909. His family owned an orange grove here (a very common sight in those days), but Leo's interests, from the age of about 13 on, was electronics, not agriculture. He had an uncle who had built a radio from parts, and that was just the kind of thing that intrigued Leo, too.

In the early 1930s a bandleader who needed a PA system to amplify his sound at dances asked Leo to build him one, and by 1938, he had opened his own "radio service" in downtown Fullerton. It wasn't long before musicians started to come around looking for help in improving the sound quality of their guitars and amplifiers, and it was in a shed behind this shop that Leo unveiled his first electric guitar in 1945.

In 1946 Fender opened his Fender Electric Instrument Company in Fullerton, and it was here that the guitars that would establish his reputation internationally—the *Telecaster* and *Stratocaster*—were made. Many people believe that these were the best electric guitar designs ever made, and they were certainly two of the most popular and successful ones ever introduced.

Fender's electric guitars have been the guitars of choice for rock musicians from Buddy Holly to Eric Clapton, and for countless garage-band musicians coast to coast.

Bob Dylan played a Fender Stratocaster when he "went electric" at the Newport Folk Festival in 1965, Jimi Hendrix played a Fender Stratocaster to make his amazing sound, and so did Keith Richards of the Rolling Stones, Bruce Springsteen, and thousands of other guitarists worldwide.

JANUARY 5

1931

Actor Robert Duvall Born in San Diego

ON THIS DAY IN CALIFORNIA HISTORY actor Robert Duvall was born in San Diego.

He never "seemed" much like a Californian. He was so adept at losing himself inside the characters he played, he always seemed like someone from the Midwest or South. Even New England or somewhere else along the eastern seaboard would have seemed more likely.

He studied acting in New York, and received positive notices for his work in the film version of *To Kill a Mockingbird* (1962), but his career didn't really take off until he played Tom Hagen in *The Godfather* (1972) and *The Godfather, Part II* (1974). After that, his stature as an actor rose dramatically—like that of many of his co-stars—and his star to truly shine.

Duvall has repeatedly received Academy Award nominations for his acting—for his portrayal of lieutenant Colonel Kilgore in *Apocalypse Now* (1979), Bull Meecham in *The Great Santini* (1980), Euliss "Sonny" Dewey in *The Apostle* (1997), and Jerome Facher in *A Civil Action* (1998). He won the Oscar for Best Actor for his portrayal of Mac Sledge in *Tender Mercies* (1983).

He is probably best known to most Americans, however, for his portrayal of retired Texas Ranger Augustus McRae in the televised western series *Lonesome Dove* (1989). The series was awarded six Emmy Awards, nominated for thirteen others, and is considered one of the finest westerns ever made.

Other films in which Duvall has played important roles include *M*A*S*H* (1970), starring Elliott Gould and Donald Sutherland, *Sling Blade* (1996), a wonderfully quirky film in which he played father to Billy Bob Thornton's son, *Secondhand Lions* (2003), *Gods and Generals* (2003), *Thank You for Smoking* (2005) and *Kicking and Screaming* (2005).

7

January 6

1971

Human Growth Hormone Synthesized

ON THIS DAY IN CALIFORNIA HISTORY chemists at the University of California at Berkeley announced that they had made the first synthetic human growth hormone (hGH).

Normally, this hormone is secreted automatically by the pituitary gland, but when that doesn't happen, some aspect or another of growth in the body is compromised, unless and until the hormone can be introduced some other way.

In young people, the primary indicator of a deficiency of hGH is a rate of development that proceeds at about half the rate usually seen in individuals that age. Severe deficiencies can even cause basic motor skills to develop late. In adults, a deficiency in growth hormone usually manifests itself as insufficient lean body mass or poor bone density.

The deficiency expresses itself differently at different ages, but whenever it is present, introducing a sufficient amount of hGH into a person's system is the best remedy. The deficiency can be a partial or complete one, but whatever its extent, it is usually a permanent condition.

Growth hormone deficiency is treated by growth hormone replacement therapy, and virtually all human growth hormone prescribed in most of the world today is synthetic growth hormone, manufactured by recombinant DNA technology (another area where California-based ingenuity has led the way).

Growth hormone has been used for a variety of purposes. The late stages of AIDS are often accompanied by the wasting of the muscles and growth hormone has been used to ameliorate that condition. It has been used to promote the healing of large burns, a condition where generating new tissue and generating it quickly is critical, to slow or reverse some of the effects of aging, and to help bodybuilders generate outsize muscle mass.

JANUARY 7

1911

First Airplane Bombing Experiments Conducted

ON THIS DAY IN CALIFORNIA HISTORY the first airplane bombing experiments using actual explosives were conducted just south of the city of San Francisco.

The experiments were carried out by Philip O. Parmelee and Lt. Myron Crissy on a test range at Tanforan Racetrack in San Bruno. Airplanes had only been around about eight years at this point and the experiments demonstrated vividly one of the more disturbing ways this new invention could be used.

Just the year before, the city of Los Angeles had hosted the first international air show ever held in the United States, a show that let the city show itself off, as well as showcase its suitability for year-round aviation. Here there were clear skies and snow-free ground, even in the middle of January. Where else were aviators going to find that?

By 1920 "boy wonder" Donald W. Douglas was turning out a plane a week at his assembly plant in Santa Monica. He had come out West to get involved in the then-rising aircraft industry there and it was his "DC" series of planes, and especially his "DC-3" aircraft, that would put commercial air transportation on the road to becoming a paying proposition in the United States.

San Diego's Ryan Aviation was also busy making airplanes in California in the 1920s, as was the Lockheed Aircraft Company. Other California-based plane makers emerged in the decades that followed, including Northrop, North American Aviation, and Convair, and there was plenty of work for everyone.

The emergence of so many major plane makers in one place was helped, in part, by the coming of World War II and the huge demand for warplanes that came with it, so it was only natural that this would be the place where many of the big breakthroughs in American aviation would be made, too.

9

JANUARY 8

1880

"Emperor Norton" Drops Dead on California Street

ON THIS DAY IN CALIFORNIA HISTORY the much-esteemed "Emperor" Joshua Norton dropped dead on California Street in San Francisco. He had been born in London in 1818 and arrived in San Francisco in 1849, with $40,000 in his pocket, an enormous sum of money at the time.

In this boomtown to end all boom towns, Norton set himself up as a wholesale grocer and then undertook the venture that would change his life—and that of the city of San Francisco—forever.

In 1854 Norton tried to corner the rice market in San Francisco, but his strategy didn't work out as planned. Instead of getting rich, he went broke, and the shock of it all drove him mad. He made a few efforts at a comeback, and even dropped out of sight for a time, but when he reappeared, it was not as Joshua Norton, familiar local businessman, but as "Norton I, Emperor of the United States, and Protector of Mexico," a totally new creation.

He wore a plumed top hat and a military uniform, strapped a sword to his side, and wandered the streets of San Francisco with his two dogs, Bummer and Lazarus, at his side. He issued "proclamations," which were published in the local newspapers, and his own currency, which local merchants took as payment.

Showing that he was as much a seer as a madman, Norton issued, in 1869, a proclamation that bridges be built across San Francisco Bay. The engineering had not yet been created to make such an enterprise feasible, of course, but as we all know today, that's exactly what would happen in the years ahead.

When the beloved eccentric died in 1880, he had become a symbol of the city itself: a cautionary tale about staking everything on the big strike, but at the same time, a fine example of surviving calamity by reinventing yourself altogether. He had become, in a word, a legend.

JANUARY 9

1959

Rawhide Premieres on CBS TV

ON THIS DAY IN CALIFORNIA HISTORY the long-running and extremely popular television show, *Rawhide*, premiered on American TV.

The show starred a very young and very "rock-and-roll-looking" Clint Eastwood, and provided the acting debut and springboard from which he would launch his career as an American entertainment icon.

The first episode ran on January 9, 1959, the final one on January 4, 1966, 217 episodes in all and all broadcast in black and white. By the mid-1960s it was one of the nation's top ten shows, and only 3 other TV westerns ever managed longer runs—*The Virginian* (9 years), *Bonanza* (14 years), and *Gunsmoke* (20 years).

Eastwood would go on to make a name for himself in what came to be known as "spaghetti westerns" (low-budget, sparely drawn and violent westerns first made by Italian studios), a group including *A Fistful of Dollars* (1964), *For a Few Dollars More* (1965), and *The Good, the Bad, and the Ugly* (1966). It was an extremely popular venture and one that made Eastwood an international star.

After doing his spaghetti westerns, Eastwood would develop the role for which he is often still best remembered—Inspector "Dirty Harry" Callahan of the San Francisco Police Department—and utter the immortal line that every dedicated moviegoer knows, "Go ahead, make my day."

As Eastwood got older, he moved from being a leading man on screen to being a leading man in real life, and was elected mayor of Carmel in 1986. He also moved from in front of the camera to behind it, producing such memorable films as *Unforgiven* (1992), *The Bridges of Madison County* (1995), *Mystic River* (2003), *Million Dollar Baby* (2004), and *Flags of our Fathers* (2006), proving he could make big things happen on both sides of the lens.

11

JANUARY 10

1950

Ben Hogan and Sam Snead Square Off

ON THIS DAY IN CALIFORNIA HISTORY legendary golfer Ben Hogan played Sam Snead in the Los Angeles Open. It was his first tournament appearance since an auto accident a year earlier.

Both men were in their prime, both just 37 years old. Hogan had shattered his legs just the year before in a collision with a bus and had spent all the time between that day and this struggling to get back on his feet. In fact, in the days just after the accident, his doctors told him that he might never walk again.

Sam Snead was not struggling with any mobility challenges that January day in 1950. He had been named the PGA Player of the Year for 1949 and was in the midst of a career that would ultimately include 3 PGA Open wins, 3 Masters wins, and a win at the British Open. He would finish his golf career as the all-time PGA career leader with 81 wins.

Hogan had discovered golf working as a caddie at Glen Garden Country Club in Ft. Worth, Texas, when he was just 15, and it was there that he lost a playoff among the course's caddies to another local boy his age named Byron Nelson. That "setback" aside, however, he would turn pro at 17 and make it on to the tour as a full-time player when he was only 19.

Though he would finish his career with fewer wins than Snead —63 to Snead's 81—Hogan was no slouch, either. He would be named PGA Player of the Year 4 times, win 9 major competitions (including 6 of the 9 he played in after his car accident), 4 Grand Slam titles, 4 U. S. Open titles, 2 Masters competitions, 2 PGA Championships, and one British Open.

Hogan shot a 34 on his first 9 holes, and would post a total score of 280 strokes through the course of the 4 games played. It was an incredible showing for a player whose ability to even walk had been in doubt less than 12 months before.

January 11

Whisky a Go Go Opens on the Sunset Strip

ON THIS DAY IN CALIFORNIA HISTORY the Whisky a Go Go nightclub opened at 8901 Sunset Boulevard in West Hollywood. Many have called it the birthplace of rock and roll in Los Angeles.

It has been called the first real discotheque in America, too, and it certainly fueled a lot of firsts in that area. The site had previously been a bank building that had been remodeled into a club called "The Party." The Party didn't last long, however, and the Whisky picked up where The Party left off.

The Whisky called itself a "discotheque," but the name was actually something of a misnomer because a *disco*theque would be a place that simply *played* records, and whatever else the Whisky was about, it was about live-band performance. This was no ultra-hip sock hop featuring DJ's and their discs. This was a place where *bands* came to play.

The first live performer to play at the Whisky was Johnny Rivers, and he was followed by a steady stream of others, including the Byrds and the Doors, who were, for a time, the *house band* here. Frank Zappa and the Mothers of Invention played here. Jimi Hendrix played here. Otis Redding played here, too.

In 1966 Smokey Robinson and the Miracles helped make the place famous with their hit song, "Goin' to a Go Go," as did the "go-go dancers" who danced suspended from the ceiling in a cage. The audience thought the dancing was part of the act and, voila!, the go-go dancer in a cage was born.

In 1971 the Whisky nearly burned to the ground and it wasn't until the late '70s that live music returned to its stage: first "punk," then hard rock, then "grunge." The Whisky actually closed its doors in 1982, but in 1986 those doors were opened once again. This time, however, the Club was a place for bands and promoters looking to *rent* a venue to showcase their talents.

JANUARY 12

1995

O. J. Simpson Trial Begins in Los Angeles

ON THIS DAY IN CALIFORNIA HISTORY the trial of the now infamous O. J. Simpson, superstar athlete, passably amusing comic actor, and TV pitchman, began in Los Angeles.

Up until the events that led to his presence in an L. A. court-room, Simpson had been an endlessly likable icon of the American sports and entertainment scenes. He had been a Heisman-Trophy-winning halfback for the University of Southern California and had completed an illustrious career as a running back for the Buffalo Bills and Oakland Raiders.

Once football was through, he created a new career for himself in show business. He worked as a sports announcer for some of the nation's major networks and also gave some memorably amusing performances in the *Naked Gun* series of films. He became a pitch-man for the Hertz Rent-a-Car organization, too, and his picture adorned billboards and TV spots all over the country.

Simpson had arrived, liked and respected as much by whites as blacks, and a familiar presence in the national media.

Then came his arrest for the murder of his wife, Nicole, and her friend, Ron Goldman. The evidence was overwhelming, but no mat-ter, the facts of the case dissolved into a microanalysis of flawed evidence-collecting techniques by the LAPD and charges of racially-motivated harassment, taking the spotlight off Simpson and the facts of the case and training it instead on the methodology followed in determining his guilt or innocence.

To the elation of blacks, and the bewilderment of whites, Simp-son was found not guilty, and his trial brought to a close. Along with it, however, Simpson's role as a warm and friendly presence in American media came to a close, too, and guilty or innocent, he is unlikely to ever grace American television or movie screens in a positive way again.

January 13

1929

Legendary Lawman Wyatt Earp Dies

ON THIS DAY IN CALIFORNIA HISTORY legendary Wild West lawman Wyatt Earp died in Los Angeles. He was 81.

His fame came largely from his days as a lawman on the American frontier, of course. He had been the sheriff of Wichita and Dodge City, Kansas, and with the help of his brothers, Virgil and Morgan, and his friend, "Doc" Holliday, faced down some of the toughest outlaws ever to ride through the Wild West.

It was in Dodge City that he met and became friends with "Bat" Masterson and "Doc" Holliday and that he established his reputation as a lawman and gambler.

He was born in Monmouth, Illinois, in 1848, and in 1864 moved with his parents to Colton, California, where he found work as a teamster and railroad worker. In 1870 he returned to the East to get married, but after his new bride died suddenly, he again drifted out West, where he worked as a buffalo hunter and stagecoach driver before beginning his career as a lawman.

Earp left Dodge City in 1878, and from there traveled to New Mexico and California, accompanied by his second wife, and even worked for a time as a Wells Fargo agent.

In 1879 he joined up with his brothers in Tombstone, Arizona, where they hoped to establish a stage line. There were already two in town, however, so the brothers acquired the town's gambling concession instead. Virgil became the town marshal, Morgan took a job with the local police department, and Wyatt met his third wife, Josie, who remained with him until his death in 1929.

Earp spent his later years on the West Coast. He ran gambling halls and saloons in Alaska during the gold rush there in 1897 and later moved to Los Angeles where he befriended some of Hollywood's early stars, including movie cowboys Tom Mix and William S. Hart. Hart was one of the pallbearers at his funeral.

JANUARY 14

25,000 Attend Human "Be-In" in San Francisco

ON THIS DAY IN CALIFORNIA HISTORY 25,000 people attended a human "Be-In" in San Francisco. The event was staged in San Francisco's Golden Gate Park during the famous "Summer of Love" (1967). It was the "Age of the Hippie" and San Francisco was the world capital of hippiedom. It was very much a sign of the times.

The *Berkeley Barb*, U. C. Berkeley's student newspaper, furnished some portentous prose to define the spirit of the day: "We shall shower the country with ecstasy and purification. Fear will be washed away; ignorance will be exposed to sunlight; profits and empire will be drying on deserted beaches; violence will be submerged and transmuted in rhythm and dancing."

A tall agenda, yes, but then again this was the dawning of the Age of Aquarius and achieving "the peace that passes all understanding" was all in a day's work.

Beat poets Allen Ginsberg and Gary Snyder recited poetry and prayers. The high priest of psychedelia, Dr. Timothy Leary, addressed the crowd. The Grateful Dead, Quicksilver Messenger Service, and Jefferson Airplane provided the day's soundtrack. Owsley Stanley the III, the legendary San Francisco drugmaker, supplied the requisite doses of LSD.

The park was a sea of long-haired kids, many stoned. There were bells, chimes, peace signs, incense, flags, flowers, multicolored clothes and the unmistakable scent of cannabis in the air.

San Francisco's 1967 Human Be-In was a turning point. After it, the Haight-Ashbury area became infinitely better-known and a magnet for disaffected kids coast to coast. Staying clear of the war in Vietnam brought them. Getting clear of their significantly more uptight parents brought them. Most of all, perhaps, the idea that this was ground zero for a completely new and free way of life, a new beginning for the family of man, brought them, too.

JANUARY 15

1913

Actor Lloyd Bridges Born in San Leandro

ON THIS DAY IN CALIFORNIA HISTORY actor Lloyd Bridges was born in the small Northern California town of San Leandro, an agricultural community directly south of Oakland that was once known best for its cherries.

His father was in the hotel business and wanted his son to be a lawyer. But what Lloyd wanted to do was go to UCLA and study acting. He did, and it was there that he also met his future wife, Dorothy, to whom he remained married for over 50 years.

Bridges started his acting career on the stage and worked his way around the country doing summer stock, but it would be on the big screen and TV that he would really make his mark. In 1941, he signed a contract with Columbia Pictures, and was cast in "B" westerns, serials, and comedy shorts there.

The big-screen movies Bridges appeared in were usually fairly routine affairs, except for his role as the traitorous deputy sheriff in *High Noon* (1952). It was on the "little screen" that he really shined, frequently guest-starring on shows from *Robert Montgomery Presents* in the 1950s to *Seinfeld* in the '90s.

Bridges's first notoriety on TV came with his starring role as diver Mike Nelson in the series, *Sea Hunt* (1958-1961), which was, for a time, the most successful show on TV. It made him famous and led to offer of the role of Captain Kirk on *Star Trek*, but he turned it down. Late in his career, he again found fame with his loopy character portrayals in the *Airplane!* and *Hot Shot* movies.

Though he was, in his prime, an athletically built man with chiseled good looks, he certainly didn't show that kind of physical promise early on. In 1914, barely a year old, he won a "fat baby contest," judged by none other than former President William Howard Taft (himself 300 plus), who thought he was as fat as he was. Now, that's fat!

17

January 16

1908
Pinnacles National Monument Established

ON THIS DAY IN CALIFORNIA HISTORY Pinnacles National Monument was established in California's Gabilan mountains southeast of San Jose.

This area east of the Salinas Valley is comprised of the remains of an ancient volcano and is estimated to be some 23,000,000 years old. It was originally formed when the Pacific Plate lurched past the North American Plate (part of California sits on one plate, part on the other, and the two meet here), transforming the earth's crust into the shapes seen here now.

The craggy rock spires, caverns and other intriguing earth formations that make up the area are the work of millions of years of earthquake activity and erosion. The experience of making your way through this bizarre agglomeration of earth formations has been likened to "rock climbing on the moon."

The vegetation found in this area is diverse, too, but only the very strong and adaptable can survive.

Chaparral predominates, covering eighty percent of the ground, but other kinds of plants can also be found. Blue oak and digger pine trees grow here, as do cattails, ferns, cottonwoods, and willows. Wildflowers also grow in the park, breaking up up the dusty green color of the chaparral in spring. But plenty of interesting colors are created simply by sunlight as it moves over the area's dark-red rocks.

Eagles and falcons roost here, but they stay high up and away from humans. And so does the California condor. This bird, a vulture with an orange head and neck and a 10-foot wingspan, is a true survivor from prehistoric times, and has been close to extinction on more than one occasion. It has been making something of a comeback in recent years, however, even though its population remains fragile.

18

JANUARY 17

1994

Northridge Earthquake Hits Southern California

ON THIS DAY IN CALIFORNIA HISTORY the Northridge earthquake rolled through the San Fernando Valley, leaving a massive trail of destruction in its wake.

The quake struck in the early morning hours of January 17, 1994 (4:30 in the morning, Pacific Standard Time). The epicenter was originally thought to be in the San Fernando Valley town of Northridge, but was later determined to be in the neighboring town of Reseda.

Damage was caused within a fifty-mile radius of the quake's epicenter, most of it occurring at the west end of the San Fernando Valley and in the city of Santa Monica. Sections of Interstate Highway 10 and California Highway 14 collapsed from the shaking and several important hospitals in the area were so badly damaged they had to be evacuated.

Fifty-seven people were killed and 1,500 seriously injured. The only reason more people weren't injured or killed was that the quake struck early in the morning and on a holiday.

The Northridge earthquake was unusually strong (a 7.5, according to most estimates, second only to the Great San Francisco Earthquake and Fire of 1906) and caused the earth to "lift up" as much as twenty inches in places. It also revealed that many of the buildings in the area were not nearly as "earthquake-proof" as many engineers had previously thought.

The Northridge earthquake was the third major earthquake to strike California in the 23-year period beginning in 1971. The first was the San Fernando earthquake that struck near the San Fernando Valley town of Sylmar in 1971, the second, the Loma Prieta earthquake that struck just south of San Francisco in 1989. The Northridge quake would turn out to be the most costly earthquake in U. S. history.

19

JANUARY 18

1777

City of San Jose Founded

ON THIS DAY IN CALIFORNIA HISTORY the city of San Jose was founded. It was one of just two *pueblos*, or towns, that the Spanish had chosen to establish in this remote province of their New World empire. (The other was Los Angeles.) For most of its history, it was the center of a thriving agricultural community, a place where acre upon acre of fruit trees and vegetables grew.

When California became American territory in 1848, San Jose had just 700 inhabitants, but was still the area's leading city north of Monterey. The discovery of gold changed that, of course, making San Francisco Northern California's leading city, but San Jose still remained an important supply center for miners bound for the gold fields and even served as the state capital from 1849-1851.

When it was officially incorporated as a city in 1850, San Jose's population had grown to 3,000, not small, but still modest compared to what was then San Francisco's population of around 25,000. It was particularly appealing to those drawn to the slower pace of life in "the country."

At the end of World War II San Jose's population stood at just 57,000, but like so much else in California, the War changed all that. By 1950 the city's population stood at 95,000, and by the mid-1970s, had swollen to 535,000.

The coming of the computer industry triggered an even bigger population boom, because this was ground zero for the industry, the heart of Silicon Valley.

The fruit trees and vegetable farms were uprooted to make way for R&D plants and the making of computers and computer-related technology. In 2005 the population of the city stood at 904,522, and San Jose had become the 10th-largest city in the nation. There was every reason to believe it would grow into an even larger city still in the years just ahead.

January 19

Notre Dame Ends UCLA's 88-Game Winning Streak

ON THIS DAY IN CALIFORNIA HISTORY UCLA's phenomenal 88-game basketball game winning streak, the longest in college basketball history, was broken by archrival Notre Dame.

Notre Dame had been the last team to beat UCLA before the streak began, too—almost exactly three years before. The Bruins were leading by a score of 70-59 with just 3 ½ minutes left to play, and it would have seemed a large enough margin to lock in win number 89.

But the Irish scored 24 unanswered points during those 3 ½ minutes, including the game-winning shot made with just 29 seconds to go. Not one of the five shots the Bruins put up during the game's final 10 seconds made its way through the hoop.

This was a team coached by the legendary John Wooden, a man who had been quite a player himself in his day, earning all-state honors three times in high school, All-American honors three times in college, and being named College Player of the Year in 1932, the year he helped lead Purdue to the national championship.

Wooden's teams did things that no other college basketball teams are likely to do again.

In addition to racking up the unprecedented 88-game winning streak, the Bruins logged four perfect 30-0 seasons, 38 straight NCAA tournament victories, 20 Pac-10 championships, and 10 national championships, seven of them in a row. On their home court, Wooden-coached teams were an incredible 149-2.

Wooden developed an impressive amount of basketball talent as a coach at UCLA, including All-Americans Walt Hazzard, Gail Goodrich, Kareem Abdul-Jabbar (Lew Alcindor), Lucius Allen, Sidney Wicks, and Bill Walton, and he was himself one of only two players ever to be inducted into the Basketball Hall of Fame as both a player *and* a coach.

January 20

1929

First Full-Length "Talking Movie" Shot Outdoors Released

ON THIS DAY IN CALIFORNIA HISTORY the movie *In Old Arizona*, the first full-length "talkie" shot completely outdoors, was released. It was a big success and inaugurated a new era in film—the era of full-length films shot on location and incorporating sound.

The film was directed by Raoul Walsh, the man who would go on to direct such films as *High Sierra* (1941), starring Humphrey Bogart, and *Band of Angels* (1957), starring Clark Gable. It was nominated for five Academy Awards, including "Best Picture of the Year." Its central character, the Cisco Kid, would also garner a considerable amount of screen time in the years ahead.

The film made a number of "breakthroughs." It was the first major "western" to use sound (it was, after all, just 3 years after sound had been introduced in *The Jazz Singer*), and it was the first "talking film" to be shot outdoors, using a variety of real-life locations, including Bryce Canyon and Zion National Park in Utah, the San Fernando Mission near Los Angeles, and various sites in the Mojave Desert northeast of L. A.

The "singing cowboy" in the film (the first western with one) was Warner Baxter, not quite 30 at the time, who won a "Best Actor" award for his work and would go on to play a variety of dashing-leading-man roles in the years ahead, including Alan Breck in *Kidnapped* (1938) and the Cisco Kid (again) in *The Return of the Cisco Kid* (1939).

Movies with sound would be a good thing for actors with voices that "translated" well to the big screen, but for those whose voices didn't, it was a disaster. Once sound came in, many Hollywood careers took off or collapsed overnight. One of the biggest beneficiaries of this change in moviemaking methods was Warner Brothers. They had bankrolled *The Jazz Singer* and it was their studio that benefited the most from its success.

JANUARY 21

1962

Snow Falls in San Francisco

ON THIS DAY IN CALIFORNIA HISTORY snow fell in San Francisco. San Francisco can feel cold, of course, colder than many places where snow is a typical part of the winter menu. But snow is not something that is *expected* to fall here.

Snow is common in the far northern part of the state, of course, at places like Mt. Shasta and at nearby Mt. Lassen.

It is common throughout the Sierra Nevada range, too, a range which runs for 400 miles along the eastern boundary of the state from Lassen Peak in the north to Tejon Pass in the south, and especially on the highest peaks in that range, like Mt. Whitney, which, at 14,495 feet, is the highest mountain in the "lower" forty-eight states.

Snow also falls in Southern California. It falls in the San Bernardino Mountains, on Arrowhead Peak (5,174 feet) and at Big Bear Lake (close to 7,000 feet above sea level), and in the San Gabriel Mountains, on "Mt. Baldy" (8,600 feet). In January of 1949, 80 inches of snow fell on Mt. Palomar (5,500 feet), northeast of San Diego.

Over the course of the past 100 years, snow has fallen in downtown Los Angeles more than 20 times. On most of these occasions, this has been nothing more than a light dusting of snowflakes, but on the morning of January 15, 1932, almost two inches of snow fell in downtown L. A., the most ever recorded in the city on a single day. Snow even covered the beaches at Santa Monica.

And though snow falling in San Francisco on this day in 1962 was a truly remarkable thing to have happened, it was not the first time snow had fallen here. Seventy-five years before, on February 5, 1887, almost four inches of snow fell in downtown San Francisco, an event which must have made the 19th-century city a truly remarkable sight to see.

JANUARY 22

1984

"Macintosh" Introduced at Super Bowl XVIII

ON THIS DAY IN CALIFORNIA HISTORY the Apple Computer Company unveiled its Apple "Macintosh" to the TV-viewing public during Super Bowl XVIII (with its "1984" commercial).

The Macintosh project had started early in 1979 and was the brainchild of a design engineer named Jef Raskin, who wanted to develop a computer for the average consumer that could be operated by clicking images, instead of inputting strings of code. With the "Mac," he accomplished that. More so than any machine before it, the "Mac" made the mouse and point-and-click operation standard features of the personal computer.

The first mouse was devised by Douglas Engelbart, a Stanford Research Institute scientist, in the mid-1960s. Raskin's innovation was to put that mouse in the hands of average users. The "Mac" also popularized the idea of storing data on a floppy disc, including built-in speakers in a personal computer, and ergonomic design, which dramatically reduced the clutter that had characterized computer set-ups up to that time.

Later versions of the Macintosh computer would introduce desktop publishing, CD-ROM drives as a standard feature, new kinds of storage devices and interesting and vivid colors for computer hardware. Still later versions would pioneer the first notebook computer with a 17-inch display monitor, the first true touchpad to be used as a pointing device on a notebook computer, and the first notebook computer with built-in Ethernet support.

The limitations of the first "Macs" were that they had insufficient memory and could not easily be expanded. They also lacked a hard drive or any means by which one could be attached. Later versions of the product came with much more memory and allowed the attachment of peripherals, as well as faster CPUs and improved graphics capabilities.

JANUARY 23

1862

First Grapevine Cuttings Arrive in San Francisco

ON THIS DAY IN CALIFORNIA HISTORY European vine cuttings, personally chosen and shipped to California by Agoston Haraszthy, the "Father of the California Wine Industry," arrived in San Francisco Harbor. It was from these cuttings that the first serious winemaking efforts in California would grow.

Haraszthy first came to California in 1849, to San Diego, and it was here that he planted his first California vineyard and made wine. Just three years later he moved to San Francisco, where he planted a vineyard near Mission Dolores, created from 160 cuttings and six rooted plants that he brought from San Diego.

In 1857 Haraszthy moved again, this time to Sonoma County, where he developed the first large vineyard ever cultivated in California and built a palatial home for himself. He called his estate "Buena Vista," a well-known vintage to this day.

In 1861 Haraszthy returned to Europe to find ways to improve California's vineyards and to collect fruit tree stock to transplant. He collected more than 100,000 cuttings of 350 different varieties of wine grapes, and also gathered up planting stock for several other kinds of fruits—and nuts—too.

In 1862 Harper & Brothers published his report of his findings in Europe entitled *Grape Culture, Wines and Wine-Making, with Notes upon Agriculture and Horticulture.* Until well into the 20th century, it remained the most authoritative work of its kind in the English language.

Despite all of the money, energy and enthusiasm that Haraszthy brought to the task of educating California grape-growers and winemakers about the best way to do their work, acceptance came slowly. In 1866 business reverses caused him to lose his vineyards and move to Nicaragua where he tried to establish a sugarcane plantation and make rum for export.

JANUARY 24

1848

James Marshall Discovers Gold in the American River

ON THIS DAY IN CALIFORNIA HISTORY a man named James Marshall discovered gold in the American River near Coloma.

Marshall had been born in New Jersey, and like his father before him, became a carpenter. At 18 he decided to head out West, going first to Indiana, then to Illinois, and finally to Kansas, where he spent a number of years trying to make a living as a farmer.

In 1844 Marshall decided that his plan to become a farmer maybe wasn't such a good idea after all, so he joined a wagon train heading to California, arriving at Sutter's famous "fort" in July of 1845.

Here things began to look up. He did some carpentry work for Sutter and soon purchased some livestock and several hundred acres of land. In 1846, however, he decided to join up with Fremont's "California Battalion" to assist in the "Bear Flag Revolt." When he returned to his home in 1847, he found that all his cattle had been stolen and was forced to sell his land.

It was this turn of events that led Marshall to contract with Sutter to build a sawmill on the American River, and it was during that effort that he spotted the gold nuggets that set off the California Gold Rush.

Ironically, Marshall did not benefit personally from the rush for riches that his discovery of gold set off. He couldn't secure good title to his own claims and the sawmill he built quickly failed when the men needed to operate it ran off to find their fortunes in the gold fields.

Marshall resented his misfortune to the end of his days, but was helpless to change the course of events that he himself had set in motion. He became a drifter and ended up living in a cabin, raising a small garden for food. He triggered one of the greatest rushes for wealth in human history, but made nothing from it himself.

January 25

1949

First "Emmys" Awarded

ON THIS DAY IN CALIFORNIA HISTORY the first Emmy Awards were presented in Los Angeles. The programs up for consideration had been aired in 1948 and the awards were presented at the Hollywood Athletic Club. A show named *Pantomime Quiz Time* won the award for "Best Show."

The awards had been established by the Academy of Television Arts & Sciences and the idea behind them was to honor "excellence in television programming," as well as to promote its "cultural, educational and research aims." Just six Emmys were presented at this first show, and to be eligible to receive one, shows had to have been produced in Los Angeles. As television became more of an international phenomenon, the requirement that shows be produced in L. A. was removed.

Today there are many more than six categories in which television shows can win an Emmy and the awards are actually made by two separate groups.

The Academy of Television Arts & Sciences in Los Angeles awards the "prime-time" Emmys, those given to shows that air between about 7:00 and 11:00 p.m. in their markets. The National Academy of Television Arts and Sciences in New York City awards the Emmys given to daytime shows and to news, sports, local, international and documentary-type shows. The two academies officially went their separate ways in 1977.

When the Emmys were first awarded in 1949, there were only 1,000,000 television sets in the land; when they were broadcast in 1955 that number had grown to 25,000,000. The 1957 show was broadcast in color, and from 1955 to 1971, simulcast from New York *and* Los Angeles, making the awards a national, not just a West Coast event. Since 1977 the West and East Coast academies have worked together to broadcast the awards.

27

JANUARY 26

1911

First Successful "Hydroplane" Flight Made

ON THIS DAY IN CALIFORNIA HISTORY Glenn Curtiss made the first successful "hydroplane" flight in the waters off the coast of San Diego.

Curtiss was an aviation pioneer and among his many contributions to this area of American life, he was the first person to pilot a plane from the deck of a ship out at sea and then successfully land the plane back on it.

He was at the controls when the first *pre*announced public flight in the U. S. was made in 1908, and was the "flight engineer" for the first trial flight of an army dirigible (same year). He built the first private aircraft in the U. S. in 1909, set the first international air speed record (a whopping 46.5 mph), and set the first "long-distance" flying record by piloting a plane between Albany, New York, and New York City.

He trained the nation's first female pilot (Blanche Stuart Scott), introduced the first dual-pilot set-up in an aircraft, the first retractable landing gear, and the first ailerons (those movable flaps on an airplane's wings that allow the pilot to control rolling and banking movements). He received the first pilot's license in the United States, and during World War I, produced biplanes for the military and trained pilots on how to use them in combat.

It was a Curtiss NC-4 "Jenny" that made the first successful transatlantic crossing in 1919 and a Curtiss plane the Navy bought when it bought its first aircraft. Curtiss also trained the first two naval pilots and established an aviation school in San Diego, on North Island, too.

Curtiss was a prolific inventor throughout his life and created more than 500 different inventions. In addition to his many contributions to aerospace technology, he also made important contributions to motorcycle design.

28

JANUARY 27

1894

Midwinter Fair Opens in San Francisco

ON THIS DAY IN CALIFORNIA HISTORY an event known as the California Midwinter Fair of 1894 opened in San Francisco.

It was the brainchild of *San Francisco Chronicle* publisher Michael de Young, who had been California's representative at the Columbian Exposition in Chicago the year before. Within just a few months of his return to San Francisco from Chicago, de Young was busy devising plans to stage a similar fair in Golden Gate Park. He organized committees, engaged architects to do the design work and started raising money to fund his new venture.

De Young wanted to capitalize on San Francisco's status as an up-and-comer among the nation's great cities. The 1890 census showed that there were 299,000 people living in the city, almost 20 percent of the people living in the entire state at the time. If there was anywhere in the state where the Fair should be held, this was the place.

He even chose to incorporate some of the exhibits that had appeared in Chicago to enhance his Fair's appeal. But despite those efforts, it was still criticized as little more than an overstated amusement park. No matter. It did what de Young wanted it to do.

Laid out on 180 acres near the eastern end of Golden Gate Park, the Fair accomplished its goals: to give San Francisco's economy a boost, show off the Bay Area's fine winter climate, persuade more newcomers to make San Francisco their home, and further *Chronicle* publisher Michael de Young's political ambitions.

It succeeded on all fronts. In fact, it was with profits made from the Fair that de Young funded the construction of the de Young Museum in Golden Gate Park, which opened its doors in March of 1895 and in time became one of the city's foremost museums, well-known for its collections of American art and handicrafts and Asian art as well.

JANUARY 28

1914

City of Beverly Hills Incorporated

ON THIS DAY IN CALIFORNIA HISTORY Beverly Hills was incorporated as a city. The area had been nothing but lima bean fields in the beginning, but by 1919, the leading names of the movie world had begun to move in, creating the first examples of what remains to this day 5.7 square miles of breathtaking residential splendor.

The homes built by Beverly Hills's original settlers—Burton Green, Charles Canfield and Max Whittier—set the tone for things to come. Green's twenty-room mansion on the corner of Lexington Road and Crescent Drive was the first of the city's truly *great* mansions. It had a 25-by-30-foot reception hall and an immense walnut-paneled dining room. It had five upstairs bedrooms, each with its own dressing room and marble bathroom.

It was Green who first subdivided the Beverly Hills bean fields into residential lots, and who gave the town its name (he had come out West from Beverly Farm, Massachusetts). When Beverly Hills incorporated itself in 1914, only 550 people were living there. By the beginning of the Great Depression its population had grown to 22,000.

In 1919 Douglas Fairbanks and Mary Pickford, Hollywood's leading man and lady, moved to Beverly Hills. Their mansion featured a screening room in which to show movies, a bowling alley, a billiard room, five guest bedrooms, quarters for servants, and a 55-by-100-foot swimming pool. It was called "Pickfair" and was the first great mansion built by movie people here.

At century's end, Beverly Hills remained one of the world's most luxurious addresses and building great mansions reached altogether new levels of excess. TV mogul Aaron Spelling built a mansion that spread out over *56,500 square feet* and included a bowling alley, a theater, and garage space enough for eight cars—all for a family of four!

January 29

1953

First Movie in CinemaScope Premieres

ON THIS DAY IN CALIFORNIA HISTORY the first widely-viewed movie to be shot in CinemaScope premiered. The movie, *The Robe*, is the story of man who wins the robe of Jesus Christ in a dice game and is transformed from a cynic into a true believer; it stars Richard Burton, Jean Simmons, and Victor Mature.

This "process" of filming wide-screen moving images had been invented by a Frenchman named Henri Chrétien. He had developed the process in the late 1920s, but his efforts to interest moviemakers did not pan out. Now, at long last, Hollywood came calling, looking for *the lenses* Chrétien had built to create his impressive big-screen effect.

That "effect" involved removing the distortion that naturally occurs when you try to project an image twice as wide as it is high, giving you a proportional result and allowing images to be "fit" onto different sizes of film. Twentieth Century-Fox secured the rights to the technique and the lenses and immediately put them to use in filming *The Robe*.

Darryl F. Zanuck announced that 20th Century-Fox would produce all future films by using this new process and invited the other studios to license its use for their productions. MGM immediately started using CinemaScope to shoot their films, as did Walt Disney, Warner Brothers, Universal, and Columbia, but Paramount, RKO, and Republic all decided to "wait and see" if it truly took hold.

The introduction of CinemaScope was a critically important event in film history. With the arrival of television, attendance had begun to fall off at the nation's cinemas and theater owners needed a way to bring customers back. CinemaScope was the first good weapon they found to get audiences back into theatre seats and the first of many big-screen innovations that would come along in the years ahead.

JANUARY 30

1847

"Yerba Buena" Renamed "San Francisco"

ON THIS DAY IN CALIFORNIA HISTORY Yerba Buena (named for the plentiful mint that once grew in abundance here—"good herb") was renamed San Francisco. The decision to make the change was that of Lt. Washington Bartlett, then mayor of this dusty little out-of-the-way settlement by the Pacific and it indicated that Bartlett felt his little village was destined for greater things.

It's believed that Yerba Buena was originally established around 1792. An Englishman named William A. Richardson arrived in 1822 and stopped off long enough to meet and marry the daughter of the presidio's *commandante*. He clearly like the place and would spend the rest of his life here.

Mariano Vallejo, the Mexican general in command of the troops guarding California's northern frontier at the time, made Richardson "Captain of the Port" of Yerba Buena in 1835, and shortly thereafter, he built the area's first permanent habitation. He later built a large rancho in the northern shores of the Bay called "Rancho Saucelito" that bordered an inlet today known as Richardson Bay, between Sausalito and Tiburon.

For most of its history, Yerba Buena was a fairly nondescript kind of place. There was a presidio located there, which the Spanish had built as a frontier defense in 1776. There was a mission located there, too, Mission Dolores, also built in 1776, but by the time the Americans arrived in the mid-19th century, the population still stood at just 800.

But these were the days when Alta California was nothing more than a largely neglected Spanish seaport on the Pacific coast, a place not all that far from the days when only Costanoan Indians lived here, and one most likely to be visited only by accident or happenstance, by ships making their way through California's coastal waters en route to other places altogether.

JANUARY 31

1974

Movie Mogul Sam Goldwyn Dies in Los Angeles

ON THIS DAY IN CALIFORNIA HISTORY movie mogul Sam Goldwyn died at his home in Los Angeles. He was the "G" in MGM and one of the true founders of the American movie business.

Like the other movie moguls, Goldwyn came from humble beginnings. He was born in Poland and left home at age 16, penniless and on foot. He went first to England, where he stayed with relatives for a few years (and changed his name to *Goldfish*), and in 1898, immigrated to Nova Scotia. From there he went to the United States, where he became a citizen in 1902 and eventually got work in the garment industry in New York City.

While in New York, the newly-emerging film industry caught his attention and it was not long before he went into the business himself, partnering with vaudeville performer Jesse Lasky and Louis B. Mayer, a theater owner who had also come to the United States from eastern Canada, in his case, New Brunswick.

But Goldfish, Lasky and Mayer didn't get along and the partnership lasted just a few years. In 1916 he entered another partnership, this time with Broadway producers Edgar and Archibald Selwyn—the "Goldwyn" Picture Corporation—and the company enjoyed moderate success. Eventually, the Goldwyn Picture Corporation was acquired by Marcus Loew and his Metro Pictures Corporation, and it was during these years that the company became part of MGM (Metro-Goldwyn-Mayer).

During his more than three decades in the movie business, Sam Goldwyn built a rock-solid reputation for excellence. He discovered Gary Cooper, used Billy Wilder to direct many of his films, and was honored with both the Irving G. Thalberg Memorial Award and the Jean Hersholt Humanitarian Award. In the 1980s Goldwyn's studios were sold to Warner Brothers, but his name will forever remain linked to the making of motion pictures.

This Day

in

February

FEBRUARY 1

1887

Lots in "Hollywood" First Go on Sale

ON THIS DAY IN CALIFORNIA HISTORY a Kansas man named Harvey Wilcox started to sell off some acreage near downtown Los Angeles that he had subdivided and named "Hollywood". He got the idea for the town's name from his wife, who had gotten it from a woman she met while traveling East.

In 1853 just one adobe house stood here, but by 1870, a small agricultural community had begun to flourish, and in 1887 Wilcox moved in and bought the acreage that would one day become one of the most famous places in the world.

Wilcox drew up a grid map for a town that he filed with the Los Angeles County recorder's office on February 1, 1887. He laid out a central avenue through his acreage and called it Prospect Avenue, lined it with pepper trees, and started selling lots.

Money was soon raised to build two churches, a school and a library for this sedate new Southern California temperance community, and by 1900, the town had a post office, a newspaper, a hotel, two markets and a population of 500 people. There was a single-track streetcar that ran down Prospect Avenue, connecting Hollywood with the nearby city of Los Angeles, but streetcar service was infrequent and the trip took a full *two hours* to make.

In 1903 Hollywood was incorporated as a town, and in 1904, a new trolley track connecting Hollywood with Los Angeles, and running up Prospect Avenue, was opened. It was called "the Hollywood boulevard" and improved travel time between the two cities enormously.

Hollywood was annexed by the city of Los Angeles in 1910. It needed a better water supply for its citizens, and a better sewage system, too, and annexation solved both problems at a stroke. After the two cities became one, Prospect Avenue's name was changed to Hollywood Boulevard, which it remains to this day.

February 2

1848

First Chinese Immigrants Arrive in San Francisco

ON THIS DAY IN CALIFORNIA HISTORY the first "shipload" of Chinese arrived in San Francisco—two men and a woman from depression-burdened China to try their luck in the New World.

It was well-known in China, as it was throughout most of the world in the late 1840s, that gold had been discovered in California and that there was at least the possibility of finding a better life there than "at home." Travel was affordable for Chinese immigrants wanting to go to California, because those costs could be repaid by having your New World employer garnish your future wages to recoup whatever amounts had been spent on your behalf.

The Chinese were hardly greeted with open arms by California's "white" community, however. Still, they managed to make a place for themselves in their newly-adopted homeland—in the mines, in factories, in the city's laundries, and as servants in the homes of the city's most prominent citizens.

"Big Four" member Charles Crocker employed them to build the western leg of the Central Pacific Railroad, making them invaluable as railroad workers, too.

When the railroad was completed in 1869, many of California's Chinese residents turned to other occupations to make their living. They became a major factor in the state's agricultural economy, as well as in the state's fisheries, canneries, and lumber mills. By 1876 California's Chinese population had grown to 116,000, more than three-quarters of the nation's total.

The efficiency with which California's Chinese community managed to make a place for itself in the state's economy upset some of its white majority and, on at least two occasions, deadly conflict broke out—in 1871 in Los Angeles and 1877 in San Francisco. It managed to thrive, however, and many prominent artists, entrepreneurs and politicians to emerge from its ranks.

FEBRUARY 3

1959

Pop Singer Ritchie Valens Dies in Plane Crash

ON THIS DAY IN CALIFORNIA HISTORY Ritchie Valens, the first Chicano rocker in American history, and a San Fernando Valley native, was killed in a plane crash near Clear Lake, Iowa. Also killed that day was Texas rocker, Buddy Holly, and deejay J. P. ("The Big Bopper") Richardson.

Valens was born Richard Steven Valenzuela on May 13, 1941. His parents divorced when he was only three and he and his father moved to Pacoima, a suburb of Los Angeles.

Music was Ritchie's passion from early on, and his musical influences included Mexican folk songs, popular songs sung by his relatives, the cowboys he heard sing at Saturday matinee movies, and country music on the radio.

By the time he entered San Fernando High School in the mid-1950s, he had begun to play at school assemblies and after-school parties. In his junior year he joined a group called the "Silhouettes," the only rock and roll band in the area, and so one that quickly became a local star.

In May of 1958 Ritchie auditioned for L. A.-based Keen Records. Keen was looking for talent to record on a new label, Del-Fi Records, and Ritchie played an instrumental number for which he had made up some lyrics. In the short nine months between this day in May of 1958 and February of 1959 Valens recorded the three songs for which he would be forever remembered: "Come on, Let's Go," "Donna," and "La Bamba."

He was only 17 when his plane crashed in Iowa, but his influence went far beyond his years. His music inspired such later Latino performers as Los Lobos, Freddy Fender, and Trini Lopez, and even influenced non-Latino musicians like the Rascals and Bob Dylan. He received a star on the Hollywood Walk of Fame in 1990 and was inducted into the Rock and Roll Hall of Fame in 2001.

FEBRUARY 4

1974

"Patty" Hearst Kidnapped

ON THIS DAY IN CALIFORNIA HISTORY Patricia ("Patty") Hearst, granddaughter of newspaper tycoon William Randolph Hearst, was kidnapped from her apartment in Berkeley by a group calling itself the Symbionese Liberation Army ("SLA").

They subsequently kept her locked up and blindfolded, and in time, some say, she actually "joined" the group, renamed herself "Tania," and became a radical revolutionary.

The group began in the fall of 1973 when about a dozen white, college-educated California kids got together to form what they styled a "liberation army." They adopted a seven-headed snake for a symbol, a black ex-con as their leader, and expressed their rallying agenda in the sentence, "Death to the fascist insect that preys upon the life of the people." Somebody wasn't too happy.

The first "revolutionary act" the SLA took credit for was the murder of Oakland Superintendent of Schools, Marcus Foster, in November of 1973.

On April 15, 1974, Patty was photographed holding a rifle during the SLA robbery of a Hibernia Bank branch in San Francisco, and just a little over a month after that, six heavily-armed members of the SLA died in a shootout and fire that destroyed their Los Angeles hideout. The only reason that Patty was not with these six was that she had previously been arrested for shoplifting and detained.

On September 18, 1975, Patty was caught by the FBI in San Francisco, and six months later, convicted of robbing the bank in San Francisco the previous April. She was sentenced to prison, but in January of 1979 President Carter commuted her seven-year prison sentence and she was released after serving just 22 months. On January 20, 2001, the last day of his presidency, Bill Clinton gave Patty a full pardon for her crime.

FEBRUARY 5

1929

They'll Do It Every Time Debuts in San Francisco

ON THIS DAY IN CALIFORNIA HISTORY Jimmy Hatlo's long-running comic strip, *They'll Do It Every Time*, made its debut in the *San Francisco Call-Bulletin*.

Hatlo was a *sports* cartoonist at the newspaper and one day when the cartoons normally supplied by a syndicate failed to arrive, he decided to draw a cartoon to fill what would have been blank space in the paper that day. Hence was born the strip that would be his making as a cartoonist.

Hatlo drew *They'll Do It Every Time* exclusively for the *San Francisco Call-Bulletin* for seven years. Then, in 1936, the King Features Syndicate picked it up and put it into national distribution and it became a national success.

The raw material for Hatlo's cartoon came from everyday life, so sources of inspiration were in endless supply. It didn't have any central characters, like *Blondie* or *Dick Tracy*, but there were a few characters that made repeat appearances, most notably "Henry Tremblechin" and his daughter, "Little Iodine."

Little Iodine was a mischievous little kid. (Hatlo called her "the embodiment of all the little brats I ever knew.") Her dad's fate was to take it on the chin from life and Iodine's role was to be the fist delivering the blow. Somehow Hatlo made her likable, though, and she found a following of her own. In 1943 he spun her off into a separate strip, and later, into a Dell comic book.

Until his death in 1963, Hatlo oversaw the drawing of his two cartoons. His principal assistant, Bob Dunn, took over the drawing duties in 1963 and others who worked on them included Al Scaduto, who eventually took over from Dunn, Bill Yates, and Hy Eisman, who drew for *Popeye* and the *Katzenjammer Kids*. *Little Iodine* stopped running in 1986, but Al Scaduto continues to draw *They'll Do It Every Time* to this day.

FEBRUARY 6

1965

"You've Lost That Lovin' Feelin'" Hits No. 1

ON THIS DAY IN CALIFORNIA HISTORY the Righteous Brothers song, "You've Lost that Lovin' Feelin'," hit *number 1* on the Billboard pop music charts. Forty years later, in May of 2005, it received a special award for being the most-played pop song in Billboard's 65-year history of tracking radio airplay; to that point, it had been played some *10 million times*.

The duo, which included Bill Medley and Bobby Hatfield, was originally formed in 1962. In the beginning they just wanted to be good enough to succeed as a Las Vegas lounge act, but what they would actually achieve would be far greater: make some of the most popular records ever recorded.

The Righteous Brothers forged a musical link between rhythm & blues & soul that actually brought a new musical term into the language: "blue-eyed soul," soul music sung by white guys. Medley had the deep, resonant bass, Hatfield the high-flying tenor, and they created a sound unmistakably their own. When a Righteous Brothers song came on, you knew exactly who was singing.

The story goes that during an early performance a black member of the audience stood up after one of the duo's songs and said, "That was righteous, brothers." The name stuck, and the rest, as they say, is history. Over the years, The Righteous Brothers recorded such classics as "(You're My) Soul and Inspiration," "Ebb Tide" and "Just Once in My Life." They parted ways in 1968, but reunited in 1974, and again found success with "Rock and Roll Heaven."

The movies *Top Gun*, *Ghost*, *Naked Gun*, and *Dirty Dancing* repeatedly put their music before the public, bringing it to the attention of a whole new generation of fans. Medley's duet with fellow Californian Jennifer Warnes, "I've Had the Time of My Life," went platinum (1,000,000 copies sold), and in 2003, the Righteous Brothers were inducted into the Rock and Roll Hall of Fame.

FEBRUARY 7

1862

Architect Bernard Maybeck Born

ON THIS DAY IN CALIFORNIA HISTORY architect Bernard Maybeck was born in New York City. It was here in California, however, that he would make his principal contributions to American life, and with the state that he would come to be associated.

Maybeck studied architecture in France and worked for design firms in New York City and Kansas City, too, but it was when he moved to San Francisco and into the firm of A. Page Brown that the real design work he was destined to do got started.

In 1892 he moved to Berkeley to take a job teaching drawing at the University of California and he also taught courses in architecture at San Francisco's Mark Hopkins Institute of Art. Just a few short years later he became the University of California's first instructor in architecture, a position he held from 1898 to 1903.

He designed the Hearst Mining Building at Berkeley, and one of his students, Julia Morgan, would design newspaperman William Randolph Hearst's wildly over-the-top "Hearst's Castle." He also managed the 19th-century competition held to come up with a comprehensive design plan for the Berkeley campus.

This was hardly the end for Maybeck, however. He would go on to design many distinctive private residences in Berkeley and San Francisco, homes immediately identifiable as "Maybecks" because of their unique blend of Gothic Revival (sheer, upswinging spires) and Bay Region Redwood Shingle (neatly rectangular pieces of the region's most distinctive wood).

But he will always be best remembered for the Palace of Fine Arts Building that he designed for the Panama-Pacific International Exposition of 1915, rebuilt with "permanent materials" in the 1960s. It remains to this day one of the most readily recognizable and most beloved buildings in all of San Francisco and one the few structural reminders left of the extraordinary exposition then held here.

FEBRUARY 8

1915

Film *The Birth of a Nation* Opens

ON THIS DAY IN CALIFORNIA HISTORY the legendary silent film, *The Birth of a Nation*, directed by D. W. Griffith, opened at Clune's Auditorium in Los Angeles.

The film's debut title was *The Clansman*, a tale of how America came to be the way it is through the struggle of heroic and hooded white Americans to save the land from the "depredations" of violent and villainous blacks. Understandably, it provoked arguments, riots and lawsuits wherever it was shown.

That said, it may well be the single most important American film ever made, and that because of the enormous effect it has had on the development of film *as an art*.

The film introduced realistic costuming to set the historical stage, original music written for the orchestra that played during the its performance, natural outdoor landscapes as scene backgrounds, cinematically effective uses of the close-up and the still shot, and the filming of scenes from multiple angles.

It's because Griffith brought all of these now-standard aspects of filmmaking together in a single film and early on in the development of the art that his film was able to exert such an enormous influence on how future films were made.

Griffith's original budget for the film of $40,000 quickly ballooned to $60,000, and eventually increased to what was for the time an incredible $110,000. It went on to become one of the biggest moneymakers in film history, however, partly due to what was, at the time, its exorbitant charge of $2 per ticket.

By the time that talkies had made their appearance in the late 1920s, *The Birth of a Nation* had made $18 million (not a bad return on a $110,000 investment) and remained the industry's most profitable film for over two decades, until Disney's *Snow White and the Seven Dwarfs* (1937) finally surpassed it.

FEBRUARY 9

1971

Earthquake in the San Fernando Valley

ON THIS DAY IN CALIFORNIA HISTORY an earthquake rumbled through the San Fernando Valley north of Los Angeles, killing 65 and causing $500,000,000 in property damage.

The epicenter of the quake was in the vicinity of the "Magic Mountain" amusement park in Valencia. A crack in the earth 12 miles long was opened up by the initial shaking and literally thousands of aftershocks were recorded in the first few days following that strong first jolt.

Preliminary indications were that a stretch of the San Gabriel Mountains that run along the eastern edge of the Los Angeles area moved "up and west" and the shock was felt strongly in Mojave, San Bernardino, and Ventura, lightly in Los Angeles and Santa Ana, and was even noticeable as far away as San Diego.

The San Fernando earthquake demonstrated once again that it is possible for a substantial earthquake to erupt in an area with no history of seismic activity and be caused by the movement of faults unknown until the moment they give way.

In 1892 a quake like this occurred in the Sacramento Valley, and in 1954 an unmapped fault gave way near Eureka, California, generating a 6.6 magnitude quake. The 7.1 magnitude quake that hit the Imperial Valley in 1940 and the 7.7 quake that hit Kern County in 1952 were also the products of previously unknown faults. Past history is no guarantee of future results.

Most of the people killed in this quake were killed when two unreinforced masonry buildings at the Sylmar Veterans Hospital collapsed, and it has been estimated that over 1,300 buildings, as well as 1,700 mobile homes, suffered serious damage. Had the quake struck a few hours later, however, when people were at school or work or the roadways filled with traffic, the damage could easily have been much worse.

FEBRUARY 10

1940

"Tom & Jerry" Make Their Debut at MGM

ON THIS DAY IN CALIFORNIA HISTORY animated cartoon characters, "Tom & Jerry," made their debut at MGM.

Tom, a cat, and Jerry, a mouse, the stars of this series of popular, short, animated cartoons were the creations of animators Bill Hanna and Joe Barbera. The success the series enjoyed was the result of two great partnerships: the one between the animated stars and the one between the animators themselves.

Each Tom & Jerry shot revolves around Tom's attempts to catch Jerry (it never works out) and the mayhem generated by that effort. Tom is motivated by hunger, simple misunderstandings and the desire to "get even," but Jerry is as cunning as he is small and always able to elude being captured.

The first "cat-and-mouse" animated cartoon the Hanna-Barbera team put together was a piece called *Puss Gets the Boot*, completed in late 1939 and released in early 1940. The cat in this piece was named Jasper and the mouse Jinx, and the plotline went a little differently, but this was the seed from which the Tom and Jerry series would grow.

Beginning in 1965 the *Tom and Jerry* cartoons began to appear on television, but in a politically-corrected form and "toned down" for TV audiences. The black "Mammy" who had been featured in some of the early episodes was taken out and much of the violence that characterized the early cartoons was edited out, too.

In 1975 Hanna-Barbera produced a new series of Tom and Jerry cartoons for Saturday morning audiences. They replaced the violent chases of the early years with a Tom and Jerry who were now "pals" and went on adventures together. The changed relationship was in response to increasingly stringent rules about violence on children's TV, but admirable as its motives were, it unfortunately drained much of the fire and fun out of the finished result.

FEBRUARY 11

1936

Construction of Treasure Island Begins

ON THIS DAY IN CALIFORNIA HISTORY the making of "Treasure Island" in San Francisco Bay began. Four hundred acres of bay shallows were enclosed by a 3-mile-long rock perimeter and filled in with sand and silt dredged out of the Bay.

The "island" was made to create a place to hold the 1939 Golden Gate International Exposition, an event designed to celebrate the city's two new bridges—the San Francisco-Oakland Bay Bridge, dedicated on November 12, 1936, and the Golden Gate, dedicated May 27, 1937. On August 24, 1937, the dredging was complete.

Perhaps the most impressive, and certainly the most dominant, structure on the grounds of the Exposition was the 400-foot "Tower of the Sun."

On the last night of the Fair, at midnight, the multicolored searchlights that were trained each day on the nighttime sky of San Francisco Bay, were slowly dimmed, so that the only light that remained was that cast by the street lamps—and by the Tower of the Sun—which remained lit until dawn the following day.

The grounds of the Exposition included magnificent garden courts that were designed to showcase California's fine year-round weather, so much in contrast to that of New York, which was hosting a world's fair at the time. Twelve hundred gardeners designed flowerbeds that corresponded with the changing seasons to make sure the point got made.

The Fair ran from February 19 through October 29 in 1939, and again from May 25 through September 29 in 1940. During its 1939 run over 10,000,000 people visited the Exposition. After it closed its doors in 1940, San Francisco considered relocating its airport to Treasure Island, but ultimately it was made a U. S. naval installation instead. In the late 1990s it became part of the Golden Gate National Recreation Area.

47

FEBRUARY 12

1916

San Francisco Mayor Joseph Alioto Born

ON THIS DAY IN CALIFORNIA HISTORY Joseph Alioto, mayor of San Francisco from 1968 to 1976, was born in the city. The year was 1916 and Alioto would live there all of his almost 82 years.

Alioto's parents were Sicilians, who, improbably romantic as it sounds, actually met on a fishing boat while escaping from the Great San Francisco Earthquake and Fire of 1906.

Alioto's college education was completed at St. Mary's College of California and the Catholic University of America, from which he graduated in 1940, with a law degree. He worked for the Justice Department during World War II, but once the war ended, returned to San Francisco to start a law practice of his own.

Alioto was a member of the San Francisco Board of Education from 1948 to 1954, and in the 1960s chaired the city's Redevelopment Agency. In 1967 he entered the race for mayor of San Francisco when the incumbent, John Shelley, bowed out. He won the race and served two terms.

In 1968 Alioto delivered the speech at the Democratic National Convention, nominating Hubert Humphrey for President of the United States. Rumors even circulated that Humphrey would choose him as his running mate.

Alioto served as mayor during a tumultuous time in the history of his city. Protests against the war in Vietnam were common, Haight-Ashbury was in its prime, and the "Zebra murders" and "Zodiac killer" cast dark shadows over the life of the city.

But despite these distractions, Alioto managed to bring about important changes in the life of the city. During his years as mayor, minorities took on a bigger role in city politics, a serious effort to reform the city's charter was launched, and two very high-profile features of modern-day San Francisco's skyline, the Transamerica Pyramid and the Embarcadero Center, were built.

FEBRUARY 13

1988

Michael Jackson Buys "Neverland Ranch"

ON THIS DAY IN CALIFORNIA HISTORY Michael Jackson bought his now-infamous "Neverland Ranch" property in the Santa Inez Valley of Santa Barbara County.

The "King of Pop" had originally become famous as the lead singer of the "Jackson Five." They sailed to the top of the American pop music charts when Michael was still just a kid and enjoyed enormous success during their years together.

Michael *was* strange, though, and had the money to indulge that strangeness, however he might choose to. He had transformed the structure of his face into something one could easily imagine a space "alien" as having, and the color of his skin has also been transformed, from the jet black it had been in the beginning to the almost-alabaster white it is now.

And he was able to do these things—and things like buying the Santa Inez Valley property that he would transform into the amazing Neverland Ranch—because he had been so successful and become so very, very rich. That's what would ultimately get Michael into so much trouble, costing him not only a lot of his money, but his reputation as well.

For Michael liked boys and found things like having them come to his Ranch and sleep in his bed as normal, "loving" behavior, nothing at all odd for a man in his mid-forties and it was that kind of thinking that got poor Michael into trouble. Most grown-ups just didn't see it that way and some of them decided to sue Michael and seek damages.

And so it was that Neverland Ranch, a place intended to conjure up the magical innocence of Peter Pan and his refusal to grow up, came to become associated instead with a very unmagical kind of exploitation, a troubled adult making unwanted intrusions into a child's world.

FEBRUARY 14

1889

First Trainload of California Oranges Heads East

ON THIS DAY IN CALIFORNIA HISTORY the first big shipment of oranges left Los Angeles for the East Coast. It was perhaps this shipment, as much as anything else, that attracted the first big trainloads of Easterners to the Golden State.

In 1884 Los Angeles shipped off a load of locally-grown fruit for display at a national exposition being held in New Orleans. The California display stole the show and set in motion even more ambitious efforts to exhibit the state's amazing fruit harvest at exhibitions around the country.

In 1889 a program called "California on Wheels" was launched to bring displays of California fruits, vegetables and nuts to Midwestern cities and fairs. The produce used in the display had to be changed out on a regular basis, of course, and most of the California cities that participated in the program initially were quick to terminate their involvement once they saw how much work it involved, making the program, in effect, "*Los Angeles* on Wheels."

The main force behind these promotions was an Angeleno named Frank Wiggins, a man who was a marketing wonder. For thirty-five years, Wiggins directed a massive national publicity campaign for the city and made sure that Southern California's extraordinary fruit, vegetable and nut harvest was seen by crowds at virtually every important exposition or fair held in the United States between 1893 and 1909.

The "California on Wheels" exhibit became an enormously effective promotional program for Los Angeles, keeping its attractions in front of millions of potential immigrants on a nearly constant basis. By 1893, the year of the famous Columbian Exposition in Chicago (celebrating the 500th anniversary of Columbus's arrival in the New World), "California on Wheels" had been seen by some ten million people.

FEBRUARY 15

1954

Bevatron Switched On at Berkeley

ON THIS DAY IN CALIFORNIA HISTORY the *Bevatron*, a machine that was, in its time, the world's largest and most powerful "atom smasher" went into operation at U. C., Berkeley. Everything about it was big—its size, its price tag, the things it could do.

The Bevatron measured 180 feet in diameter, required a building bigger than a football field to house it, and cost $9,000,000 to build. It took its name from the size of the charge it could impart to the particles it "accelerated"—six billion electron volts or "BeVs." At top speed, it could make a proton revolve four million times in less than two seconds.

The point of all of this was to make breakthroughs in the study of matter that would be of use in areas as diverse as theoretical physics, nuclear medicine, and warfare. The Bevatron was a *super* cyclotron. The first workable cyclotrons had been built in Berkeley back in the early 1930s and the radioisotopes created in them were used to diagnose and treat disease, as well as to create powerful new sources of energy.

Radioisotopes created in these high-powered "atom smashers" were used to treat tumors, diagnose and treat thyroid disorders, and to see what was going on inside the brain, bones, liver, and other internal organs. Some, like uranium-235, were used to power nuclear power plants, some to power satellites, and some to make nuclear bombs. They were also used to test everything from airplane parts to pipeline welds, as well as to date fossils.

In 1993 the Bevatron was retired from service. New technologies had come along to take its place and this massive machine perched above the U. C., Berkeley campus had to be dismantled and removed—along with all the radioactive waste that had accumulated through the years. It took more than $70,000,000 and more than seven years to do the job.

FEBRUARY 16

1996

Former Governor "Pat" Brown Dies

ON THIS DAY IN CALIFORNIA HISTORY Governor Edmund G. "Pat" Brown died quietly at his home in Beverly Hills. He was 91 and had been governor of the state during some of its most turbulent and dynamic years, 1959 to 1967.

Brown was born in San Francisco in 1905. He got the nickname "Pat" as a twelve-year-old, while selling Liberty Bonds on the streets of San Francisco. He ended his pitches to each passerby with a quote from Patrick Henry, "Give me liberty, or give me death," and the nickname stuck. He was "Pat" from then on.

Brown graduated from San Francisco's Lowell High School, but didn't have the money to go on to college. His father owned a cigar store and it was there that Pat worked while studying law at night. He also took some University of California extension courses, and in 1927, received his degree from the San Francisco College of Law.

After completing law school, Brown started his own practice in San Francisco and affiliated himself with the Republican party. In the early 1930s, however, he became a Democrat, and in 1943, was elected District Attorney of San Francisco. In 1950 he was elected Attorney General of the state, and in 1958, governor. In the 1962 race for governor, he defeated Richard Nixon, but in the 1966 race, was defeated by Ronald Reagan.

Brown was a very popular and successful governor. He played a major role in developing California's water resources and university system, and in supporting legislation that mandated fair employment practices for all. During his administration a state economic development commission was estabished and California's highway system doubled in size, too. All told, Brown sponsored some forty major proposals during his years as governor, only five of which failed to pass the legislature.

FEBRUARY 17

1878

First Telephone Exchange Established in San Francisco

ON THIS DAY IN CALIFORNIA HISTORY the first telephone exchange was established in the city of San Francisco. It was comprised of just 18 phones and it was the seed from which the city's massive future phone system would grow.

Almost ten years later, in 1887, a particularly unique and interesting part of the city's phone system, the *Chinese* Telephone Exchange, emerged, the only Chinese-language telephone exchange outside China.

In the 1850s Chinese residents represented a full ten percent of California's population. By 1853 journalists had begun to refer to the area of the city where most of the city's Chinese citizens lived as "Chinatown," and by the 1870s, twenty-four percent of all the state's Chinese residents lived in this area.

By 1880 San Francisco's Chinese population had grown to 22,000, all of them packed into tenements and rooming houses covering twelve blocks in a north-central area of the city. It had its own merchants, its own houses of worship, and its own gambling parlors and opium dens. What it didn't have was an efficient way for members of the community to communicate with one another.

Little is known about the early days of the Chinese Telephone Exchange; most of its records were destroyed in the 1906 earthquake and fire. What is known is that the operators knew the numbers of all of the Exchange's subscribers by heart, and that when a caller asked to speak to someone, the operator could not only connect them immediately, they even knew their probable whereabouts.

The Exchange lasted until 1949. Direct-dial phone systems had become widespread by then and the time when an operator was needed to connect two callers had passed. When it closed, the Exchange employed twenty operators, all of whom, like the Exchange's first ones, were fluent in five Chinese dialects.

FEBRUARY 18

First Church of Scientology Established

ON THIS DAY IN CALIFORNIA HISTORY the First Church of Scientology was established in Los Angeles.

The Church's founder, L. Ron Hubbard, had been born in the Midwest in 1911, his father a naval officer, his mother a feminist. He spent a couple of years at George Washington University in the early 1930s studying engineering, but soon turned to writing fiction instead. He went on to become a well-known writer of science fiction and fantasy novels.

Six months prior to the outbreak of World II, Hubbard joined the United States Navy. He held a variety of different assignments as a naval officer, but repeatedly fell out with his superiors. In his autobiographical writings, he has made a variety of colorful claims about his military career, none of which appear to be true.

In May of 1950 Hubbard published the book that would ever after be associated with his name, *Dianetics: The Modern Science of Mental Health*, in which he talks in great detail about the process of getting "Clear."

"Scientological techniques" can, he says, eliminate drug abuse and mental illness, crime and illiteracy, improve care for the aged, and conditions in prisons, and are therefore powerful agents for social change. Never one to understate his case, Hubbard called the creation of Dianetics the greatest milestone in the history of man.

Predictably, a system making such dramatic and sweeping claims for itself has elicited a great deal of criticism.

Hubbard had no luck interesting mainstream publishers and medical professionals in his manuscript, but it did interest the editor of the magazine *Astounding Science Fiction*, and it was there that the book received its first promotion. Whatever its scientific validity, Scientology continues to minister to a large army of true believers, as promises of "new beginnings" so often do.

FEBRUARY 19

1888

The Hotel del Coronado Opens in San Diego

ON THIS DAY IN CALIFORNIA HISTORY the Hotel del Coronado opened its doors on Coronado Island in San Diego. Its creators, Elisha Babcock and H. L. Story, wanted to build a seaside resort that would be "the talk of the Western world."

Ground was originally broken to build the hotel in March of 1887, and for opening day in 1888, thirty thousand trees were brought over from the San Diego mainland by barge, including the Australian star pine that graces the hotel's main lawn. In 1904 that pine became the first tree ever to be lighted with electric lights.

Originally, ferries were used to carry passengers from the San Diego mainland out to the Island, but in February of 1967 construction began on a bridge that would connect the Island with the mainland, a bridge that would be over two miles long and 200 feet high. When it was completed, the Coronado Bridge immediately became a landmark of the San Diego skyline.

Quite a number of celebrities have spent time at the Del through the years, including novelist Henry James, Oz book author L. Frank Baum, and 10 U. S. presidents, starting with Benjamin Harrison in 1891. The Duke and Duchess of Windsor stayed at the Del, too, as did Babe Ruth, Charles Lindbergh and Thomas Edison.

The hotel has long been a favorite of the Hollywood crowd (the first movie shot at the hotel was made here in 1901) and silver-screen luminaries from Charlie Chaplin to Humphrey Bogart to Brad Pitt have spent time here.

The hotel even has its resident ghost. On November 24, 1892, a rich young woman named Kate Morgan checked into the resort and never checked out again. Rumors of mysterious happenings connected to her "ghostly presence" here, including unexplained voices, the sound of strange footsteps, and televisions turning on and off by themselves, have been circulating ever since.

February 20

1915

Panama-Pacific Exposition Opens in San Francisco

ON THIS DAY IN CALIFORNIA HISTORY the Panama-Pacific Exposition opened in San Francisco. Its principal purpose was to celebrate the anticipated opening of the Panama Canal in July of 1915, but it marked another important new beginning, too.

And that was the beginning of the modern history of San Francisco itself, a history that officially began with the 1906 earthquake and fire that leveled the old 19th-century city made of wood, and made way for an entirely new city, one of stone and brick and altogether new architectural styles, to be built in its place.

Plans for the Exposition had first been laid out in 1904, but the events of 1906 put those plans on hold. In 1909 the plans were once again brought out, and in 1911, Congress officially blessed the idea. By the summer of 1913, construction had begun.

The Exposition was a celebration of the opening of the Panama Canal, a truly momentous event in the history of sea travel, since it allowed ships to pass from the Atlantic to the Pacific Ocean, and back again, without going all the way around South America.

But it was also a celebration of civilization's best material achievements circa 1915, not the least of which was the new city of San Francisco itself. From the ashes of 1906 San Francisco had rebuilt itself into a major metropolis by the time the Exposition began, and as much as anything displayed on the Exposition's grounds, provided convincing testimony to how extraordinary the achievements of man could be.

The Exposition was held on San Francisco's bayside marina between February 4 and December 4 of 1915, and over 19,000,000 people visited it during the 10 months it remained open. The city of San Diego held a similar, nearly-parallel celebration in 1915-1916, the Panama-*California* Exposition, and the buildings built for it still stand in Balboa Park today.

FEBRUARY 21

1874

Oakland Daily Evening Tribune Begins Publication

ON THIS DAY IN CALIFORNIA HISTORY the *Oakland Daily Evening Tribune*, a newspaper that would in time become the leading newspaper in the Oakland/East Bay area, began publication. The paper's founders were George Stanford and Benet A. Dewes. Two years later, a man named William H. Dargie bought the paper from them and continued publishing it until he died in 1911.

In 1915 the Knowland family of Oakland bought the paper. Several generations of Knowlands would be active in the management of the *Tribune*, including Joseph R. and William F. Knowland, and under them it would become an evening newspaper, which it would remain over the course of the sixty-two years the family owned it. It was only after they sold it in 1977 that it became a morning newspaper.

Joseph R. Knowland was a big supporter of research into California history and a man active in California and national politics. He served in the California state assembly from 1899 to 1903, the California state senate from 1903 to 1904, the U. S. House of Representatives from 1904 to 1913, and was a candidate for the U. S. Senate from California in 1914.

Like his father, William *F.* Knowland was active in California and national politics, too. He served in the California state assembly from 1933 to 1935, the California state senate from 1935 to 1939, the U. S. Senate from 1945 to 1959, and ran for governor of the state in 1958.

The *Oakland Tribune* was noted for its thorough coverage of regional and national news and, like the state's other major newspapers, it was long associated with and dominated by a single family. In the Valley, that family was the McClatchys, in San Francisco and Los Angeles, the Hearsts, de Youngs and Chandlers, in San Jose and Long Beach, the Ridders, and in San Diego, the Copleys.

57

FEBRUARY 22

1860

Organized Baseball Debuts in San Francisco

ON THIS DAY IN CALIFORNIA HISTORY organized baseball began being played in San Francisco for the first time.

The first two teams formed were the "Eagles" and the "Pacifics." More teams were formed in the years that followed, and during the 1880s, an organized league emerged (the California League) that included teams from San Francisco, San Jose, Sacramento, Oakland, Fresno and Los Angeles.

In the 1880s baseball was big stuff in San Francisco, so big that a young California newspaper editor named William Randolph Hearst decided to feature it on the front page of his newspaper. This was also the paper that first published the poem "Casey at the Bat," written by Hearst's Harvard friend, Ernest Thayer (June 1888).

The successor to the California League was the Pacific Coast League, which remained active from 1903 until 1958. It included teams from the original California League, as well as teams from Portland and Seattle. The most famous of these were the San Francisco Seals, the Sacramento Solons, the Oakland Oaks, the Hollywood Stars, and the Los Angeles Angels.

In 1958 the Pacific Coast League was replaced by major league baseball in California. The Giants went to San Francisco, the Dodgers to Los Angeles, and teams were later formed in Oakland, Anaheim, and San Diego, too.

A variety of baseball firsts can trace their roots to California. It was a California transplant named Jackie Robinson who broke the color barrier in major league baseball. Ted Williams, normally associated with Boston and the last player to hit .400 or above in a regular season was a Californian (born and raised in San Diego). Joe DiMaggio, another of baseball's legendary players, was born in the East Bay, but raised, like his brothers Vince and Dom, also major leaguers, in San Francisco.

FEBRUARY 23

1883

Director Victor Fleming Born in Pasadena

ON THIS DAY IN CALIFORNIA HISTORY legendary Hollywood film director Victor Fleming was born in Pasadena. Pasadena had not even been officially incorporated as a city yet, but Hollywood, the place where he would have his greatest career triumphs, was just 15 minutes away.

Victor Fleming directed his first film, *When the Clouds Roll By* in 1919 and his last one, *Joan of Arc*, in 1948, but it was the films he made in between these two that would make his reputation, films like *The Virginian*, (1929), *Treasure Island* (1934), *Captains Courageous* (1937), *The Wizard of Oz* (1939) and *Gone with the Wind* (1939), all masterpieces of the moviemaker's art.

Fleming began his march to stardom in 1910 as an assistant cameraman at the American Film Company. He was just 21. In 1915 he was hired as the director of photography at Triangle Pictures and during World War I served with the "photographic unit" of the United States Army. He was the cameraman for Hollywood producer Walter Wanger at the Versailles Peace Conference in 1919.

Fleming won an Oscar for his work on *The Wizard of Oz*, which, ever since its release in 1939, continues to run neck and neck in popularity with his other 1939 masterpiece, *Gone with the Wind*. *The Wizard of Oz* was an "event" when it was first shown on television in 1956, and has become one of the most beloved and most shown films of all time.

The popularity of Fleming's films has endured. *Gone with the Wind* ranks fourth on the American Film Institute's list of "the 100 greatest American movies of all time" and *The Wizard of Oz* ranks sixth. But despite his towering achievements on the silver screen, Fleming is largely a forgotten man. It would be hard to find a person today who didn't recognize the names of the films he made, but not one in a thousand could tell you his name.

FEBRUARY 24

1857

First Meeting of the Los Angeles Vineyard Society

ON THIS DAY IN CALIFORNIA HISTORY the first recorded meeting of the Los Angeles Vineyard Society took place in San Francisco. The main order of business was to choose a tract of land on which the Society's members could plant vineyards.

A surveyor named George Hansen suggested that he had found the ideal place to launch the Society's new venture: a tract of land in Southern California about 26 miles southeast of Los Angeles, and today occupied by the city of Anaheim.

The group knew next to nothing about growing grapes or making wine, but they had a big dream and were determined to make a go of it, so they dutifully packed up and headed south. When they got there, there were only two American communities in the entire area—one at El Monte and one at San Bernardino.

During the 1850s wine-grape growers all over California caught "wine fever" and saw planting vineyards as the way to get rich. In 1855 one source listed the number of vines growing in California as 324,234; in 1857 the number of vines had grown to 2,000,000; in 1858, to 4,000,000; and in 1859, to 6,500,000 vines.

The Anaheim group was a big part of this growth. They divided the plot of ground they acquired into fifty twenty-acre plots and planted each plot with eight to ten thousand grapevines. By 1858 they had 500,000 vines growing and were preparing to plant many thousands more. By 1860 they had become a leader in grape and wine production, a position they would maintain for another twenty-eight years.

In 1888, however, a plant disease attacked the many thousands of vines then growing at Anaheim and killed them all in the space of a year. Suddenly, the vast vineyards of Anaheim were gone, and orange and walnut trees planted in their place. Like the vines, the Los Angeles Vineyard Society disappeared into history.

FEBRUARY 25

1904

Nutritionist Adelle Davis Born

ON THIS DAY IN CALIFORNIA HISTORY nutritionist Adelle Davis was born. She was not a native Californian (she had been born in Indiana), but it was here that she would spend most of her life, and here that she would make her mark.

Davis studied dietetics and nutrition at the University of California, Berkeley, and got a masters degree in biochemistry from the University of Southern California. She spent her life promoting healthy eating, and laid out her often controversial ideas on nutrition in four best-selling books: *Let's Cook It Right* (1947), *Let's Have Healthy Children* (1951), *Let's Eat Right to Keep Fit* (1954), and *Let's Get Well* (1965).

The fundamental premise of Davis's advice was that to eat "right," you had to eat a "natural" diet, one in which the nutritional value of your food had not been "processed" out, and in which nutritional supplements—vitamins, minerals and "health foods"—had been brought in.

"Repeatedly we are told that the 'gullible public' annually 'wastes' 400 million dollars on 'nutrition nonsense,'" she said. They buy "stone-ground flours, whole-grain breads and cereals, pressed oils, unhydrogenated nut butters, mineral and vitamin supplements, and fresh fruits and vegetables grown without chemical fertilizers and insecticides." But it was those who didn't consume these things who were the real fools, Davis insisted.

She didn't stop there, either. She linked the rise and fall of entire civilizations to their dietary habits, seeing in France's fall to Germany during World War II a kind of dietary Armageddon, the fall of a people nurtured on white bread and wine to a people nurtured on dark bread and beer. She saw in mid-20th-century America's dietary habits a situation equally calamitous, one trending, in her view, to the dietary equivalent of "the fall of Rome."

61

FEBRUARY 26

1933

Groundbreaking Ceremony for the Golden Gate Bridge

ON THIS DAY IN CALIFORNIA HISTORY a ceremony to celebrate the start of work on the Golden Gate Bridge was held at Crissy Field in San Francisco, even though construction on the bridge had actually begun the month before.

Some said bridging "the Golden Gate" would bottle up San Francisco's celebrated harbor and compromise the nation's maritime security. Some said building it would bankrupt the six Bay Area counties funding the construction. Some said a suspension bridge as long as the one needed (over a mile) was an engineering impossibility. None of these things would turn out to be true, but the fear that they might be was strong.

The idea of bridging San Francisco Bay raised almost as many eyebrows. Bridging it would require a bridge *four-and-a-half miles long* and piers that sometimes stretched down more than two hundred feet below the Bay's surface. But these challenges would be overcome, too, and by the end of the 1930s, the San Francisco Peninsula would be linked by bridge to Marin and the East Bay.

When it was done, the Golden Gate Bridge stretched for 1.22 miles, had a central span of 4,200 feet (the distance between its two towers), and "towers" that were 746 feet high (191 feet taller than the Washington Monument).

The bridge was officially opened on May 28, 1937. Population and business booms in Marin quickly followed and have shown little sign of slowing since.

The bridge was built under the direction and plans of engineer Joseph B. Strauss and it was the crowning achievement of what had already been a very distinguished career. There is a dark side to this world-famous bridge's history, however. Over 1,300 people have jumped to their deaths from it, more than from any other structure in the world.

FEBRUARY 27

1902

John Steinbeck Born in Salinas

ON THIS DAY IN CALIFORNIA HISTORY novelist John Steinbeck was born in Salinas, the county seat of Monterey County.

His father was in county government, his mother a teacher. He entered Stanford University in 1919 and attended until 1925, but ultimately dropped out and moved to New York City, where he hoped to find a publisher for his work. He found no takers, however, and decided to return to California.

Steinbeck married in 1930. His wife was a Marxist and her politics clearly influenced his own political beliefs, which became increasingly evident in his writing, giving it much of its depth of feeling about the struggles of disadvantaged people. These portrayals of the ugly side of capitalism predictably made him few friends among the rich and powerful.

In California Steinbeck found his voice writing novels about the people that the Dust Bowl had driven out West. The best of them depict people with rural backgrounds trying to get a foothold in their newly-adopted home. Two of them in particular, *Of Mice and Men* (1937) and *The Grapes of Wrath* (1939), are frequently hailed as modern-day masterpieces.

Most of Steinbeck's books are set in the Salinas Valley, and areas nearby, a region commonly referred to as "Steinbeck country." To get his "message" across, he frequently lapsed into sermonizing —not the way good novelists tell their tales—and for that he has often been criticized.

But that said, he was undeniably one of the most important American novelists of the 20th century, an importance officially acknowledged by the powers that be when he was awarded the Nobel Prize for literature in 1962. He remains an enduring and vivid voice for a difficult time in American history, and for that reason alone his work deserves to live on.

FEBRUARY 28

1960

End of the Eighth Winter Olympics

ON THIS DAY IN CALIFORNIA HISTORY the Eighth Winter Olympic Games came to a close in Squaw Valley, California. The process that had led to the Valley's selection for the games had begun over 10 years earlier when a man named Alexander Cushing moved there to develop it into the finest ski resort in the West.

He had come with the money to get the job done, too. He poured $400,000 into a new ski lodge, built a parking lot for 1,000 cars and laid a two-and-a-half-mile paved road through the wilderness. He also built a giant new chair lift—the world's largest—that could transport skiers to the top of Squaw Peak at the rate of 600 an hour. In the spring of 1949 Squaw Valley was still pristine, "undeveloped"; by fall, that look was gone.

The staging of the Eighth Winter Olympics near Lake Tahoe gave area development an enormous boost and made winter sports more popular in the United States than they had ever been before. Virtually overnight, Squaw Valley was transformed into a place with wide highways, new restaurants, ski lodges, and building after building shaped by the latest trends in architecture.

Women's speed-skating made its debut at these games, as did the biathlon, but it was the U. S. hockey team that stole the show. The lightly-regarded American team beat both Canada and the Soviet Union and got themselves into a tie-breaker for the gold medal. They needed to beat Czechoslovakia to win the gold outright, and trailing 4-3 at the end of the second period, help came from a very unlikely quarter.

During half time, Soviet team captain Nikolai Sologubov visited the American team's locker room and suggested that they inhale concentrated oxygen to give them more energy when they returned to the rink. The Americans took the Russian's advice and went on to score six goals in the third period to win the gold.

FEBRUARY 29

1939

Hattie McDaniel Wins an Academy Award

ON THIS DAY IN CALIFORNIA HISTORY actress Hattie McDaniel became the first African-American to win an Academy Award—for her portrayal of the unforgettable character, "Mammy," in the 1939 film masterpiece, *Gone with the Wind.*

She had started performing in 1915, as a vocalist for an itinerant band, and in time, became the first African-American singer to sing on network radio in the United States. When things were slow, she took work as a cook or "domestic" to make ends meet.

In 1931 Hattie decided to take her performance career in a new direction and went out West to try her luck with the movies.

She initially got work as an "extra," as black female actresses then typically did, and in 1932, made her first appearance on the big screen. Though she could hardly have known it at the time, it was her work as a "domestic" that would turn out to be her most important training for her movie career, for it was that work that readied her for the role of "Mammy," the role for which she would ever after be remembered.

In the movie, playing opposite Clark Gable and Vivien Leigh, Hattie found an opportunity to really shine on the big screen. Any number of black actresses no doubt could have played a "southern maid," but not the way Hattie McDaniel played one, and she won an Academy Award for her efforts. As she later said herself, "Why should I complain about making $7,000 a week playing a maid? If I didn't, I'd be making $7 a week being one."

Hattie McDaniel died at age fifty-seven at the Motion Picture House in Woodland Hills. To honor her contributions to the singing and performing arts, she was awarded two stars on the Hollywood Walk of Fame: one for her contributions to radio (at 6933 Hollywood Boulevard) and one for her contributions to motion pictures (at 1719 Vine Street).

This Day

in

March

MARCH 1

1909

"Lucky" Baldwin's Luck Runs Out

ON THIS DAY IN CALIFORNIA HISTORY Elias J. ("Lucky") Baldwin died in Los Angeles. He had been born in Ohio in 1828 and started out working in the grocery, hotel and saloon businesses.

Like everyone else in mid-19th-century America, Baldwin had heard that fortunes were being made in the California gold fields, but he decided that the big money for him would come, not from panning for gold, but from selling things to those who did. He arrived in San Francisco in 1853.

In San Francisco Baldwin set himself up in business and started dabbling in real estate, too, and it wasn't long before he was making his way up the city's economic ladder. He also made a lot of money from the silver mines that were brought in in western Nevada in the late 1850s.

But it was something that would happen to him in 1867 that would be the real making of his fortune—and of his legend for being "lucky." That year, prior to embarking on an around-the-world trip, he left very explicit instructions with his stockbroker in San Francisco to sell his silver-mining stocks during his absence. But the broker couldn't do it, because Baldwin forgot to leave him the key to the safe where the stock certificates were kept.

And a good thing, too. During Baldwin's absence, the stock's value shot up into the millions, far more than the price for which he had expected to sell it for, and the delay made him considerably richer than he already was.

In 1875 Baldwin moved to Southern California and bought Rancho Santa Anita in the San Gabriel Valley where he raised thoroughbred horses and built a track for them to run on (today's Santa Anita Racetrack). But no winning streak runs forever and Baldwin's was no different. He *lost* most of his money during these years, though he never stopped trying to hit it big one last time.

MARCH 2

1982

Science Fiction Writer Philip K. Dick Dies

ON THIS DAY IN CALIFORNIA HISTORY science fiction writer Philip K. Dick died in Santa Ana, at the age of 53. He had been born in Chicago in 1928, but had spent most of his life out West.

Shortly after the death of his twin sister, Jane, in January of 1929, Dick's family moved to California, where he attended high school and the University of California at Berkeley, briefly, too. He sold his first story in 1952, and from that time forward, he wrote, more or less, full-time.

Dick sold his first novel in 1955 and like many people with liberal leanings was associated with the pre-1960s counterculture of California, as well as the Communist Party. In 1963 he won the Hugo Award, science fiction's highest honor, for his book *The Man in the High Castle*.

Throughout his novels, Dick explored the nature of reality and what it meant to be human, and his books are principally populated by common people in the process of discovering that those closest to them are not who they think they are.

In 1968 Dick's *Do Androids Dream of Electric Sheep?* (made into the movie, *Blade Runner*) was published. A dark vision of California life "just after the final war," this book presents a world whose remaining citizens are just barely alive, slowly suffocating amidst the corroding remains of what had once been a high-point example of American life.

In Dick's dark vision of the American future the quality of technology is high, but the quality of human life itself is quite low. As was the quality of Dick's own life throughout his career. Hailed as a genius by devotees of science fiction, he had a very limited following during his lifetime, and always had a hard time getting by. It was only after his death that significant public recognition came his way.

MARCH 3

1851

Act Passed to Settle Land Claims

ON THIS DAY IN CALIFORNIA HISTORY Congress passed an act designed to settle land ownership claims in California. The area had not been a state six months yet, but deciding who owned what needed to be resolved as soon as possible.

It was a complicated matter. To begin with, the holdings of many citizens had been given to them by Spain or Mexico and the exact boundaries of each parcel were not easy to establish.

The first grants were made in 1784 to three retired Spanish soldiers: "Rancho San Pedro," which went to Juan José Dominguez (43,000 acres), "Rancho los Nietos," to Manuel Nieto ("all the land between the San Gabriel and Santa Ana Rivers, and from the mountains to the sea"), and "Rancho San Rafael," to José Maria Verdugo (36,000 acres in what is today East Los Angeles).

Title, however, remained with the crown. It was not until California became a *Mexican* territory that outright grants of land were made and not until after California's missions were secularized in 1834 that there were a truly significant number of them. Only fifty grants were made before 1834, but between 1834 and 1848, 600 grants were made.

The problem for Mexican landowners when the Americans took over was that the *evidence* of title to much of this property was difficult to establish. Not only were Mexican standards of title evidence looser than those in the United States, the evidence on the California grants was loose even by Mexican standards.

This led to a long period of haggling over who owned what and the loss of a significant amount of the land that had been granted to Spanish and Mexican citizens during the pre-Conquest period to ambitious Americans pressing their claims in American courts. Some cases dragged on for decades and the average time required to establish clear title was *17 years*.

MARCH 4

1887

George Hearst Gives the *Examiner* to his Son

ON THIS DAY IN CALIFORNIA HISTORY high roller George Hearst made a gift of the *San Francisco Examiner* to his son, William Randolph Hearst.

Like tens of thousands of others, the elder Hearst had come out West to make a fortune in the Gold Rush, but things didn't work out that way. His big opportunity came years later, mining for silver in Nevada, and it was silver that made him rich.

Hearst invested his money in a variety of enterprises, one of which was the *San Francisco Examiner*. In the hands of his son, it became the seed from which a media empire would grow, one that included the *New York Daily Journal*, the *Boston American*, the *Chicago Examiner* and *Harper's Bazaar*.

The younger Hearst is best remembered today as the man who made sensationalist journalism into big business, and it was that approach to the "news"—focusing on crime, gore, pseudoscience and just about anything that would move papers off the newsstand—that made him into a very rich man.

One of the things Hearst did with all that money was build a huge and imposing residence for himself on the central California coast, one known around the world as "Hearst's Castle."

Perched on a hillside in the Santa Lucia Mountains, 30 miles northwest of Morro Bay, the Castle was built over the course of 28 years. It has 38 bedrooms, 31 bathrooms, 14 sitting rooms, two libraries, a dining hall, an assembly hall, a billiard room, a movie theater, 3 guesthouses and 2 pools.

Legendary Irish dramatist George Bernard Shaw, himself once a guest at the Castle, had this to say about the place: "This is probably the way God would have done it if He had had the money." It is a summing-up of this monument to success and *ex*cess that will most likely never be improved upon.

MARCH 5

1870

Novelist Frank Norris Born

ON THIS DAY IN CALIFORNIA HISTORY novelist Frank Norris was born in Chicago. He would move to San Francisco with his parents in 1884 and it was there that he would make his mark.

Norris wrote during the late 19th and early 20th century and is principally remembered for three novels: *McTeague* (1899), *The Octopus* (1901), and *The Pit* (1903). He was also the nation's first important *naturalist* writer.

Like many writers who came of age when he did, Norris was profoundly influenced by Darwin. He was preoccupied with the idea that there was a basic struggle in life between the forces of civilization and darker forces deep within the human mind and this struggle emerges again and again in his fiction.

He also sympathized with the basic principle underlying socialist thought: sharing the wealth rather than letting the strong take all, a sympathy which influenced several writers who came after him, including Upton Sinclair, author of *The Jungle* (1906) and one-time candidate for governor of California.

Norris spent two years studying painting in Paris, and between 1890 and 1894, was a student at Berkeley, though he did not graduate with a degree.

He worked as a news correspondent in South Africa from 1895-1896, as editorial assistant for the *San Francisco Wave* from 1896 to 1897, and as a war correspondent for *McClure's Magazine* in Cuba in 1898. In 1899 he joined the publishing firm of Doubleday & Page in New York City.

In 1902, while living in New York City, Norris had an appendix attack and was operated on. Unfortunately, there were complications and he developed a condition known as peritonitis, an inflammation of the membrane that lines the abdomen, from which he later died. He was just 32.

March 6

Rate War between Southern Pacific and Santa Fe

ON THIS DAY IN CALIFORNIA HISTORY a rate war broke out between the Southern Pacific and the Santa Fe Railroads for travel from the Midwest to Los Angeles, dropping the cost of making the trip from the $125.00/passenger it had been to just *$1.00*/passenger.

The rate fell first to $12.00, then to $8.00, then to $6.00, then to $4.00, and finally, at noon on March 6, 1887, to $1.00/passenger. The $1.00 rate lasted just one day, but it was a sign that California—and the nation's railroads—were deadly serious about luring newcomers to this exciting new Shangri-la out West.

The nation's first transcontinental railroad had been completed in 1869, and for the first time in its history, California was easy to get to. This, coupled with the appearance of some vividly-written books about the state (Charles Nordhoff's, in particular) inspired thousands who might have confined their "California dreamin'" to a good read about the Golden State to take a train west and see California first-hand. Many who came decided to stay and spread the word about it in their letters back home.

With prices so low, many who might otherwise have stayed home decided to pack their bags and take a train ride to this amazing new place out West. Newcomers praised the area's climate, its picturesque landscape, and its "easy" way of life; in countless letters "back home," they commented on its suitability as a place for new business enterprise, too.

The railroads were quick to add their voices to the chorus of praise and distributed pamphlets promoting California's charms at railway stations all over the United States. The strategy worked like a charm, drawing Americans coast to coast to the nation's far western edge. In 1887 the Southern Pacific brought 120,000 people to Los Angeles and the Santa Fe unloaded three to four trains a day there.

MARCH 7

1849

Famed Horticulturalist Luther Burbank Born

ON THIS DAY IN CALIFORNIA HISTORY famed horticulturalist Luther Burbank was born in Lancaster, Massachusetts, just six weeks after James Marshall first discovered gold in the American River. He moved to Santa Rosa in 1875 and it was there that he would remain for the rest of his life.

Burbank bought a 17-acre plot of land in Santa Rosa, and inspired by Darwin's "The Variation of Animals and Plants under Domestication," conducted cross-breeding experiments on plants for fifty years. In fact, were it not for the efforts of this one man, it's unlikely that the nation's rich harvest of fruits, vegetables and flowers would ever have become as rich as it has.

Burbank introduced more than 800 new varieties of plants, including more than 250 new varieties of fruit and 90 new vegetables, and hundreds of ornamental flowers.

Among his creations were the "Shasta lily," the "Santa Rosa" plum, the "Flaming Gold" nectarine, and the "Burbank potato," once the dominant variety found on American dinner tables. Thanks in large part to Burbank, California became the nation's principal producer of almonds, artichokes, dates, olives, and walnuts, and the producer of a third of all the fruit consumed in the land.

Burbank described the results of all of this experimenting in a series of catalogues he published between 1893 and 1901 (*New Creations*) and in several books that made him a towering figure in the world of plant science. His work was so extraordinary one writer called him "a one-man Renaissance in horticulture."

Burbank's birthday is celebrated as "Arbor Day" in California and certainly no one thought more highly of California as a place to cultivate plants than he did: "I firmly believe, from what I have seen, that this is the chosen spot of all this earth as far as Nature is concerned."

MARCH 8

1971

Comedian Harold Lloyd Dies

ON THIS DAY IN CALIFORNIA HISTORY silent-movie comedian Harold Lloyd died at his home in Beverly Hills. He was 77.

During the course of a career that stretched from 1912 to 1947, Lloyd made nearly 200 films. He is best remembered today for the character he developed who wore horn-rimmed glasses and was an ambitious and resourceful go-getter. That character provided a common thread throughout the films he made, including *Grandma's Boy* (1922), *Safety Last* and *Why Worry?* (1923).

Lloyd was one of the three great film comedians of the silent era—the other two being Charlie Chaplin and Buster Keaton—and it was in *his* films that such things as thrilling chase scenes and daredevil physical feats (many of which he did himself) really came into their own.

In 1924 Lloyd began producing his own films and it was during this period that much of his best work was done: *Girl Shy* (1924), *The Freshman* (1925), *The Kid Brother* (1927), and *Speedy* (1928), the last silent movie he made. These were all extremely successful films and ones that made Lloyd a very rich man.

Lloyd made some films during the "sound era," including *Movie Crazy* (1932) and *Milky Way* (1936), but his films had fallen out of tune with the times and audiences in the 1930s didn't respond to him as enthusiastically as previous ones had. He stopped making movies and instead turned his energies to charity work—and to the work of tending his Beverly Hills estate.

And that estate, "Green Acres," was quite a showplace for the times. The main house had 44 rooms, 26 bathrooms, 12 fountains, kennel facilities for 77 dogs, and quarters for 33 servants. There was an Olympic-sized swimming pool, a lighted tennis court, a lake to canoe on, and an indoor handball court. Soon other high-profile movie people began to erect estates nearby.

76

MARCH 9

1959

The First "Barbie Dolls" Debut

ON THIS DAY IN CALIFORNIA HISTORY the first generation of Barbie dolls went on sale.

California companies have always been big contributors to the American toy chest, and on this day in 1959, Mattel, Inc., made one of the biggest contributions to that chest that any American toy company would ever make. For it was on that day that Mattel debuted "Barbie," a doll unlike any doll before it—a "grown" woman, with permanent makeup, fancy clothes, and a physically impossible figure.

The doll's creator, Ruth Handler, thought the doll would be a hit with little girls right away, but top management at Mattel did not at first agree. The doll was such a departure from what dolls had been in the past, they feared it might not find a market.

However, by the time "Barbie" turned 31 in 1990, over 500 million of the dolls had been sold, which was twice the nation's total population at the time.

In fact, Barbie would go on to be not just Mattel's best-selling doll, but the best-selling doll in history. Every second of every day, two Barbies are sold somewhere in the world, and placed head to toe, all the dolls sold since 1959 (including her plastic friends) would encircle the earth more than seven times.

Over the years, Barbie's maker has created a neighborhood full of plastic friends for her, too—friends like "Ken" and "Skipper" and "Scooter" and "Tutti." Mattel makes a Barbie to suit just about every taste and ethnic identity imaginable—black Barbies, brown Barbies, and Asian Barbies, too.

Barbie's clothes have continued to change with the times. When Bob Mackie gowns were all the rage in the '70s, Barbie wore Mackie gowns. When Harley-Davidson leathers were the thing to wear, Barbie donned them, too.

MARCH 10

1933

Big Earthquake Hits Long Beach

ON THIS DAY IN CALIFORNIA HISTORY an earthquake struck the city of Long Beach, rocking that city to its foundations and causing $50,000,000 in damage.

The shaking started at 5:54 p.m. Pacific Standard Time and was measured at 6.3 on the Richter scale. The epicenter turned out to be just offshore between Huntington and Newport Beaches, on the Newport-Inglewood fault line which runs parallel to the California coastline.

The shaking was extremely violent and aftershocks persisted for *three years* after the initial jolt. Six of these additional tremors were in excess of 5.0 magnitude and struck within twenty-four hours of the first big jolt.

Buildings that had been properly reinforced during their original construction faired well during the shaking; those that hadn't been, didn't. Buildings built of unreinforced masonry—most of the schools then standing in Long Beach—failed badly. Luckily, the quake hit when most kids were not in school or the final death toll of 120 would have been much higher.

Most of the buildings that crashed to the ground that March day in 1933 had "irregular" shapes, were built of brick, and weren't designed to resist any sudden shaking movements. But it wasn't just design flaws that caused these buildings to collapse. They hadn't been built too well to begin with.

So many school buildings failed during the 1933 Long Beach earthquake, legislation was passed mandating earthquake-resistant design for elementary, secondary, and community college school buildings throughout the state. This legislation also required that all public school plans and specifications be reviewed and approved by the state prior to construction. No school built in compliance with these directives has ever failed.

MARCH 11

1889

Orange County Carved Out of L. A. County

ON THIS DAY IN CALIFORNIA HISTORY Orange County was carved from what was then "southern Los Angeles County." Back then "Los Angeles County" included not only what is today Los Angeles and Orange counties, but also parts of modern-day Ventura, Kern, San Bernardino and San Diego counties as well.

The county's oldest city is Anaheim, which sits about twenty-six miles southeast of downtown Los Angeles. Just to the north of Anaheim is the city of Fullerton, known for its affluence and the high concentration of doctors who live there; about seven miles to the south of Anaheim sits Santa Ana, the county seat. A little to the southeast of Santa Ana the master-planned late-20th-century city of Irvine can be found.

But what makes Orange County part of the mental furniture of the average modern American has nothing to do with these inland communities. It has do with the cities that line the Orange County coast.

Beginning with Seal Beach on the north end and stretching down to San Clemente on the south, the Orange Coast is where all the communities that typically make Orange County of interest to people who don't live there are—Seal Beach, Huntington Beach, Newport Beach, Corona del Mar, Laguna Beach, Dana Point and San Clemente. Here the nation's fantasies about living well at the beach are routinely brought to life.

Orange County has grown by leaps and bounds since its original creation in the late 19th century. In 1900 a mere 19,696 people lived here, by 1920 that figure had only increased to 61,375, and by 1940 the county's population stood at 130,760. But by 1960, it had leaped to 703,925, and by 1980, to 1,932,709. In 2006 it was estimated to have a population of over 3,000,000 people (3,002,048), with more coming in every day.

MARCH 12

1928

St. Francis Dam Bursts

ON THIS DAY IN CALIFORNIA HISTORY the St. Francis Dam in northern Los Angeles County's Santa Clarita Valley burst, creating the second worst disaster in the state's history. It had been designed by L. A.'s legendary city engineer, William Mulholland, and had apparently been faulty from the start.

The dam began to give way just prior to midnight on this day in 1928, in the remote San Francisquito Canyon area of far northern Los Angeles County. It was just two years old, and had only recently been filled to capacity, but there was already evidence it wasn't sound. Serious leaks had appeared even before it was full.

The floodwaters raced through San Francisquito Canyon and all the way to the Pacific, some 54 miles away. They destroyed the towns of Castaic Junction, Piru, Fillmore, Santa Paula and Saticoy, and before they had spent themselves, killed over 600 men, women and children. (The initial wall of water was 140 feet high.)

Reporters and photographers were quickly on the scene and their papers ran pictures of almost unbelievable devastation, long lists of the dead, and stories of miraculous survival.

One such story was that of Frank Maier and his wife and three children who lived on a ranch in the area. As the waters swirled in around the home in which they had been living, the Maiers apparently made their way to the attic. Once there, Frank shot a hole through the roof, through which he passed his wife and two of his children.

But as he was about to follow them with his third child, the house began to move. A nearby stand of sycamore trees caught it, however, and rocked it from side to side without turning it over or letting it be carried away. The house floated, like a leaky boat, then dropped, essentially intact, back to the ground. Remarkably, it never had more than eighteen inches of water in it.

MARCH 13

1897

San Diego State University Founded

ON THIS DAY IN CALIFORNIA HISTORY San Diego State University was founded.

It started out as the "San Diego Normal School" and its mission was to train elementary school teachers. Initially, there were seven faculty members and ninety-one students and classes were held in rooms above a downtown drugstore. Later a 17-acre campus was constructed on Park Boulevard.

In the beginning, the range of classes offered at the school was very limited, but that began to change under the leadership of Samuel T. Black, who had been California's state superintendent of public education.

From 1910 to 1935 Black's successor, Edward L. Hardy, oversaw the development of the school. In 1921 it was renamed "San Diego State Teachers College" and San Diego Junior College became a branch of the school. This lasted until 1946.

By the 1920s "San Diego State" had grown so much that it needed larger facilities and a campaign was launched to build a new campus on the eastern border of the city. In early 1931 those facilities were ready to be occupied.

In 1935 "San Diego State Teachers College" became "San Diego *State* College" and Walter R. Hepner became the college's president. He was succeeded by Malcolm A. Love in 1952, who served until 1971, by which time the university's enrollment had swollen to over 25,000.

In 1960 San Diego State became part of a chain of California colleges referred to as the California State College "system," which in 1972 became known as the California State *University* system. The institution's name was also changed from San Diego State University to *California* State University, but the decision was so unpopular, it was promptly changed back.

MARCH 14

1896

Sutro Baths Open

ON THIS DAY IN CALIFORNIA HISTORY 7,000 people gathered at San Francisco's Ocean Beach to celebrate the official opening of the Sutro Baths, an extravagant public bathhouse developed by the fabulously wealthy one-time mayor of the city, Adolph Sutro.

Fifteen years earlier Sutro had bought most of the western headlands of the San Francisco peninsula and built his home there and it was here that he intended to build his baths.

The original complex covered over three acres. It included a fresh water tank, five saltwater tanks, each set at different temperatures, and a saltwater tank left at ocean temperature. The pools were enclosed in glass, held 1,685,000 gallons of seawater, and could be filled or emptied in an hour by the high or low tides. And there were "toys," too—slides, springboards, trapezes to swing from, and a high dive that could accommodate up to 1,600 divers at a time.

If you wanted to stay dry, there were natural history exhibits, painting and sculpture galleries, displays of artifacts from around the world, and three restaurants that could seat up to 1,000 people at a time.

The Sutro Baths could handle up to 25,000 people in a day and the cost of admission was just ten cents (twenty-five, if you wanted to swim). Getting out to the far western shores of the San Francisco peninsula was no problem, either. For just five cents, San Franciscans could take one of three railroads that connected the Bay side to the Pacific Ocean side of the city.

The Baths endured from their opening in 1896 until 1937, when one of Sutro's grandsons converted them into an ice-skating rink. Revenues from the rink didn't support the facility, however, and in 1964, the property was sold to developers who wanted to put up high-rise apartments in its place. In 1966 a fire demolished the Baths and their ruins are what remain at the site today.

MARCH 15

1991

Four Officers Charged in Rodney King Beating

ON THIS DAY IN CALIFORNIA HISTORY four members of the Los Angeles Police Department were charged with felony assault in the beating of motorist Rodney King.

On March 3, 1991, Mr. King was pulled over by police for driving recklessly through the Lake View Terrace neighborhood of northeast Los Angeles. When the police ordered him out of his car, King initially refused to comply, and when he did get out of the car, he charged the officers, knocking a couple of them to the ground. That's when the trouble began.

The police tried twice to subdue King with a Taser gun, but that didn't work, so they switched to clubbing him with nightsticks. He was kicked or clubbed some fifty-six times. In addition to the three officers who were personally involved in this incident, twenty-four others allegedly stood by and watched it, some helping to hold King down.

The officers' defense team got their trial moved from Los Angeles County, where many African-Americans live, to the suburban Simi Valley area of Ventura County, where a large number of police officers live.

On April 29, 1992 three of the four indicted officers were acquitted by a jury composed of ten whites, one Hispanic, and one Asian, and the verdict set off rioting in Los Angeles, which resulted in hundreds of buildings being severely damaged or destroyed and dozens of people being killed.

On May 1 President George Bush announced that the officers should at least be charged with having violated King's civil rights. Charges were filed, a trial held, and on August 4, 1993, officers Stacey Koon and Laurence Powell were sentenced to thirty months in prison. The other two officers were acquitted and no additional rioting occurred.

MARCH 16

1901

Governor Gage Signs California Redwood Park Bill

ON THIS DAY IN CALIFORNIA HISTORY Governor Henry T. Gage signed the "California Redwood Park Bill."

Redwood trees are a big deal in California, of course. They are the largest living things on the planet and the most spectacular stands still in existence all are found in California. Governor Gage's action stopped loggers in their tracks who were, at the time, busy leveling the last remaining stands of redwoods.

In the 1880s a man named Ralph Sidney Smith, editor of the *Redwood City Times and Gazette*, used his paper's pages to advise his readers that California's unique redwood forests needed to be preserved. It was a small start in a small town, but it got the ball rolling, and it was thinking like Smith's that ultimately resulted in the creation of California's first redwood state park.

A number of different groups lent their support to this effort to save the redwoods. Governor Gage's bill authorized the use of state funds to purchase a property in Santa Cruz County that was literally covered with redwoods. The year after that the California Redwood Park Commission acquired 2,500 acres in an area today known as "Big Basin Redwoods State Park." These acts sent clear signals that a serious effort to save the redwoods had begun.

The "Native Sons and Daughters of the Golden West" were also instrumental in the effort to get California's redwoods set aside as state and national parkland, and in the 1920s, the "Save the Redwoods League" worked hard to protect these trees, too.

In 1968 the Redwood National Forest, a national park located on California's far northern coast between Eureka and Crescent City, was established, comprising 112,430 acres in all. It included forty-five percent of all the "old-growth" Coast Redwood trees still in existence, as well as the world's tallest Coast Redwood, a tree almost 368 feet high.

MARCH 17

1948

"Hells Angels" Motorcycle Club Formed

ON THIS DAY IN CALIFORNIA HISTORY the Hells Angels motorcycle club was formed in the predominantly blue-collar Southern California city of Fontana. The original "Angels" were ex-World War II paratroopers, an elite group trained to drop behind enemy lines and kill as many enemy combatants as possible.

In addition to riding heavily-modified Harleys and proudly displaying "their colors," the Angels are also notorious for busying themselves in less savory ways.

It has been estimated that the Hells Angels take in $1 billion a year worldwide from drug trafficking, prostitution, and money laundering. They have long been associated with most forms of capital crime in the United States, too. Over the course of the past 50 years they have grown to include a worldwide membership now estimated to be in the thousands.

Though the Angels publicly profess to be "just a motorcycle club" and often claim that their membership consists mostly of law-abiding citizens who have been misrepresented by the media, there is ample evidence that that's not the case. They even refer to themselves as "1%-ers," to acknowledge the fact.

The name was originally inspired by a phrase used by the American Motorcycle Association, which once claimed that 99% of motorcycle riders were law-abiding citizens. Leaving, of course, the 1% who weren't.

Perhaps the most notorious event in Hells Angels history involved the 1969 Rolling Stones concert at the Altamont Speedway in northern California. The Angels had been hired to provide security for the Stones and a shoving match erupted near the stage during the course of one of the songs they were playing that resulted in the death of a fan named Meredith Hunter. The Angel who killed the fan, Alan Passaro, was later acquitted.

MARCH 18

Nation's First Wildlife Preserve Established

ON THIS DAY IN CALIFORNIA HISTORY legislation was passed in the California state legislature paving the way to establish the first wildlife preserve in the United States at Lake Merritt in Oakland. In the years to come citizens coast to coast would establish similar preserves to keep the natural world around them as pristine as possible, too.

The lake was not always a lake. Originally it was simply an arm of San Francisco Bay, but in 1869 a man named Dr. Samuel Merritt decided to dam it up. The result was "Lake Merritt," which remains to this day the largest urban saltwater lake in the nation.

The legislation put in place by the California legislature specified the terms by which fish could be caught and taken from Lake Merritt, prohibited the taking of waterfowl, and generally prohibited the taking of "any wild animal or game" from the Lake Merritt area. Violations of the provisions of this legislation could result in fines or imprisonment.

In 1925 a display of lighting called the "Necklace of Lights" was lit for the first time during a celebration known as the "Dons of Peralta Water Festival." The display was made up of 126 lampposts and 3,400 light bulbs, which remained on until 1941 when war-related blackouts on the West Coast required them to be dimmed. Years later, they were turned back on and remain on today.

The parkland that surrounds Lake Merritt is a busy center of social and athletic life for the city of Oakland, too.

In addition to enjoying the soothing beauty of the lake and the birds that roost here, visitors can play golf, walk, jog, or bike along paved pathways, play tennis at the Athol Tennis Courts, kayak or feed geese, lawn bowl, or just read a good book from a nearby library. In 1963 the Lake Merritt Wild Duck Refuge was designated a National Historic Landmark.

MARCH 19

1891

Earl Warren Born in Los Angeles

ON THIS DAY IN CALIFORNIA HISTORY prominent American lawyer, California state governor and Supreme Court jurist Earl Warren was born in Los Angeles. It was still a fairly small town in those days, with a population of around 50,000.

Warren didn't grow up in Los Angeles, however. He grew up in a railroad town near Bakersfield called Kern City and would go on from there to attend the University of California at Berkeley, from which he would earn both his B. A. and law degrees.

After law school, Warren worked for five years in private practice in the San Francisco Bay area, left private practice in 1920 to work for San Francisco County, and in 1925 was appointed District Attorney of Alameda County, just across the bay. He developed a reputation for being tough on crime and never had a conviction overturned. He held this position for twelve years, getting himself reelected three times.

Warren's political star continued to rise. He became California's attorney general in 1939, and in 1943, became the 30th governor of the state. As governor, he was able to lower taxes, and still fund everything from public education to public highways, which made him very popular. He was reelected three times.

He ran for Vice President of the United States in 1948, on a ticket that paired him with Thomas Dewey for President. They narrowly lost the election to Harry Truman and Alben Barkley, but Warren had found his way into the national spotlight, and he would stay there the rest of his life.

In 1953 President Dwight D. Eisenhower chose Warren to be the fourteenth Chief Justice of the United States Supreme Court, a position he would hold until 1969. During his years on the Court important rulings in such areas as civil rights, separation of church and state, and racial segregation were made.

MARCH 20

L. A. Lakers Retire Kareem Abdul-Jabbar's #33

ON THIS DAY IN CALIFORNIA HISTORY the Los Angeles Lakers retired the number of one of the best players to ever play the game. His name was Kareem Abdul-Jabbar, and though he was a New Yorker by birth, it was as a Californian that he would do the things that would make him famous in American life.

Kareem played his college ball at UCLA. During his years there (1965-1969), he was voted to the first team All-America basketball team three times, national player of the year twice, and led UCLA to three national championships (on the strength of an incredible 88-2 record), becoming in the process the leading scorer in the school's history.

In the pros Kareem's accomplishments were equally staggering. He became the first professional basketball player to play 20 seasons, and when he retired, held NBA records for most minutes played (57,446), most field goals attempted (28,307), most field goals made (15,837), and most points scored (38,387).

Kareem excelled in every area of the game. He led the league in scoring twice (in 1971 and 1972), in rebounding once (1976), and in blocked shots four times (in 1975, 1976, 1979 and 1980). He was named Rookie of the Year in 1970, played in 18 NBA All-Star games (1970-1977 and 1979-1989), and was elected to the All-NBA first team ten times (1971-1974, 1976-1977, 1980-1981, 1984 and 1986). He led the Lakers to the NBA championships five times (1980, 1982, 1985 and 1987-1988) and was the league's MVP six (1971, 1972, 1974, 1976, 1977 and 1980).

Kareem was one of those athletes who come along once in a lifetime in a sport. Other players have excelled in one area or another of basketball—Wilt Chamberlain and Michael Jordan come to mind —but no other player excelled for so long in so many, and it is that that really sets him apart.

MARCH 21

1963

Alcatraz Prison Officially Closed

ON THIS DAY IN CALIFORNIA HISTORY the Alcatraz federal prison in San Francisco Bay was emptied of its last inmates by order of United States Attorney General Robert F. Kennedy.

The San Francisco Bay island on which Alcatraz prison was built was discovered in 1775. Before the Spanish arrived pelicans were the island's principal residents and it was the pelicans that inspired the island's name. In 1865, when the U. S. Army decided to build its first fort on the Pacific Coast, it was on Alcatraz that it chose to put it.

But no sooner had the army finished building the fort than the place began to evolve into a prison. The army, it turned out, had little use for an island *fort* out West, but it did need a prison, especially a remote and isolated one. Alcatraz fit the bill perfectly and for many years remained just that—a military prison.

But in 1933 things began to change, for that was the year that the military prisoners here were removed and, beginning in 1934, civilian criminals put in their place. This group included Al Capone, "Machine Gun" Kelly, and Arthur "Doc" Barker, men who would make the word "Alcatraz" signify a kind of ultimate in incarceration, the place where the hardest cases did the hardest time.

Over the course of its life as a high-security prison, Alcatraz was home for 1,545 hard-case criminals. Most did their time, but there were some who tried to escape. It is believed that five successfully did so, but whether they actually made it to shore and freedom is unknown.

In 1963 Alcatraz was closed, and during the ten years that followed, it simply sat abandoned. From 1969 to 1971 a group of Indian activists occupied the island, and in 1973, it became part of the Golden Gate National Recreation Area. In recent times, almost a million people a year have visited this storied place.

MARCH 22

1891

David Starr Jordan becomes Stanford's First President

ON THIS DAY IN CALIFORNIA HISTORY David Starr Jordan accepted an offer to become the first president of Stanford University.

Starr had been born on a farm in Gainesville, New York, in 1851. In 1866 he entered what was then the newly-established campus of Cornell University, where he received both a B. A. and an M. A. in botany. Beginning in 1870 Jordan taught botany at Cornell, but later moved to Indianapolis where he earned a medical degree from the Indiana Medical College there.

In 1878 Jordan earned a Ph.D. from Butler University in Indianapolis, and in 1879, was offered a professorship at Indiana University. From 1879 through 1891 he helped gather critical data about the Pacific Coast's marine industries.

In January of 1885 Dr. Jordan was chosen to be the president of Indiana University, and six years later, asked if he would be willing to become the first president of newly-established Stanford University. He accepted the offer and remained the president of Stanford from 1891 to 1913.

Jordan was president of the California Academy of Sciences from 1896 to 1904 and president of the World Peace Foundation from 1910 to 1914. In 1913 he accepted the position of "chancellor" at Stanford, so that he could put more energy into his efforts to promote world peace, in 1915 chaired the "World Peace Conference" and, in 1916, retired from the university.

David Starr Jordan was an extremely prolific writer during his academic career and wrote some 650 articles and books on ichthyology alone. By 1881 he had already published about 250 papers on North American ichthyology, as well as the *Manual of the Vertebrates of the Northern United States*. He would remain actively involved in science and in efforts to bring about world peace until his death in 1931.

MARCH 23

1868

University of California, Berkeley, Established

ON THIS DAY IN CALIFORNIA HISTORY the University of California, Berkeley, was established. The state's 1849 constitution envisioned an institution of higher learning that would foster the "intellectual, scientific, moral and agricultural improvement" of the state's citizens, and this was it, created by the merger of two others already in operation at the time.

The first of these was a private institution called the College of California that was located in Oakland. It had been founded in 1855 by a former Congregational minister named Henry Durant who had come to the Bay Area from New England. The courses the college offered were modeled on the offerings at Harvard and Yale, though in addition to the "classical curriculum," it also offered courses in "modern languages." Anticipating expansion, it bought 160 acres north of the campus, which it called "Berkeley."

Despite the existence of this *private* institution of higher learning, the state still felt the need to establish a *public* institution of higher learning, so in 1868 it decided to take advantage of the federal land grant act passed six years before (the Morrill Act) to establish a separate institution to be called the "Agricultural, Mining, and Mechanical Arts College." The idea was to offer courses in several practical pursuits not taught at the "College of California."

Initially, the newly-merged college used the College of California facilities in Oakland for its campus, but in September of 1873, the University, and its then student body of 191 students, moved north to Berkeley.

With able leadership and increasing streams of public and private funding, Berkeley continued to grow in stature through the years that followed. It developed distinguished faculties in virtually all of its subjects, and by the 1960s, was generally regarded as the finest public university in the United States.

MARCH 24

1769

"Sacred Expedition" Sets Out for San Francisco

ON THIS DAY IN CALIFORNIA HISTORY the "Sacred Expedition," the name given to the first Spanish expedition to set out from what is today Baja California to establish towns, forts and missions in what is today the *state* of California, began.

The Spanish had at least a couple of different motives for launching this expedition. For one thing, they didn't want the Russians to gain a foothold here. For another, they wanted to convert the area's Indians into "good Christians" and put them to work in enterprises that would establish new revenue streams for the crown.

In any case, the expedition was dispatched in 1769, led by Gaspar de Portola, at that time governor of *Baja* California, and Father Junipero Serra, in charge of overseeing spiritual matters for Spain in this new place.

Two parties left Baja California by land—one headed by Portola and Serra, one by Captain Rivera y Moncada and Father Juan Crespi—and one by sea, consisting of three locally-built ships that sailed from Cabo San Lucas and La Paz. The first of the three ships, the *San Antonio*, made the trip in 45 days. The last of the three, the *San José*, was lost at sea, along with its entire cargo and crew.

In all, about half of the 300 men who made up the expedition died en route. The half who survived went on to establish missions at San Diego and Monterey, as well as other missions, towns and even forts in between, blazing in the process the coastal route that would come be known as "El Camino Real" ("the road of kings").

Portola would go on to become governor of *both* Californias—"Baja" and "Alta" (the area that today comprises the state of California); Serra would go on to great fame as the iron-willed Franciscan cleric responsible for establishing the first nine of the California missions; and Crespi would gain fame for his work in supporting the work of Serra.

MARCH 25

1895

De Young Museum Opens

ON THIS DAY IN CALIFORNIA HISTORY the original main building of the de Young Museum opened in Golden Gate Park.

The museum was established by newspaperman Michael de Young with $75,000 he made from the city's Midwinter Fair of 1894. He had originally come to the city with his older brother Charles as a child (in 1854), and in partnership with him, founded the newspaper that would eventually evolve into the *San Francisco Chronicle*.

The de Young's original collection came from three sources: the city's 1894 Midwinter Fair; Mr. de Young's personal art collection; and a group of Gold-Rush-era items which had been donated by San Francisco families who wanted them to be preserved in some sort of public and permanent way.

The original main building was damaged badly by the 1906 earthquake and fire and in 1926 was condemned by the city as unsafe. Nonetheless, the museum continued to grow during the years between the Great Quake and its condemnation. De Young himself donated funds to build the first wing in 1917, a second wing was built in 1925, and a third one in 1931.

The "de Young" contains an impressive collection of American art and is particularly strong in American decorative crafts. There are paintings here by such well-known American artists as Gilbert Stuart, James McNeill Whistler, Winslow Homer and Thomas Eakins, as well as paintings by artists like Georgia O'Keefe.

In addition, the de Young houses galleries devoted to silver plate and furniture from Great Britain, art from Africa, and art objects from the South Pacific, Asia, and Central and South America, too. For the most part, the collection is arranged chronologically and the pieces on display range from the 17th century to modern times.

MARCH 26

1874

Robert Frost Born in San Francisco

ON THIS DAY IN CALIFORNIA HISTORY poet Robert Frost was born in San Francisco. It's believed that his family lived in seven different homes before they left the state in 1885, and today, near the site of one of them, a "Robert Frost Plaza" has been established.

Frost finished growing up in the East, and it is typically with New England, not California, that he is associated. He attended both Dartmouth and Harvard universities, though he didn't receive a degree from either school. As an adult, he bought a farm in New Hampshire, and it is typically with the New England countryside that he and his verse are associated.

In March 1894 Frost's first published poem, "My Butterfly: An Elegy," appeared and he was paid $15.00 for it. In 1912 he sold his farm in New Hampshire and moved to England. The very next year, his first book of poetry, *A Boy's Will*, was published.

In England Frost met some of that era's leading figures in English poetry, including poet and critic Ezra Pound, who was the first American to review his work favorably. In 1915 he returned to America, bought another farm in New Hampshire, and launched a career as a full-time writer and teacher. From 1916 to 1938 he taught at Amherst College.

Frost is widely regarded as one of the four or five greatest American poets of the 20th century and his work was once widely memorized and recited by American schoolchildren. He was President John F. Kennedy's favorite poet and at Kennedy's inauguration, recited his poem "The Gift Outright."

Over the course of his almost seventy-year-long career as a poet, Frost won four Pulitzer Prizes, in 1924, 1931, 1937 and 1943. He preferred to write traditional verse with readily recognizable meter and rhyme. Of "free verse" he once said, "I'd just as soon play tennis with the net down."

MARCH 27

1850

Act Passed to Incorporate City of San Diego

ON THIS DAY IN CALIFORNIA HISTORY an act to incorporate the city of San Diego was passed; Joshua Bean, a former soldier, was chosen as mayor. California hadn't been a state for seven months yet and the town was just a raw, provincial seaport, nothing like the kind of place it would one day become.

In fact, it would not be until shortly after the Civil War that Yankee ingenuity would really begin to work its magic here, for that was when a man by the name of Alonzo E. Horton came to town and made it his business to bring the city to life.

From the very beginning, the city's founders emphasized the natural landscape over "development."

In 1868, at a time when the city was nothing more than a remote and undistinguished southwestern seaport, they had the foresight to set aside a centrally-located 1,440-acre tract of land that would eventually be transformed into a magnificent city park and become the geographic and aesthetic center of the city. By any standard, Balboa Park is one of the *great* parks of the world.

In 1870, when Horton opened his 100-room "Horton House" in downtown San Diego, the city had just 3,000 residents, no railroad service, poor roads, and an as-yet-unimproved harbor. Thirty-five years later, when it was torn down, and the 437-room U. S. Grant Hotel opened up on the same site, San Diego was linked by rail to the rest of California, just a few years away from being linked by rail to the rest of the nation, and not far from the day when it would have its own thoroughly modern deep-water harbor.

Today San Diego is the second largest metropolitan area in the state of California, the sixth-largest metropolitan area in the nation, and continues to grow at a furious pace. The day when it was of interest only to the handful of Mexican soldiers and friars stationed there now seems impossibly long ago.

MARCH 28

Mary Pickford and Douglas Fairbanks Get Married

ON THIS DAY IN CALIFORNIA HISTORY silent-movie heavyweights Mary Pickford and Douglas Fairbanks were married in the Los Angeles home of minister J. Whitcomb Brougher.

Fairbanks had found it difficult to get Mary to commit to a specific date for the wedding, but discovered that telling her the day was a good choice, "astrologically speaking," was the way to do it. After the ceremony, they honeymooned at Fairbanks's hunting lodge in Beverly Hills.

When they married in 1920, Pickford and Fairbanks were two of Hollywood's biggest stars, the leading man and leading lady in a place filled with leading men and leading ladies. Their Beverly Hills home, "Pickfair," was the social center of the movie world and their marriage, the first celebrity marriage in what would prove to be a long list of celebrity marriages to come.

Pickford had begun her acting career in her native Toronto, but her ambitious mother soon moved her to New York to give her a shot at the big time, and it was there that she came to the attention of D. W. Griffith and began what would be a fabulously successful career in film. By 1916 she was making $500,000 a year.

Fairbanks had been born in Denver and it was there that he began his acting career. He quickly became a hit and decided, as Pickford had, that his future lay in New York. He debuted on Broadway in 1902, and in 1915, moved to Hollywood, where he soon made a name for himself as a "matinee idol."

Pickford and Fairbanks had met in 1916 and shortly thereafter began having an affair. Pickford and Chaplin were then the two highest paid stars in Hollywood, but Fairbanks was ambitious, and within eighteen months of his arrival out West, became the third highest paid one. In 1919 Pickford, Fairbanks, Griffith and Chaplin joined forces to form "United Artists."

MARCH 29

1919

Bob Simmons Born in Los Angeles

ON THIS DAY IN CALIFORNIA HISTORY Bob Simmons, the inventor of the modern, lightweight surfboard was born in Los Angeles. Simmons was one of the true pioneers of the sport and his work nothing short of revolutionary.

During his early teens Simmons developed a tumor on his left ankle that was serious enough for doctors to consider amputating his leg. He recovered, however, through good treatment and a change in diet, and even took up riding a bicycle to regain his strength. Unfortunately, he had a serious cycling accident, another setback from which he had to find the strength to recover.

While in the hospital recovering from his injuries, Simmons was advised to try surfing. It would still be a few years before he was truly well, but once he was, he took the advice. In 1939 he got up on a surfboard for the first time at Newport Beach and was immediately hooked. He would surf the rest of his life.

Simmons was a smart guy, too. Though he had been forced to drop out of high school when he had had the problems with his leg, he nevertheless went on to get himself admitted to Caltech, where he got a first-rate education in areas like aero- and hydrodynamics. After leaving Caltech, he continued to keep up with the latest thinking on watercraft design and ways to maximize maneuverability, lift and speed, and translated that thinking into his own innovative work with surfboard design.

Simmons was a loner and typically surfed alone. He surfed all kinds of places long before they had drawn the attention of other surfers and the opportunity to do that was no doubt a big part of the appeal of a sport like this to a guy like him. But surfing alone has its risks, and it was while doing this, at Windansea Beach on the San Diego coastline in 1954, that Simmons tragically drowned. He was just 35.

MARCH 30

1962

Rapper M. C. Hammer Born in Oakland

ON THIS DAY IN CALIFORNIA HISTORY rap music artist M. C. Hammer was born in Oakland.

In his early teens, Hammer was hired by Oakland "A's" baseball team owner Charlie Finley to keep him up-to-date on what was going on with team members when they were at the park. Finley didn't live in Oakland, but Hammer did, and after a chance meeting between the two outside the A's Oakland stadium, where Hammer performed for those headed in and out of the park, the two struck up a friendship. Finley called him his "executive vice president."

Hammer's real name was Stanley Kirk Burrell, but he got the name "M. C. Hammer" (and later just "Hammer") because of his resemblance to baseball great, "Hammerin'" Hank Aaron. He had ambitions to become a professional baseball player, but was unable to get himself picked up by a major team, so he joined the Navy instead. When he got out, he began performing in Oakland-area clubs and even established his own record label, "Bust It."

Hammer's debut album, *Feel My Power* (1987), sold 60,000 copies, and with an opening act like that, he quickly attracted the interest of major record labels. Capitol Records wanted to record him, but he initially turned them down. Until a hefty signing bonus was included. Capitol re-released his debut album under the title *Let's Get It Started* in 1988, and under that name, the album went triple platinum (over three million copies sold).

His second album, *Please Hammer, Don't Hurt 'Em* (1990), included the song that is still the song by which he is best known today: "U Can't Touch This." The album eventually went "diamond" (over ten million copies sold), the first hip-hop record album to do that. Though Hammer's financial success was beyond question, his songs were often criticized for being too repetitive and for relying too much on lyrics created by others.

MARCH 31

1922

KFI-AM Begins Transmitting in Los Angeles

ON THIS DAY IN CALIFORNIA HISTORY radio station KFI-AM began transmitting its broadcasts in Los Angeles. The original station used a 50-watt transmitter built by local mogul, Earle C. Anthony, who operated it from his garage.

Anthony was an ambitious guy. He built a working electric car when he was 17 and a motion picture camera, too. Working with his father, he built a local Packard dealership into a Los Angeles institution and has even been credited with inventing the "filling station" itself, as well as opening the first two in the state. When radio came along, Anthony was quick to see its possibilities, too.

In the early days, KFI was typically on the air only four and a half hours a day, and for many years, it was the Los Angeles area affiliate of the NBC radio network, most particularly the NBC *Red* Network, which was known for having the most powerful signals of all American radio stations. It carried sporting events like the World Series and the Rose Bowl, and from 1960 to 1972, was the flagship station of the Los Angeles Dodgers radio network.

During the 1970s and '80s KFI broadcast one of the most listened-to radio shows in radio history, *The Lohman and Barkley Show*, starring Al Lohman and Roger Barkley. Other hosts of the show included Bob Hudson and Ron Landry, creators of the hilarious "Ajax Liquor Store" routine, and "America's d. j.," Gary Owens, who not only was one, but played one on TV. Easy-to-listen-to music with comic hosts, that was KFI's style.

Today KFI broadcasts from its Burbank, California studios on a 50,000-watt AM transmitter located in nearby La Mirada. It is a strong transmission signal and allows KFI to be heard throughout Southern California and even some distance into Arizona, Nevada, and northwestern Mexico, as well as, at night, some parts of Hawaii and other parts of the western United States.

This Day
in
April

APRIL 1

City of Palm Springs Incorporated

ON THIS DAY IN CALIFORNIA HISTORY the city of Palm Springs incorporated itself. It had been little more than a sleepy Indian village just fifty years before, but a very different future lay just ahead, and it was now taking steps to ready itself for that future.

The first non-Indian residents of the community had arrived in the late 19th century, including those who would open the area's first hotels—Welwood Murray, who opened the "Palm Springs Hotel," and Nellie Coffman, who opened the "Desert Inn."

Hollywood headliners were quick to follow. Fatty Arbuckle and Rudolph Valentino partied here in the 1920s. Silent-screen star Charles Farrell and his wife came in the 1930s, and, in partnership with actor Ralph Bellamy, opened the Racquet Club. Clark Gable and Errol Flynn, Rock Hudson and Cary Grant, Liberace, Gloria Swanson, and a laundry list of others came in the 1940s, '50s and '60s.

Golf quickly became the city's dominant recreation and it is said that there are more golf courses here (per capita) than any other place on earth. There are also more swimming pools here per capita than anywhere else, reportedly one for every four residents.

The primary purpose of Palm Springs, at least in modern times, has been to provide a getaway for the rich, and in places like "Sunnylands," once the estate of media magnate and philanthropist Walter Annenberg, the most extravagant of Palm Springs's many extravagant estates, the essential features of Palm Springs living at its best hit high relief.

But big changes have swept over Palm Springs in more recent times. The pace of development accelerated dramatically and this once sleepy getaway has found itself filling up with condos, hotels, shopping malls and bumper-to-bumper traffic and on the way to becoming a high-desert version of the urban aggravation its visitors so often once came here to escape.

103

APRIL 2

1902

First Motion Picture Theater in America Opens

ON THIS DAY IN CALIFORNIA HISTORY the first motion picture theater in America designed specifically to exhibit *films* opened in Los Angeles: "Tally's Electric Theatre." Its creator, Thomas L. Tally, would later propose that an organization of film exhibitors be created, one from each major city, which would make or buy the films they showed, and distribute them, too.

Tally presented his idea to another American exhibitor, John D. Williams, who liked it enough to join forces with him and create a company called the "First National Exhibitors Circuit," the forerunner of the many different film distribution organizations that would pop up in the years ahead.

One thing Tally discovered early on was that it was not going to be easy to attract and hold a motion picture audience. To begin with, projectors were difficult to run and hard to repair, and the films themselves were expensive, typically poor in quality, and few. But perhaps the most important thing Tally discovered was that customers simply didn't want to enter a darkened room in order to view a few minutes of pictures in motion.

So he reasoned that if he couldn't lure customers into his theater directly, he might have more success luring them in *indirectly*, and to accomplish this, he punched some holes in the wall that separated the entry area of his theatre from the area where the motion pictures were shown and invited customers to look in through the peepholes while standing in the well-lighted entry.

It worked. Curiosity to see what was on the other side of that peephole eventually drew people inside; putting the price of regular admission at five cents, and the price for looking through a peephole fifteen helped, too. The original theater opened at 311 South Spring Street, but there were also theaters at 428 South Broadway, 262 South Main, and at 904 State Street in Santa Barbara.

APRIL 3

1860

Pony Express Makes Its First Run

ON THIS DAY IN CALIFORNIA HISTORY the Pony Express began its first run between St. Joseph, Missouri, and Sacramento. It began this day in 1860, and ended, in Sacramento, ten days later, on April 13th. The mayor of St. Joseph presided over the "kickoff" of the service and a boy named Johnny Fry was the first rider.

"Stations" providing fresh mounts were spaced out about ten miles apart all along the 1,966-mile trip from St. Joseph to Sacramento. At each station the rider changed horses and off he'd go again. Every 100 miles, *riders* were changed out, too.

The mail pouch was thrown over the saddle and sat on by the rider. It had pockets built into each of its four corners into which mail was stuffed and each one was padlocked to keep it secure during the trip. Each mail pouch could hold about twenty pounds of mail and since the total weight the horse carried could not exceed 165 pounds, everything else, including the rider, had to total 145 pounds, or less.

Being a Pony Express rider was a dangerous job and the service lasted just eighteen months. The advent of the telegraph made it unnecessary for riders to risk life and limb on horseback to get messages from one side of the continent to the other, but the Express did demonstrate that mail could be moved overland across the continent year-round, and that was something that up until this time no one believed possible.

The other big change that came seven years after that was the completion of the transcontinental railroad, which still permitted mail to be sent, but now more quickly, more safely, and in greater quantity yet. Still, the Pony Express became the stuff of romance during the brief time that it lasted, and another example of an enduring American theme: the ability of the individual to master any challenge.

APRIL 4

Creation of Golden Gate Park Authorized

ON THIS DAY IN CALIFORNIA HISTORY the city of San Francisco issued city order #800, authorizing the creation of Golden Gate Park.

This wonderful urban park literally had to be raised from sand dunes, for when the city bought this land in 1868, that's all it was. In fact, San Franciscans at the time called it "The Great Sand Park," and even Frederick Law Olmsted, the foremost landscape designer of the day, did not think the area could support trees and be successfully transformed into parkland.

The first plan to transform these dunes was laid out by the Park's first superintendent, William Hammond Hall. The actual landscaping work was done by his assistant, however, John McLaren, and it was McLaren, a man commonly referred to as the "Father of Golden Gate Park," who was primarily responsible for making the park into the kind of place it is today.

The buildings in the Park dedicated to culture and sport are located in its eastern half—the "Conservatory of Flowers" (a gift from well-heeled city fathers James Lick and Charles Crocker), the California Academy of Sciences, including the Steinhart Aquarium and the Morrison Planetarium, the M. H. de Young Memorial Museum, and Kezar Stadium.

This is also where the Park's most exotic vegetation can be found, things like the prehistoric-looking glade of tree ferns that stand across the street from the Conservatory of Flowers, and the memorable mix of Japanese exotics and native California plants in the Japanese Tea Garden.

The western half of the Park is composed of less complex vegetation and has more open space than the eastern half, making it more suitable for activities like soccer, fly casting, flying kites, and riding horses. It is also where the Park meets the Pacific, the common boundary of the city's far western edge.

APRIL 5

1916

Actor Gregory Peck Born in La Jolla

ON THIS DAY IN CALIFORNIA HISTORY actor Gregory Peck was born in the exclusive south coast community of La Jolla.

Peck's mother had been born in Missouri; his father was a pharmacist whose mother an immigrant from County Kerry in Ireland. They divorced when Peck was just five and left him with his grandmother to be raised.

He attended both San Diego High School and San Diego State (for one year), and later enroll himself in the pre-med program at the University of California, Berkeley. He would later change his major to English, however, and get involved in acting, appearing in five plays his senior year.

After graduating from Berkeley in 1939, Peck went to New York to try to make it as an actor. He studied at the Neighborhood Playhouse there, was often broke, and even spent some time sleeping in Central Park. He eventually did find work on Broadway, however, and in 1944, found his first work in films.

Acting on the big screen was clearly what Peck was born to do. He was nominated for "Best Actor" by the Academy of Motion Picture Arts & Sciences five times, four nominations coming during his first five years in the business. But he didn't win the award until his fifth nomination in 1962. Appropriately, it was for what he himself regarded as his best performance, lawyer Atticus Finch in *To Kill a Mockingbird*.

Peck was one of the true Olympians of the American film industry, those figures who routinely come to mind whenever there is talk of the business's true "stars." In 1979 he was inducted into the "Western Performers Hall of Fame;" in 1989, was awarded a "Lifetime Achievement Award" by the American Film Institute; and in 1996, received a "Crystal Globe" for his contributions to world cinema. He died in 2003, at the age of 87.

APRIL 6

1937

Musician Merle Haggard Born in Oildale

ON THIS DAY IN CALIFORNIA HISTORY country-western music super-star Merle Haggard was born in the in the tiny Bakersfield suburb of Oildale. His family had come to the San Joaquin Valley during the dark days of the Dust Bowl and it was not all that long after their arrival that Merle was born.

He taught himself to play guitar on a guitar his older brother gave him when he was twelve.

Like many another country singer of his generation, Haggard lived the life he sang about, one that included jail time, lost love, hard drinking, wandering around, and making a living doing a lot of different things. He ran away to Texas at 14, returned home only to run away again, and along the way got himself involved in a variety of robberies to make ends meet, one of which landed him in San Quentin prison.

It was while at San Quentin that Haggard got the opportunity to hear Johnny Cash play live. Cash provided him with a living example of a man gone wrong who used his guitar and voice to get right, and it was his example that Haggard took to heart.

Playing honky-tonks and bars, in Bakersfield and elsewhere, Haggard and Bakersfield neighbor, Buck Owens, developed a country-music style that would come to be known as "the Bakersfield Sound," and also come to be regarded as two of the most influential country singer-songwriters in the business.

Over the course of his career, Haggard has written well over 300 songs, including "The Bottle Let Me Down," "Okie from Muskogee" and "The Fightin' Side of Me," and 40 number one country hits. In 1977 he was inducted into the Nashville Songwriters Hall of Fame, and in 1994, into the Country Music Hall of Fame, and has continued to tour and record throughout what has now become a forty-plus-year career.

APRIL 7

1967

"Progressive Radio" Born in San Francisco

ON THIS DAY IN CALIFORNIA HISTORY a radio format that came to be known as "Progressive Radio" was born in San Francisco. Its creator was KMPX-FM disc jockey Tom Donahue.

Donahue's first job as a disc jockey was in the late 1940s, in Charleston, West Virginia. He would go on from there to work at a variety of stations before landing the job at KMPX, where he would build his broadcast around live music, album cuts, and commercials and announcements judged to be of interest to his audience ("public service announcements").

Donahue arrived in San Francisco in 1961 to take the job at KYA, and in early 1964, in partnership with fellow disc jockey Bobby Mitchell, formed a recording label called Autumn Records. The new label's principal producer was Sylvester Stewart ("Sly Stone"), who later achieved a little rock-and-roll fame of his own as the lead singer of "Sly and the Family Stone."

In 1964 Autumn Records recorded Bobby Freeman's "C'mon and Swim," a minor-league hit for them, and the "Beau Brummels," the first major group to come out of mid-1960s San Francisco. It also recorded the "The Great Society," fronted by superstar-to-be Grace Slick, before "Jefferson Airplane" took off. Donahue and Mitchell produced the city's first rock concerts in Golden Gate Park, including the Beatles final public concert on August 29, 1966.

Donahue's radio format proved to be a popular one and soon radio stations across the country were imitating it.

In May 1968 Donahue and most of his staff moved over to station KSAN-FM, and once there, made it into a Progressive Rock powerhouse. In 1972 he became the station's general manager, and just three years later, was close to becoming general manager and part owner of KMPX. On April 28, 1975, however, he died suddenly of a heart attack.

APRIL 8

1910

Los Angeles Motordome Opens

ON THIS DAY IN CALIFORNIA HISTORY the Los Angeles Motordome opened near Playa del Rey. Buying, driving and racing cars was just as big a deal back then as it is today, and there were even more American carmakers, all of them looking for buyers.

For most people, of course, owning a car in the early days was simply an impossible dream, an extravagance indulged in only by the wealthy.

The early racers, guys like Louis Chevrolet (who designed the first ones), Barney Oldfield (for whom the Oldsmobile was named), and "Willie K." Vanderbilt the II (whose racing attire included fur-lined pants and a fur-lined overcoat), were all rich guys, professional racers, or both.

Carmakers were quick to realize that winning races sold cars. If one car did better than another in a race, then that car got the attention of the car-buying public. The saying went that if "you win on Sunday, you sell on Monday," and that certainly seemed to be the case. At least until even more effective ways of reaching the nation's car-buying public emerged, like television.

Car-racing also gave carmakers a way to see how well their cars held up under hard use and where they needed to make improvements. Things like the rearview mirror, disc brakes, fuel injection, computer controls and radial tires all grew out of efforts to improve racecar performance.

The Los Angeles Motordome was one of these early racetracks. It was a mile long and a *board* track, and remained open for three years, until 1913. It was also a track that inspired hundreds of similar tracks to be built all across the county. A board track known as the "Los Angeles Motor Speedway" was even built in Beverly Hills, at the intersection of Rodeo Drive and Wilshire Blvd., and remained in operation from 1920 to 1924.

APRIL 9

1966

Angel Stadium Opens

ON THIS DAY IN CALIFORNIA HISTORY "Angel Stadium," the home of the California Angels baseball team, and, for a time, the Rams and Raiders of the NFL, opened its doors.

On opening day in 1966 the Angels hosted the San Francisco Giants in an exhibition game. Ten days later, the Angels played the Chicago White Sox in the first American League game they ever played.

The original stadium seated 43,204 and seating capacity was later increased to 43,250. Additional construction was undertaken during 1979 and 1980 so that the stadium could adequately accommodate the fans of the Los Angeles Rams football team, too. When this new construction was completed, the stadium could seat 65,158 fans (later reduced to 64,593).

Ultimately, the NFL football teams basing themselves here moved on—the Rams to St. Louis in 1995, the Raiders that same year back to Oakland—and on October 1, 1996, a new set of renovations to Angel Stadium were begun in order to convert it back into a baseball-only facility. On September 15, 1997, it was announced that the stadium would henceforth be known as the "Edison International Field of Anaheim."

That was more than a mouthful, and so it came as no surprise on December 29, 2003, when the Angels organization announced that the field had again been renamed, this time to "Angel Stadium of Anaheim."

The new stadium included three restaurants for those who wanted something other than what they could get in the stands: a sports bar at the Club Level (the "Knothole Club"), an upscale eatery with outdoor seating located at Field Level behind home plate (the "Diamond Club"), and an indoor restaurant that overlooks the main entrance to the park (the "Home Plate Club").

111

APRIL 10

1882

Matson Shipping Lines Founded

ON THIS DAY IN CALIFORNIA HISTORY Captain William Matson began a shipping service between San Francisco and Hawaii. He had first arrived in California in 1867 and had been engaged in trading on the bays, rivers and coast of northern California between that time and this. Now, fifteen years later, he was establishing the shipping lines on which his lasting fame would rest.

In 1901 the "Matson Navigation Company" incorporated itself. In the beginning, "Matson Lines" focused on moving cargo, but in 1908 Matson ships began carrying passengers, too. In time, larger freight and passenger ships were put into service, and when Captain Matson died in 1917, the fleet boasted fourteen of the largest, fastest, and most modern ships afloat.

During World War I, most of the Matson Lines's ships were taken over by the U. S. Navy and used for military purposes. When the war was over, they were returned to the company and resumed doing what they had been doing before. Two of them, the "Manulani" and the "Manukai," were the largest freighters then hauling cargo in the Pacific.

In 1926 Matson added three ships that had been sailing for a company called the "Oceanic Steamship Company," and in 1927, took over its Southern California rival, the "Los Angeles Steamship Company." By the early 1930s Matson added three more ships to its fleet—the "Mariposa," the "Monterey," and the "Lurline"—which replaced some of the company's older vessels.

During World War II, Matson ships were again drafted into the war effort. They survived the war, and once it was over, resumed passenger and freight service. Until 1970, that is, when the Matson Lines stopped offering passenger service altogether. From that time to this, the Matson Lines have operated as a freight-only line and maintained a sizable fleet of container ships.

APRIL 11

Pasadena & Los Angeles Electric Railway Incorporated

ON THIS DAY IN CALIFORNIA HISTORY Moses Sherman and a man named Eli Clark incorporated the Pasadena & Los Angeles Electric Railway, rolling up the then-existing horsecar and cable-car systems into a single company.

The tracks of this state-of-the-art urban railway ran from 4th Street in downtown Los Angeles to Chestnut Street in Pasadena, and there was still actually *space* between the city of Los Angeles and the city of Pasadena. Of course, there wouldn't be much "space" for long. The coming of the railroad marked the beginning of the end of the area's identity as open countryside.

The creators of this rail line had been major players in the development of Greater Los Angeles, but financial difficulties in 1898 forced them to sell the line to a group headed up by president of the Southern Pacific Railroad, Collis P. Huntington, and his nephew, Henry E. Huntington.

This new group would roll up the line that had been created by Sherman and Clark into a company that would acquire a variety of other locally-developed lines, including the "Santa Ana, Orange and Tustin Street Railway Company" and the "Santa Ana & Orange Motor Company," and consolidate them all into the "Pacific Electric" Railway Company, an enterprise that ran its rails throughout the length and breadth of what are today Los Angeles, Orange, San Bernardino and Riverside counties.

Sherman was well aware that what making an area accessible to public transportation did for land values. Twelve years after he sold his railway interests to Huntington, a home building company in which he was a partner, purchased 47,500 acres in the southeastern part of the San Fernando Valley. From that parcel, Sherman purchased 1,000 acres for himself, and in 1927, sold that acreage for $780 per acre, making himself a very wealthy man.

APRIL 12

1988

Sonny Bono Elected Mayor of Palm Springs

ON THIS DAY IN CALIFORNIA HISTORY Sonny Bono was elected mayor of Palm Springs, a development that struck many as odd because he had made his name completely outside the political arena, in the world of popular entertainment.

He had gotten his start in the music business back in the late 1950s and early '60s in Los Angeles, writing or cowriting songs that other people made into hits and learning about promotion and arrangement, working with the legendary Phil Spector.

But what Bono was really after was a spot on the main stage himself and that opportunity came in 1963 when he teamed up with future wife, "Cher." Sonny could write and Cher could sing, and by combining those skills with a "sixties look" that made them really stand out from other acts the duo's star quickly rose.

Sonny & Cher's success as a singing act brought them to the attention of some major players in other parts of the entertainment industry, most notably Fred Silverman at CBS, who decided to build a television variety show around them. Having found a following on the airwaves, they now set out to find one on TV, and from 1971-1974, they did.

But all was not well with the couple, and in 1975, they divorced. After the split, Sonny played some minor parts on TV and in the movies and married again. He divorced again in 1984, but in 1986 married for a third time. He became a Scientologist, fathered two children, and tried to open a restaurant in Palm Springs.

It was while working through the municipal red tape that went with trying to open a restaurant that Sonny got interested in politics. He was elected mayor of Palm Springs in 1988, and four years later, made an unsuccessful run for the U. S. Senate. In 1994 he made a successful run for the House of Representatives, where he served with distinction until his death in a skiing accident in 1998.

114

APRIL 13

Wallace Stegner Dies

ON THIS DAY IN CALIFORNIA HISTORY distinguished teacher and writer Wallace Stegner died. Though he was born in Iowa and did his undergraduate work at the University of Utah, it was as a Californian that he would make his lasting mark.

Stegner wrote a number of well-regarded books during his long career as a writer and teacher, including *Angle of Repose*, which won the Pulitzer Prize in 1972, and *The Spectator Bird*, which won the National Book Award in 1977.

In 1992, the year before his death, he was awarded a "National Medal" from the National Endowment for the Humanities, but refused to accept it, because he didn't believe in government involvement in the arts and didn't want anyone to think he did.

The Big Rock Candy Mountain, an autobiographical piece of work, was his first big writing success and appeared in 1943. In 1954 a nonfiction book entitled *Beyond the Hundreth Meridian: John Wesley Powell and the Second Opening of the West* appeared. *Wolf Willow: A History, a Story, and a Memory of the Last Plains Frontier* appeared in 1962, *Angle of Repose* in 1972, *The Spectator Bird* in 1976, and *Crossing to Safety* in 1987.

Stegner established the Creative Writing Program at Stanford University during his years as a professor there, a program that at one time or another included Edward Abbey (*Desert Solitaire*), Wendell Berry (essayist, poet, and novelist), Ken Kesey (*One Flew Over the Cuckoo's Nest*), Ernest J. Gaines (*The Autobiography of Miss Jane Pittman*), and Larry McMurtry (*Lonesome Dove*).

Stegner was also an active environmentalist and in the mid-1960s served on the board of the Sierra Club. He also worked for a time as a Special Assistant to Secretary of the Interior, Stewart Udall. Tragically, he died on this day, at age 84, from injuries sustained in a traffic accident in Santa Fe, New Mexico.

APRIL 14

1895

Hotel Raymond Burns Down

ON THIS DAY IN CALIFORNIA HISTORY the lavish 200-room Hotel Raymond in South Pasadena burned to the ground. It was the creation of Walter Raymond, owner of the Boston-based travel firm "Raymond and Whitcomb," who had first visited Pasadena in 1882 and immediately saw the appeal it would have for well-to-do Easterners looking for a pleasant place to while away the winter.

The Raymond originally opened its doors for business in 1886 and was very much of a piece with the small but elegant South Pasadena community that surrounded it. South Pasadena itself would not be officially incorporated as a city until 1888, but these were the years during which the elegant and exclusive community it is today began to take form.

Present-day Pasadena, Altadena and South Pasadena occupy an area that had once been part of a tract of land granted to Colonel Manuel Garfias (in 1843) by the government of Mexico. Between 1843 and 1846 Garfias built the home known as "El Adobe Flores" here, the oldest home in South Pasadena.

The Cawston Ostrich Farm opened here in 1896 and quickly became a popular tourist attraction. For a small fee visitors could stroll around the farm's grounds and even buy souvenir postcards to commemorate their visit. The farm did have a very specific practical mission, though. The feathers of the birds here were harvested to manufacture and sell a variety of "feather" products, including feather boas and plume trimmings for women's hats.

In 1900 South Pasadena had only 1,001 residents, but it had begun to grow. Henry Huntington's "Big Red Cars" rolled into town in 1902, the first bank opened up in 1904, and the first high school opened in 1907. In 1908 home delivery of mail began and the new city library opened. By 1950 the city's population had grown to 16,935, and by 2000, had reached 24,292.

APRIL 15

Alonzo E. Horton Arrives in San Diego

ON THIS DAY IN CALIFORNIA HISTORY pioneer San Diego settler Alonzo Erastus Horton arrived in town. He acquired 960 acres for $264 and shortly thereafter began to transform it into an area that has been known since that time as "New Town."

Horton was a promoter and an entrepreneur and had come to San Diego with the idea of building a great city where only a tired little seaport then stood.

He had been born in Connecticut in 1813 and grew up in upstate New York. He showed great promise as an entrepreneur, but poor health forced him, as it forced so many others, to move out West. The far western edge of the United States at the time was Wisconsin, so in 1836 Horton moved to Milwaukee.

In 1847 he moved to St. Louis, and in 1851, decided to join the flood of adventurers then headed West to find their fortunes in the California gold fields. He sold off the property he then owned in the Midwest and headed to northern California.

In 1857 he returned to Wisconsin, but by 1862 was back in California, this time going to San Francisco. In San Francisco he sold furniture and household goods for a time, and it was while doing that that he learned about what was then an up-and-coming little community called San Diego.

San Diego was known for its fine climate, but, Horton noted when he arrived, it had been built pretty far inland and was not really taking advantage of its location.

It seemed to him that it would make more sense to lay it out along the Bay, so he acquired some acreage, built a home for himself on one of the lots in the tract, and then sold the surrounding lots to others. He then acquired another tract, did the same thing, and repeated this process until he'd managed to get a fairly good-sized city hammered together.

APRIL 16

Architect Richard Neutra Dies at Age 78

ON THIS DAY IN CALIFORNIA HISTORY architect Richard Neutra died. He was born in Austria, and died in Germany, but in his professional prime worked extensively in California, designing the buildings for which he will long be remembered.

Neutra moved to the United States in 1923, still in his early thirties. In 1929 he became a U. S. citizen and initially worked in partnership with some of the leading architects of his time, including Frank Lloyd Wright and Rudolf Schindler. Eventually, he would establish a practice with his wife, Dione.

Unlike most architects, who are often preoccupied with imposing their own artistic vision upon whatever project comes to hand, Neutra took great pains to understand what his clients had in mind, and even went so far as to have them fill out questionnaires to guide his designs. He, too, was an artist, but it was also important to him that each property be fitted to its setting and work the way its owner wanted it to work.

When you think of Neutra's work—Barnsdall Lodge and the Lovell house in Griffith Park, the Strathmore Apartments in Westwood, Dr. Robert Schuller's original drive-in church in Garden Grove—you think of modern architecture at its best, buildings composed of concrete panels, plenty of windows and a highly functional interior. When you look at a building and say it "looks modern," it is probably a Neutra-inspired design you're looking at.

In fact, it was Neutra more than anyone else who articulated the structural themes that eventually came to dominate California architecture. His clients were known to "give him his head" so that he could create some daringly-designed structure for them to live in, and it was this "openness to the new" that made his work so fresh, and the state such an ideal staging ground for innovative architectural design in the early 20th century.

APRIL 17

1924

MGM Pictures Formed

ON THIS DAY IN CALIFORNIA HISTORY MGM Pictures was formed out of three motion-picture-making companies that had been operating independently up to that point: Metro Pictures, Goldwyn Pictures, and the Louis B. Mayer Company.

Metro Pictures had originally been formed in 1916 by Richard A. Rowland and Louis B. Mayer. They started out by distributing the films of a company called Solax Studios, but the enterprise wasn't all that Mayer had hoped it would be, and so, in 1918, they went their separate ways. In 1920 the company was purchased by theater-chain-owner Marcus Loew so that he would have a reliable source of films for the many theaters he owned.

Goldwyn Pictures had been formed in late 1916 by Sam Goldfish and four others. Two years before, Goldfish had been a founding partner of the Jesse L. Lasky Feature Play Company. In early 1916 he was forced out at the Lasky Company, however, and in 1920, was forced out at Goldwyn.

Louis B. Mayer formed the Louis B. Mayer Company in Los Angeles in 1918. He had grown up in very humble circumstances in the East, living first in St. John, New Brunswick, Canada, and by his late teens, in Boston.

In Boston he got involved with Nickelodeons, and by the mid nineteen-tens, was bankrolling the New England ticket sales for movie blockbuster *The Birth of a Nation*. It was the financial success he had doing that that put him into a position to make and distribute films on his own.

At MGM, Loew and Mayer created the "star system," making film after film with a relatively fixed stable of actors who came to be strongly associated with the studio, making many of them, including Greta Garbo, Clark Gable, Joan Crawford and Elizabeth Taylor, very famous.

APRIL 18

1906

Great San Francisco Earthquake and Fire

ON THIS DAY IN CALIFORNIA HISTORY the Great San Francisco Earthquake and Fire struck the city of San Francisco.

The initial jolt lasted less than a minute, but the force released was powerful enough to buckle roadways and sidewalks, throw thousands of buildings off their foundations, and break gas lines all over the city. Chimneys and wood-burning stoves were toppled and bottles containing flammable chemicals shattered from one end of the city to the other. The city's water mains broke, too, stopping the flow of water through the city and making it impossible to fight the many fires the quake set off.

Just three days after the quake and fires hit, most of 19th-century San Francisco had burnt to the ground.

Fire claimed City Hall, the Palace Hotel, the opera house and the mansions that the city's railroad barons had built on Nob Hill. It swallowed police stations and prisons, some thirty schools, the city's main library and seventeen fire stations. The devastation was mind-boggling—478 dead (the "official" death count), 250,000 homeless, and 28,000 buildings completely destroyed.

The Quake played a major role in making San Francisco into the beautiful city it is today, however. In the 19th century it was known for its ugliness, not its beauty, and the Great Quake and Fire cleared the way for new construction.

Efforts to rebuild began almost immediately after the fires that the Quake triggered were put out.

San Franciscans loved the picturesque, if unpredictable, spot on which their city was perched, and whatever might befall it, there was no doubt but that raising it up again was the only thing most residents wanted to do. Besides, "experts" insisted that the city could be built "safer" this time around, heading off the kind of devastation seen in 1906. As always. time would tell.

APRIL 19

1987

Last California Condor Captured

ON THIS DAY IN CALIFORNIA HISTORY the last free-flying California condor in the wild, a 19-pound, 7-year-old adult male, was captured. For the first time since the Pleistocene Era, these ancient, orange-headed, black-feathered birds with a ten-foot wingspan, and native to this area, stopped flying though its skies. Their remaining population, now all in captivity, stood at just 27.

Back before the first Europeans arrived, a large number of these birds thrived along the North America coastline and they were even a deity for some native California tribes. They first came to the attention of "white men" when a Spanish cleric traveling with Vizcaino saw one flying over the waters of Monterey Bay in 1602.

In 1937 just 1,200 acres of wilderness, the "Sisquoc Condor Sanctuary," had been set aside for the bird's habitat, and in 1946, it was estimated that only 60 to 100 California condors remained in the wild, almost all of them confined to the southern part of the state.

In 1947 this situation was improved dramatically when the U. S. Forest Service set aside 35,000 acres within the Los Padres National Forest for the bird's use (the "Sespe Condor Sanctuary" in Ventura County). In 1951 this sanctuary was expanded by fifty percent, to 53,000 acres.

In 1953 the bird officially received legal protection for the first time when it became "unlawful to take any condor at any time or in any manner." In 1975 a "recovery plan" for the condor was adopted, and in 1979 the United States Congress passed legislation to help expedite the "California Condor Recovery Plan."

In 1983 the first wild condor chick was captured, making it one of only three condors then in captivity. Many more would be captured in the years just ahead. California's population of condors is now significantly larger than it was just a few decades ago, but how long that trend will continue, no one knows.

APRIL 20

1949

Willie Shoemaker Wins His First Horse Race

ON THIS DAY IN CALIFORNIA HISTORY, in Albany, California, 17-year-old Willie Shoemaker won his first horse race.

It was the first of 8,833 wins he would have over the course of his long and successful career. He would win 11 Triple Crown races, including four Kentucky Derbies, five Belmont Stakes races, and three Preakness Stakes races, and become the first jockey to win over $100 million in a racing career.

Shoemaker was born on August 19, 1931, in the small West Texas town of Fabens. He was so small at birth—just two and one-half pounds—that he wasn't even expected to live for more than a few hours. He somehow managed to pull through, however, though he would only grow to be 4 feet, 11 inches tall, and weigh just 95 pounds.

Two of the most notable rides of Shoemaker's career were at the Kentucky Derby. He would have won the 1957 Derby, aboard "Gallant Man," but misjudged the finish line and stood up too soon, allowing "Iron Liege" to take the race. At the 1986 Derby he became the oldest jockey to ever win the race, riding an 18-1 long shot named "Ferdinand." (He was 54.)

Shoemaker broke the win record of his longtime competitor, Johnny Longden, in September of 1970, but in 1999, his own record of 8,833 victories was broken by Laffit Pincay, Jr. The last race in which he ever rode was, fittingly, at the Santa Anita Racetrack, but he finished out-of-the-money, on a horse by the name of "Patchy Groundfog."

Soon after retiring from racing in 1990, Shoemaker became a trainer. Unfortunately, on April 8, 1991, a car accident left him paralyzed from the neck down and confined to a wheelchair. He still remained involved in the sport as a trainer until 1997, however. He died October 12, 2003, at the age of 72.

APRIL 21

ON THIS DAY IN CALIFORNIA HISTORY fashion designer Rudi Gernreich died at the age of 62. He left Austria at the age of 16 to pursue a career in fashion design. He initially found work as a dancer and later worked his way into the world of fashion design. In time, he also became a high-profile gay activist.

Gernreich started out designing fabric and, one thing leading to another, found his way into designing *fashion*. He spent three decades pushing the boundaries of what can only be called "futuristic fashion" and what he had in mind is easiest to see by simply looking at the photos photographer William Claxton took of his clothes being worn by model Peggy Moffitt.

Though he did not make the first ones, Gernreich contributed mightily to making the bikini a fashion phenomenon in America. It was created by the French during World War II and first worn in numbers on the French Riviera in the 1950s. But it had generally fought an uphill battle to gain acceptance outside France. Except in America. In America it caught on quickly, thanks to designers like Gernreich who helped make it the chic thing to wear.

But the bikini went nowhere near as far as Gernreich wanted to go. In 1964 he introduced the "No Bra" (a soft, sheer, almost weightless piece of apparel that created a boom in "little nothing" lingerie boutiques across the nation) *and* the topless bathing suit as fashion possibilities for America's bold and beautiful.

In time, Gernreich would give the nation the "*micro*miniskirt," unisex clothing, and the thong, too (around 1979), but in 1964 it was all about taking it all *off* in American fashion, and Rudi Gernreich was the designer leading the way. In 2003, at an exhibition of his work at the Phoenix Art Museum, he was called "one of the most original, prophetic and controversial figures of the 1950s, '60s and '70s" and whatever else he was, he was certainly that.

APRIL 22

ON THIS DAY IN CALIFORNIA HISTORY an organization calling itself the San Gabriel Orange Grove Association named their newly-founded agricultural cooperative "Pasadena" (from a Chippewa word said to mean "crown of the valley").

During its formative years, *two* Pasadenas would emerge. There was the "artistic Pasadena," a place of artists and intellectuals, the place of Caltech, the Mt. Wilson Observatory and the Pasadena Playhouse (1916). This was the group that "did research," wrote novels, collected art, and generally pursued the higher life of the mind in affluent and refined circumstances.

The other Pasadena, equally affluent, and composed largely of financially successful immigrants from Indiana and Illinois, were a bit more "outer-directed," more interested in outdoor life for its own sake, not necessarily one filled with artistic and intellectual challenges, but one in which things like building, landscaping and tending an elaborate home, as well as riding and hunting, was the proper business of daily life.

This "other Pasadena" was best represented by the people who belonged to the Valley Hunt Club and the gentlemen orchardists who came here because it was such an agreeable place for a person with money to retire, the people who built the extraordinary mansions that still line South Orange Grove Boulevard.

But most of Pasadena was a blend of these two worlds. It was generally a high-toned, tree-lined, well-heeled kind of place overall, one where a capitalist like David Gamble (of Proctor & Gamble fame) and Caltech scientists like George Ellery Hale and Albert Michelson could all feel at home. It was a place where elegant art collections (many of which would one day fill the local Norton Simon Museum) and celebrations of the athletic life like the Rose Bowl both had a place.

APRIL 23

ON THIS DAY IN CALIFORNIA HISTORY legendary farm labor leader Cesar Chavez died in his sleep.

He was born near Yuma, Arizona, in 1927, to a family of migrant farm workers who had lost its farm during the hard years of the Great Depression. Like other children of migrant farm workers, he attended many different schools during the course of his academic career—in his case, over thirty of them—but got no further than the 8th grade.

In 1946 Chavez joined the United States Navy and served in the western Pacific and it was during his time that he had the experience that would set him on the path to becoming a civil rights leader. One time on leave he decided to sit in the "white" section of a racially-segregated movie theater, but when asked to move, he refused.

After Chavez left the Navy, he began working as an "organizer" for the Community Services Organization, a Latino civil rights group. By the late 1950s he had become its national director, but was determined to pursue his civil rights interests in a different way, and resigned in 1962 to form the National Farm Workers Association, which later became the United Farm Workers.

In 1965 Chavez led the strike that would put his name in the nation's history books and make it known throughout the land: the strike of grape-pickers in the Central Valley farm town of Delano, demanding higher wages for grape-pickers and a national boycott of California table grapes.

Throughout the remainder of his life, Chavez would lead efforts to create better working and wage conditions for California's migrant farm workers, going on hunger strikes and leading grape boycotts. He would become a hero in the American farm labor movement and his name known across the land. Many American cities have named streets in his honor.

APRIL 24

1912

Officials Misled about "Need" to Flood Hetch Hetchy

ON THIS DAY IN CALIFORNIA HISTORY the city of San Francisco received a report from one of its engineers making the case for using the Mokelumne River in northern California as a source of new water for the city.

A controversial alternative to doing this was to dam up the Hetch Hetchy Valley in Yosemite National Park, a choice that would create an immense reservoir in the High Sierras, but also drown out the beauty of a place that many thought to be nearly the equal of the Yosemite Valley.

Since the early 1860s San Francisco had gotten its water from the Crystal Springs Reservoir located in the mountains south of the city. But as good a source of water as these lakes were, they were not sufficient for the city's future water needs and so alternatives had to be found.

One such alternative was the Hetch Hetchy Valley, and though it was not actually *necessary* to dam Hetch Hetchy for the city to have a new reservoir, doing so was of enormous financial benefit to the people who wanted to make that happen. And they were clearly prepared to do whatever it took to get the job done, including suppressing information supporting any other choice.

And so, on this day in 1912, a chain of events was set in motion that would ultimately lead to damming up the Hetch Hetchy Valley in Yosemite National Park and allowing the waters of the Tuolumne River to rise up along its walls until they finally swallowed all the trees and flowers that then covered the valley's floor.

Before all was said and done, a national controversy would rage for over a decade about what the right thing to do was, making the fight over Hetch Hetchy the first truly national conflict over the environment in the nation's history, and the first of many many more to come.

APRIL 25

1961

Robert Noyce Patents the Integrated Circuit

ON THIS DAY IN CALIFORNIA HISTORY high-tech pioneer Robert Noyce received a patent for the integrated circuit. (Jack Kilby of Texas Instruments had a similar application pending at the time and the two men were ultimately deemed its *co*inventors).

Noyce was born in Grinnell, Iowa, where he earned his undergraduate degree in physics, and it was here that he first learned about transistors, in the classroom of a professor who had gotten two of the first ones. After graduation, Noyce went on to do his Ph.D. at MIT, where he quickly realized that he was more knowledgeable about transistors than anyone around him.

After completing his studies at MIT, Noyce took a job with electronics giant Philco, and it was there that he decided he wanted to go to work for the Shockley Semiconductor Laboratory in Mountain View, where electronics pioneer William Shockley was trying to "build a better transistor."

Shockley was no picnic to work for, and in 1957 Noyce and seven other engineers at the Shockley Lab resigned to start their own firm. They got their start-up capital from a company named Fairchild Camera and Instrument, and together created one of the early giants of the high-tech industry, Fairchild Semiconductor.

Noyce became the general manager of the new enterprise, and it was here at Fairchild that he designed the first integrated circuit. He stayed on until 1968, when he left with a man named Gordon Moore to found modern-day software giant, Intel.

At both Fairchild and Intel Noyce fostered a very casual working environment, the kind of environment now thought of simply as "the way people at high-tech companies work"—casual dress, freeform work schedules, informal collaborations among work groups to generate ideas. The creation of this kind of working environment was another of Noyce's contributions to high-tech.

APRIL 26

ON THIS DAY IN CALIFORNIA HISTORY Hollywood screenwriter Anita Loos was born in the tiny far northern California town of Sisson (later renamed Mt. Shasta). Her father was a humorist, journalist, editor and screenwriter, skills that he had clearly passed on to his middle child.

In 1892 the family moved to San Francisco, where Loos's father ran a tabloid newspaper. It must have been a fascinating place for a future writer and also provided young Anita with an opportunity to try her hand at acting.

Following their time in San Francisco, the Loos family moved to San Diego, and not all that long after that, Anita was off to Hollywood, where she found work writing screenplays for D. W. Griffith. Her first one was used to make a movie starring two of the headliners of the day, Lionel Barrymore and Mary Pickford.

In 1919 Loos moved to New York City, where she collaborated with her second husband on the screenplays for several movies, some plays, and a couple of books, *Breaking into the Movies* (1919) and *How to Write Photoplays* (1922).

But where she really hit her stride was with the advent of the "talkies," for it was then that she could write dialogue for the characters on the screen and that was where that she really shined. She wrote the screenplays for *Red-Headed Woman* (1932), starring Jean Harlow, *San Francisco* (1936), and *Susan and God*, starring Joan Crawford, Fredric March, and Ruth Hussey (1940).

Loos is perhaps best remembered for her short novel, *Gentlemen Prefer Blondes* (1925), which was an overnight best-seller, and its many spin-offs, including her stage adaptation of the book and the 1953 film starring Jane Russell and Marilyn Monroe. She would write a sequel entitled *But Gentlemen Marry Brunettes* (1928), which was also made into a successful film.

APRIL 27

Angelus Temple Designated a National Historic Landmark

ON THIS DAY IN CALIFORNIA HISTORY Angelus Temple in Los Angeles was designated a National Historic Landmark. It had been one of the most famous churches of its day and the place where evangelist Aimee Semple McPherson became a media sensation in the 1920s and '30s.

Sister Aimee had only arrived in L. A. just before Christmas of 1918, but by 1923 had managed to erect one of the leading religious centers in Southern California, and by the end of that decade, was enjoying an influence that was truly worldwide.

"Sister" Aimee used stage props and radio like no evangelist before her, and when radio broadcasting became available, acquired her own radio station, KFSG ("Kall Four Square Gospel"), extending the influence of her ministry over the entire western United States. Beginning in 1927 she established a series of satellite churches, too, churches that still count their membership in the millions.

When she needed a way to make sure her church was full every Sunday, she introduced what she called "illustrated sermons," sermons conceived and presented as full-blown theatrical productions. And she drew upon a wide variety of sources for her inspiration. Even the occasion of being stopped for speeding was grist for her mill, once inspiring her to appear before her congregation holding up a motorcycle and dressed as a policewoman, proclaiming, "Stop! You are breaking God's law."

Like all great evangelical dynamos, Sister Aimee was one of a kind and it is daunting to think what she might have been able to do had she had television at her disposal. She certainly sensed its power, and even applied for a television license in 1944, but died before she could put it to use. But even without it, she was able to make herself into the most publicized preacher of her time and the spiritual leader of millions the world over.

APRIL 28

1999

Actor Rory Calhoun Dies

ON THIS DAY IN CALIFORNIA HISTORY actor Rory Calhoun died at St. Joseph's Medical Center in Burbank. He had starred in more than 80 films, and appeared in over 1,000 TV shows, and was a familiar face to the moviegoing public of the 1950s.

Calhoun was born in Los Angeles in 1922 and in the late 1930s dropped out of high school. In 1940 he was arrested for car theft and served three years in prison. After his release, he worked as a boxer, a lumberjack, a truck driver and a cowpuncher, not knowing at the time he was getting experience he would later put to use in film.

In 1944 Calhoun was spotted by actor Alan Ladd's wife, Sue Carol, riding a horse in a Los Angeles park. He hadn't done too well in life just yet, but he was 6'3" and had Hollywood-style good looks and that would prove to be his making. Mrs. Ladd arranged for him to have a screen test at 20th Century-Fox and he soon made his film debut in *Something for the Boys* (1944).

Calhoun went by his real name, "Frank McCown," in his first few films, but that name really didn't have the kind of big-screen pizzazz his managers were looking for, and so, in 1947, producer David O. Selznick changed it to "Rory Calhoun."

In 1949 he appeared in his first two westerns: *Sand*, a 20th Century-Fox release, and *Massacre River*, an Allied Artists release. From this point on he starred in more and more bigger-budget films, including *With a Song in My Heart* (1952), *How to Marry a Millionaire* (1953), and *River of No Return* (1954).

But it will be for his roles in westerns that Calhoun will be best remembered: *The Domino Kid* (1957), *Apache Territory* (1958), and the TV series, *The Texan* (1959-1960). For his work in movies and television, Calhoun has been honored with two stars on the Hollywood Walk of Fame, one at 7007 Hollywood Blvd., for his movie work, one at 1752 Vine Street, for his work on TV.

130

APRIL 29

1992

Massive Riot Breaks out in "South Central"

ON THIS DAY IN CALIFORNIA HISTORY a huge riot broke out in South Central Los Angeles. Before it was over, more than 50 people had been killed, as many as 2,000 injured, and the damage done to property had soared to nearly a billion dollars.

The spark that lit this flame was the acquittal, by a mostly white jury, of four Los Angeles policemen who had been tried for the beating of black motorist Rodney King the previous April 3.

But the King beating wasn't the only factor involved. There was an extremely high unemployment rate in the South Central area of the city and a pervasive and enduring perception on the part of neighborhood residents there that the police went out of their way to harass blacks and Hispanics.

South Central was a different kind of place in 1992 than it was when the 1965 riots broke out. In 1965 South Central was predominantly black area and the animosities driving the riot largely a matter of conflicts between the LAPD and the area's predominantly black community.

By 1992, however, the area included a significant number of Hispanic residents, as well as a sizable Korean community. There was a significant amount of animosity between these groups, especially between the area's black residents and Korean merchants, who, the black community said, treated them poorly and overcharged them for the things they bought.

The riots began the evening after the King verdict was announced, but ultimately took several days to play themselves out.

Television coverage broadcast vivid images of L. A. going up in flames, area stores being looted, bystanders being beaten, and rioters shooting at police with assault weapons. Initially, California National Guard troops were sent in to control the situation, but eventually federal troops were needed to restore order.

APRIL 30

Alice B. Toklas Born in San Francisco

ON THIS DAY IN CALIFORNIA HISTORY author and all-around-bohemian Alice B. Toklas was born in San Francisco. Her fame came from her association with another Bay Area native, avant-garde writer Gertrude Stein—and from a cookbook that bore her name, and that included a recipe for "hash brownies."

Alice B. Toklas was an adventurous soul and the West Coast wasn't all that exciting a place for someone who wanted to drink in the cream of world culture in those days, so in 1907 she headed off to Paris where, on her first day there, she met Gertrude Stein.

In Paris Toklas and Stein's apartment became a gathering place for the artistic elite of the day, a place where writers like Ernest Hemingway and Thornton Wilder could at times be found, as well as Europe's leading painters of the day, including Pablo Picasso, Henri Matisse and Georges Braque. Alice was the grease that made it all go: Stein's lover, secretary, cook, editor, critic and general personal support system.

Gertrude would return the favor by immortalizing Alice in the title of her own autobiography, which she called *The Autobiography of Alice B. Toklas* (1933), and, according to people in a position to know, the book really was "Alice's book," one that reflected the way she thought, talked, and viewed Gertrude Stein.

After Stein's death in 1946, Toklas published a memoir of her own that was a mixture of reminiscences *and* recipes entitled *The Alice B. Toklas Cook Book* (1954).

The recipe for "hashish fudge," which called for fruit, nuts, and an assortment of spices, as well as *cannabis sativa*, or marijuana, was the one most responsible for immortalizing her name. They came to be known as "Alice B. Toklas brownies," and the book in which she first described how to make them has not been out of print since it first came out.

This Day

in

May

MAY 1

1965

Bandleader "Spike" Jones Dies

ON THIS DAY IN CALIFORNIA HISTORY bandleader "Spike" Jones died in Beverly Hills. He had been born in Long Beach fifty-three years before, the son of a Southern Pacific Railroad agent. His given name was "Lindley Armstrong," but he was so thin, people often compared him to a railroad spike. The name stuck.

Spike's life was all about music. He got his first set of drums at 11 and as a teenager played in bands he put together himself. He learned from a chef friend how to "make music" with pots, pans, knives, forks and spoons, and he got some experience playing in theater orchestras, too.

In the 1930s Jones joined up with the "Victor Young Band," a decision that would result in offers to play on some of the leading live radio shows of the day, including the *Al Jolson Lifebuoy Show*, *Burns and Allen*, and Bing Crosby's *Kraft Music Hall*.

In the 1940s he put together a backup band he called "The City Slickers." They recorded five records for RCA-Victor, and between 1942 and 1949, managed to come up with seven "top ten" hits. In 1945 Spike even got his own radio show and people like Groucho Marx, Hank Williams and Burl Ives all made appearances.

What "Spike" and his band became famous for were the parodies they did of the work of other musicians. In 1948 they even made a recording of "(All I Want for Christmas is) My Two Front Teeth" that became a number one hit. In the late 1940s and early '50s, Jones made several appearances in films (playing himself).

"Spike" Jones is in that wonderfully screwball part of the entertainment business that includes the Marx Brothers, Stan Freberg and "Weird Al" Yankovic, and his entire career was devoted to making the kind of music that connoisseurs of the comic and oddball never tire of. The rock band Aerosmith once even considered calling themselves "Spike Jones."

MAY 2

1925

Kezar Stadium Opens in Golden Gate Park

ON THIS DAY IN CALIFORNIA HISTORY Kezar ("Key' czar") Stadium in San Francisco's Golden Gate Park opened its doors. It is located in the southeast corner of the park, and named for Mary Kezar, a woman who had left money to the city to build a "playground." A San Francisco judge ruled that a football stadium met the test.

In the beginning, a variety of area schools used Kezar Stadium as their "home" football stadium, including San Francisco Polytechnic High School (now closed), the University of San Francisco, Santa Clara University and St. Mary's College in Moraga. The East-West Shrine Game, a postseason matchup of college all-stars, was played here from its beginnings in 1926 until 1974, too.

Between 1946 and 1970 the San Francisco 49s professional football team played in Kezar Stadium, subsequently moving to San Francisco's Candlestick Park. In 1960 the Oakland Raiders football team played their games in this stadium, and on January 3, 1971, the National Football Conference's championship game was played here, the last NFL game played in this facility.

Golden Gate Park was a beautiful place to build a stadium. It is the largest park in San Francisco and within easy walking distance of the Strybing Arboretum, the Japanese Tea Garden, the M. H. de Young Museum, the California Academy of Sciences, and the Conservatory of Flowers. It was also just a stone's throw away from the city's Haight-Ashbury district.

In 1989 the original 59.000-seat stadium in which all of this football history was made was torn down. What was put up in its place was a modern, 10,000-seat stadium intended for the use of area high schools, and which has also become the site of the annual San Francisco City Championship Game known locally as "The Turkey Bowl." In 2004 Kezar Stadium became the home of the "San Francisco Freedom," a professional cricket team.

MAY 3

1942

Evacuation of Japanese-Americans Ordered

ON THIS DAY IN CALIFORNIA HISTORY Lt. General John DeWitt issued "Civilian Exclusion Order No. 346," calling for the Japanese-American population on the West Coast to report to designated "assembly centers" from which they would be moved to internment camps in the nation's interior.

Almost 112,000 people were affected, and of that number, approximately two-thirds were American citizens. The remaining one-third came under the jurisdiction of the "Alien Enemies Act," part of the Alien and Sedition Acts passed back in 1798 to protect the nation from the acts of "dangerous aliens" who were citizens of a nation the U. S. was at war with.

Once rounded up, these people were first sent to temporary "relocation centers" and then shipped to one of ten permanent centers located in the far western interior of the country. They had been forcefully removed from their homes in California, Oregon, Washington and Arizona, and as a group, constituted the single largest forced relocation in U. S. history.

The camps to which these people were sent were located in some of the bleakest parts of the nation. Their "housing" amounted to little more than "tarpaper-covered barracks . . . without plumbing or cooking facilities" and the camps themselves were enclosed with barbed wire and guarded by soldiers. Food was strictly rationed and served military-style, 250-300 people at a time.

In early 1944 the government began to release internees so that they could put their lives back together, and in January 1945, the order was rescinded altogether. All detainees were released in 1945, but the last camp was not closed until August of 1948. The forced detention of all these people failed to make the nation more secure, of course, and many prominent public officials later admitted as much.

MAY 4

ON THIS DAY IN CALIFORNIA HISTORY English author Aldous Huxley ingested a tablet of mescaline at his home in the Hollywood Hills, beginning one of the more notable episodes of drug-taking in world history. He had first visited Southern California in 1937, and in 1938, came to stay. Huxley's long-term interest in the mind and how it worked had now taken a new turn.

Though he had already produced several remarkable books before he arrived in L. A. (most notably his internationally-renowned novel, *Brave New World*), Huxley would produce several more during his twenty-five years as a Southern Californian.

The first of these was *After Many a Summer Dies the Swan* (1939), a novel set in the San Fernando Valley community of Tarzana (founded by long-time local resident Edgar Rice Burroughs, author of the Tarzan books), and one that satirized, among other things, the idea of "living long by eating right."

Huxley also spent his California years ringing changes on a subject that would fascinate him throughout his life: wisdom East, wisdom West, and man's dark fate if he didn't wise up. Always interested in science, technology and the "direction" in which human life was headed (he was concerned about ecology and overpopulation long before most people), Huxley was also interested in the mind, and the drugs that had the power "alter" it.

And so in May of 1953 he initiated the first of what would be several experiences that he would have with the drug mescaline, experiences memorably recounted in his books *The Doors of Perception* (1954) and *Heaven and Hell* (1956). By the time of his death in 1963, he could legitimately lay claim to having contributed enormously to the effort to understand the human condition and to having raised an army of issues that would be debated long after his passing.

MAY 5

California Chronicler H. H. Bancroft Born

ON THIS DAY IN CALIFORNIA HISTORY Hubert Howe Bancroft, the man who would become California's leading 19th-century chronicler, was born in Granville, Ohio. In 1852, just 20 years old, he moved to San Francisco, and it was there, from the 1856 to 1868, that he ran a bookstore at 2898 Jackson Street. It was also during these years that he started his own publishing company.

During this period Bancroft also accumulated a substantial library of historical materials related to the Far West, and it was these materials that provided the research base from which his staff of writers would compose such volumes as *Native Races of the Pacific States* (5 volumes, 1874-1876) and the *History of the Pacific States of North America* (21 volumes, 1882-1890).

Bancroft approached the writing of history the way Henry Ford would later approach the building of cars. It was clearly too large a task for one man, so he gathered together a *team* of writers to "assemble" his histories, each contributing their part to the whole. And because his histories were made this way, most moderns would not be inclined to consider him their "author," at least in the way we normally use that term today, but he certainly saw himself as the author of these books.

This was not history-making in a traditional sense, but it was history-making nonetheless.

Bancroft's compilation ran to thirty-nine volumes altogether and preserved a great deal of material that would otherwise have been lost. It and the many other volumes he collected during his lifetime survived the fires that swallowed San Francisco in 1906 and became the "seed" collection for the library at U. C. Berkeley that was named in his honor. In time, this collection would grow from the 50,000 volumes it was at the beginning to almost 500,000 volumes, and continues to grow to this day.

MAY 6

Olympic Club Opens in San Francisco

ON THIS DAY IN CALIFORNIA HISTORY the Olympic Club, the *first* athletic club in the U. S., was founded in San Francisco.

Artist Charles C. Nahl and his half brother, Arthur, had maintained an outdoor gym in the backyard of their home on Bush Street since 1855. The equipment they installed there was intended for their own use, but it attracted so much interest from friends and neighbors, they soon found themselves installing more. Soon they needed a separate building, too.

And so it was that on this day in 1860 Charles Nahl, his half brother Arthur, and some members of San Francisco Fire Department (the Lafayette Hook and Ladder Club on Broadway Street) decided to establish the "San Francisco Athletic Club." The original membership came to twenty-seven and the club's establishment predated that of the New York Athletic Club by six years.

In 1912 a new, five-story club building was built on Post Street, just above Mason, at a cost of $430,000. (The furnishings alone cost $40,000.) It was said to be the finest facility of its kind in the United States and it was easy enough to see why.

The front was built of pressed brick and trimmed in marble. On the first floor were the main gymnasium, the clubroom, a reading room, a library and a trophy room. On the second floor there was a main dining room, private dining rooms, a billiard room, a room for playing cards and a kitchen. The club's handball courts extended from the building's third floor to its fifth.

In a mezzanine area located between the first floor and the basement there were 328 dressing rooms and 560 lockers, as well as a rifle range. In the basement itself there was a steam room, showers, a barber shop, physicians' offices and a swimming pool that was 100 x 35 feet, had a depth that varied from 3 ½ to 9 feet, and was filled with water pumped straight from the ocean.

MAY 7

1939

Union Station Opens in Los Angeles

ON THIS DAY IN CALIFORNIA HISTORY Union Station in downtown Los Angeles opened. It was the last of the great train stations built in the United States, and was built on land that had once been occupied by the city's first Chinatown.

Union Station was designed by John and Donald Parkinson, a father-and-son team of architects, whose firm had been responsible for designing some of the more important and recognizable buildings in the city from the late 19th century on, including earlier facilities for the Southern Pacific and Union Pacific Railroads and the Los Angeles City Hall.

The Parkinsons incorporated a variety of architectural styles into their design for Union Station, a blend composed of Spanish Colonial elements, Mission Revival elements, and elements of a style that was popular at the time the Station was completed in 1939, "Streamline Moderne." Moorish and Aztec design features were incorporated, too.

As you would suspect, Union Station originally served the Southern California area's principal railroads, including the Atchison, Topeka and Santa Fe, the Southern Pacific, and the Union Pacific Railroad. And as you would also suspect, it saw its heaviest usage in the early days, especially during the first ten years after it opened, when rail travel was the most efficient and luxurious way to move between L. A. and other parts of the nation.

In more recent times Union Station has again seen a burst of passenger traffic through its doors. A variety of forces have been driving this, including the introduction of a subway system into the downtown area of the city, a light rail system "on top," and the routing of some Amtrak lines here as well. The Station will no doubt play a crucial role in the high-speed rail system many planners see rolling through the whole of California one day.

MAY 8

ON THIS DAY IN CALIFORNIA HISTORY Paramount Pictures was officially incorporated. It had originally been created by a man named
W. W. Hodkinson to distribute films nationally, an indispensable
first step in getting movies seen by the American public.

In 1912 a man named Adolph Zukor established his Famous
Players Film Company, and the following year producer Jesse Lasky
launched his Lasky Feature Play Company. Lasky's first hire was an
inspired one. His name was Cecil B. De Mille.

Initially, both Zukor and Lasky distributed their films through
Paramount, but it wasn't long before Zukor saw the benefit in getting
all aspects of production and distribution under the same roof, so in
1916 he engineered the merger of Paramount, Famous Players, and
the Lasky Feature Play Company into a single firm, "Famous
Players-Lasky." Lasky and DeMille took care of production, and
Zukor managed everything else, constantly dreaming up new ways
to make the enterprise larger.

Zukor believed that the key to making successful films was
promoting "stars" and he was the man who made Hollywood's "star
system" the force it became. He signed and developed many of the
leading ones of his day, too, including Mary Pickford, Douglas
Fairbanks, Gloria Swanson, Clara Bow, Rudolph Valentino and
Wallace Reid.

In the teens and twenties Zukor kept two production companies
busy, built up a chain of nearly 2,000 theatres, and became an early
investor in radio, buying a fifty-percent interest in the Columbia
Broadcasting System (CBS) in 1928. He consolidated his power as
he went along. His distributor, W. W. Hodkinson, was out of the
partnership by 1917 and he let Lasky go in 1932. By the early 1930s
the firm was known as the Paramount Pictures Corporation and fully
under Zukor's control.

MAY 9

1841

First Wagon Train Leaves for California

ON THIS DAY IN CALIFORNIA HISTORY the first wagon train headed to California left Independence, Missouri. It was led by a man named John Bidwell, who would, in time, become a soldier, a politician, a statesman and a philanthropist. It arrived in the Sacramento Valley in early November of 1841.

Bidwell did a variety of different things in the course of getting himself established in California. He worked as a ranch hand for a time. He became a Mexican citizen and secured a large land grant. He even discovered some gold on the banks of the Feather River. In 1849, however, he decided to focus his efforts on agriculture, and became, over the course of the half century still left to him to live, the best-known farmer in the state.

Bidwell saw action during the Mexican-American War and worked himself up to the rank of major before the war was over. After the war, he turned his hand to politics and got himself elected to the California State Senate (1849). He had become a man to be reckoned with and built an impressive mansion for himself in the northern California town of Chico.

Bidwell supervised the state census in 1850 and 1860, served as a delegate to the Democratic Party's national convention in 1860, was made a brigadier general in the "California Militia" in 1863 and was a delegate to the Republican Party's national convention in 1865-1867. In 1875 he ran for governor on the "Anti-Monopoly Party" ticket, but was defeated by Democrat William Irwin.

In 1880 Bidwell again ran for governor, this time on the Prohibition Party's ticket, but was defeated by Republican George Perkins. In 1892 the Prohibition Party fielded him as their candidate for President, but that bid for office was also unsuccessful. After a long and successful life, Bidwell died in Chico (which he also founded) on April 4, 1900.

MAY 10

1869

Union Pacific & Central Pacific Join Rails

ON THIS DAY IN CALIFORNIA HISTORY the Union Pacific and Central Pacific Railroads joined rails at Promontory Point, Utah.

The Union Pacific had been incorporated on July 1, 1862, the same day President Lincoln signed the Act authorizing the Union Pacific and the Central Pacific to build a railroad that would run from Omaha to the ocean. To link up on this day in 1869 with the tracks being built by the Central Pacific from its starting point in Sacramento, the Union Pacific had to lay some 1,087 miles of track west from its starting point in Omaha, Nebraska.

The Central Pacific Railroad was incorporated June 21, 1861. It was the brainchild of a man named Theodore Judah and financed by California's "Big Four"—Leland Stanford, Collis P. Huntington, Charles Crocker and Mark Hopkins. Its backers had gotten their starts in California as retail merchants and all four became fabulously wealthy building the railroad. Stanford contributed the political savvy, Huntington a ruthless management style, Crocker the hands-on skills of a good field general, and Hopkins the sharp eye and balanced judgment of a good accountant.

Groundbreaking ceremonies for the building of the Central Pacific Railroad were held in Sacramento on January 8, 1863, on the Sacramento riverfront near the foot of K Street. Later this same year, on October 26, the first actual rail was laid. Almost six hard years of work lay ahead.

With the completion of these efforts by the Central Pacific and Union Pacific Railroads, the eastern and western halves of the country were connected by rail for the first time. The railroad made it possible to go from one side of the nation to the other with relative ease, and because it did, the American West became settled and developed at an increasingly rapid pace, especially its far western edge, California.

MAY 11

1927

Academy of Motion Picture Arts & Sciences Founded

ON THIS DAY IN CALIFORNIA HISTORY the Academy of Motion Picture Arts & Sciences was founded in Los Angeles. Its original membership included thirty-six members of the motion picture community, including many of the major industry figures of the time.

To become a member of the Academy of Motion Picture Arts & Sciences, a person must, naturally enough, distinguish themselves in some area of the industry. This can be through acting, art direction, direction, cinematography, editing, music, production, public relations or studio management, documentary work, work in short films or animation, writing, or work with sound or visual effects.

From the time it was founded in 1927 until 1946, the Academy rented the space it occupied. In 1946 it moved into its second home at 9038 Melrose Avenue in Hollywood, and in December of 1975, relocated to its third, a seven-story headquarters at 8949 Wilshire Boulevard in Beverly Hills. As the motion picture industry grew in importance, so too did the importance of the Academy.

Within ten years, however, the Academy had again outgrown its facilities and was forced to find new space.

The historic "Waterworks" building in La Cienega Park seemed to be a good fit, so in 1988, a new lease was signed for that. But even this space didn't contain the Academy for long. In just ten years, a building that had originally been the first Hollywood television studio on Vine Street was purchased and converted into a new home for the Academy's film archive.

The list of those who have led the Academy of Motion Picture Arts & Sciences is a distinguished one and has included Douglas Fairbanks, Sr., William de Mille, Conrad Nagel, Frank Capra, Walter Wanger, Bette Davis, Jean Hersholt, George Stevens, Wendell Corey, Arthur Freed, Gregory Peck, Walter Mirisch, Karl Malden and Arthur Hiller.

145

MAY 12

1848

Sam Brannan Waves around a Bottle of Gold Dust

ON THIS DAY IN CALIFORNIA HISTORY pioneer Sam Brannan waved around a bottle of gold dust in Portsmouth Square that he had collected from Mormon miners working the shallows of the American River. It was the act, say many, that turned "gold fever" in mid-19th-century California into a gold *epidemic*.

On February 4, 1846, Brannan and some 240 of his fellow Mormons had set sail from New York harbor aboard the ship *Brooklyn*, bound for California. On July 31, 1846, they landed at the tiny village of "Yerba Buena," effectively tripling its size.

Brannan established the village's first newspaper, *The California Star*, a weekly that first appeared in January of 1847 and that did things like attack prominent Californians of the day—Walter Colton and Robert Semple, for example, founders of a rival paper, *The Californian*, and Yerba Buena's mayor Washington Bartlett (for changing the village's name from "Yerba Buena" to San Francisco).

The same year that Brannan got *The California Star* off the ground, he also opened a store at Sutter's Fort and it was that venture that would bring him into contact with the gold dust that he was waving around in Portsmouth Square on this day in 1848.

Early in 1848 some of Sutter's employees were in Brannan's store paying for goods they bought with gold that they had collected at Sutter's Mill. Naturally, Brannan was curious about what was going on at the mill and so he made a visit there. As a representative of the Mormon church, he also felt compelled to collect tithes on the value of the gold the Mormon miners had found.

Once he'd collected the tithes from the miners, Brannan took them back to San Francisco, bought every shovel in the city, and then ran through the streets shouting, "Gold, gold from the American River," creating an instant demand for his exclusive supply. The rest, as they say, is history.

MAY 13

1846

War Declared on Mexico

ON THIS DAY IN CALIFORNIA HISTORY the United States formally declared war on Mexico, an act that would ultimately result in California becoming the thirty-first state in the union.

But even though the declaration of war was signed by President Polk this day in 1846, it took some time before the Californians even knew that war had been declared. Getting news of this kind to a disbursed population of Americans residing in a remote Mexican province in 1846 was no simple task.

In any case, Texas had been seized from Mexico ten years before and had become a state just the year before. The Mexicans and Texans didn't agree where the southernmost border of Texas ended, however—the Texans said the Rio Grande, the Mexicans the Nueces—and to resolve the matter engaged each others forces in the disputed territory between the two rivers.

Even as late as July 7, American naval officer John D. Sloat, his ship at anchor in Monterey Bay, had yet to *officially* hear that a state of war existed between the United States and Mexico. But fearing that the British might stake their claim before he could, he decided to issue a proclamation to the Mexican government in Monterey that "henceforward California will be a portion of the United States."

Later that month Commodore Robert F. Stockton took over Sloat's command and quickly moved to take control of the political and military situation.

By early 1847 Stockton had succeeded and California was firmly in American hands. By early 1848 the war with Mexico was concluded and California, along with a good deal of the rest of the American Southwest, ceded to the United States. Just weeks before, gold had been discovered in the American River and "California" was, unbeknownst to its former owners, on its way to international stardom.

MAY 14

1887

Cornerstone of Stanford University Laid

ON THIS DAY IN CALIFORNIA HISTORY the cornerstone of Stanford University was laid.

The date chosen for the event was the birthday of the school's namesake, Leland Stanford, Jr., son of the former governor. The boy had died in Italy of typhoid fever in 1884, just 15, and the Stanfords decided to build the university to honor his memory and provide for the future of California's "other" children.

In order to design the school he had in mind, Stanford met with the president of M.I.T., Francis A. Walker, and the man who had created New York's Central Park, landscape architect Frederick Law Olmsted. Olmstead developed the general plan and Charles Allerton Coolidge, just 28 years old and a partner in the Boston firm of Shepley, Rutan and Coolidge, drew the plans.

On this day in 1887, with 300 guests in attendance, a sandstone block and accompanying bronze plaque were laid into the corner of the first building in what would in time become the school's "Inner Quad." A month after the cornerstone was laid 100 men were at work laying the school's foundations, and a little over four years later, on October 1, 1891, Stanford University opened its doors.

Many of the university's original buildings were destroyed by the Great Earthquake and Fire of 1906, but despite the damage wreaked by that calamity, the Inner Quad, the Chemistry Building and Encina Hall, the dorm where John Steinbeck lived during his time here, survived.

The school's administration chose to rebuild the university in the Spanish Colonial style used to often in modern California architecture, making it all red-tile roofs crowning buff-colored sandstone blocks. The result was a pleasingly uniform and very "California" kind of look, and a fittingly "native" reincarnation for the state's premier university.

MAY 15

1948

Original "McDonald's" Opens in San Bernardino

ON THIS DAY IN CALIFORNIA HISTORY Dick and Mac McDonald, brothers and fast-food entrepreneurs, opened the first McDonald's restaurant in San Bernardino. They didn't invent "fast food" or the hamburger, but when you hear those words today, it's typically their name that first comes to mind.

In 1937 the McDonald brothers opened a hot-dog stand in Arcadia which they called the "Airdome." The venture was profitable and the brothers used the money they made from it to open their first "true" restaurant, a drive-in barbecue place that they decided to open in San Bernardino and call "McDonald's."

It wasn't long before they realized that where they were making all their money selling hamburgers, not barbecue, however, and so in 1948 they decided to shut down their San Bernardino restaurant for a few months and completely remodel it.

The *new* "McDonald's" restaurant offered a simple menu of hamburgers, French fries, and milkshakes, produced on an assembly line, not made-to-order, and permitted no substitutions. What was available was what was listed on the menu.

Carhop service was stopped, customers had to order and retrieve their food from an order/pick-up window and the area where the food was prepared was opened up so that customers could see how the whole process worked. Traditional plates and utensils disappeared and food was served in paper bags.

A milkshake-machine salesman named Ray Kroc first saw the McDonald brothers' assembly-line food-service during the course of a sales call, and in 1955, bought the operation from them. It was in *his* hands that it would become the familiar chain that now encircles the globe and can claim that it has "served billions." What Kroc saw here was "America's eating future" and he changed forever what it meant in America to "go out to eat."

MAY 16

First Workable Laser Demonstrated in Malibu

ON THIS DAY IN CALIFORNIA HISTORY Ted Maiman, a physicist, electrical engineer and native Angeleno demonstrated the world's first workable laser. The process that would make such a device work had been known since 1917 when Albert Einstein first proposed the idea, but no one realized the range of uses such a device could be put to until the 1950s.

Maiman first became interested in the idea of building such a device while doing research for his Ph.D. at Stanford. In a 1984 interview he recalled that several scientists, most of them with large research budgets, were working on prototypes in August of 1959. Some, in fact, had been at it for almost a year and he had yet to even begin whatever effort he might be able to launch.

One of the big points of contention in this process centered on the kind of material the laser should be made of. Cases were made for this material and that, but what Maiman thought would work best was a synthetic ruby. Most researchers didn't agree, giving his choice about a 1% chance of working, but he felt confident he was right and pressed ahead.

Even his bosses at the Hughes Research Lab didn't think the synthetic ruby was the material to use, and when the day came for Maiman to demonstrate his "Ruby Laser System," May 16, 1960, his work on the project had been all but cancelled.

But, as we now know, Maiman had it right. Working with just a $50,000 research budget (as opposed to the $500,000 to $1,000,000 budgets that had been available to his competitors), he was able to make the world's first workable laser, make it using a synthetic ruby, and complete the entire process in a mere nine months. Since then, laser research and development has flourished and the making of lasers for a wide range of uses has become a multibillion-dollar business.

MAY 17

1947

Legendary Racehorse Seabiscuit Dies

ON THIS DAY IN CALIFORNIA HISTORY legendary racehorse Seabiscuit died on the Mendocino County ranch to which he had been retired in April of 1940. He was not all that old for a horse, just 14. He had been horse racing's all-time money winner and one of the most famous figures in the America of his day.

Seabiscuit did not start out on the West Coast. He started out where most racehorses start out, on a farm in Kentucky. And though he had top-of-the-line racing genes in his blood—his "grandfather" was racing great "Man O' War"—he didn't look like much of a race-horse, either. He was small, knobby-kneed, and much more inter-ested in eating and sleeping than racing, so in 1936, he was sold, to San Francisco auto dealer Charles Howard.

That's when things started to get interesting, because Seabiscuit didn't just get a new owner in 1936, he got a new trainer, too, and it was that trainer that would make the difference.

In November 1936 he ran his last two races of the year at Bay Meadows in San Mateo. In the first race he started out badly, but quickly "righted" himself and ran past the competition in a time just two-fifths of a second off the world record; in the second race he won easily. Then came the "Santa Anita Handicap" in February of 1937. Seabiscuit won the warm-up race with no trouble, but was edged out by a nose in the race itself.

But over the course of the next three years Seabiscuit routinely won the races he ran, including a race held on November 1, 1938, pitting him against "War Admiral" in what was promoted as "The Race of the Century." War Admiral, favored by 4-1, was expected to win easily, but it didn't happen that way. Seabiscuit led by a length after twenty seconds and was ahead by four lengths by the time the race was over. With this achievement behind him, he became one of horse racing's true immortals.

151

MAY 18

1927

Grauman's Chinese Theatre Opens

ON THIS DAY IN CALIFORNIA HISTORY Grauman's Chinese Theatre opened at 6925 Hollywood Blvd. The movie shown that night was Cecil B. De Mille's *The King of Kings* and the theatre had cost more to build than any theater before it.

Its creator was Sid Grauman, who also built the nearby Egyptian Theatre, as well as the Million Dollar Theater on Broadway. Grauman had been born in San Francisco in 1879 and has been credited with originating the idea of the "spectacular movie premiere," something he did when he opened the Egyptian in 1922.

One of the things that "Grauman's Chinese" is famous for, of course, is its forecourt, where stars of all kinds have "left their mark" in cement. The most common way of doing this has been by having a star leave a hand- or footprint behind, but other ways of leaving an impression have been managed, too.

Groucho Marx and George Burns left impressions of their cigars in the cement here, Betty Grable an impression of her legs, and Jimmy Durante and Bob Hope impressions of their noses. Tom Mix's horse "Tony," Gene Autry's horse "Champion" and Roy Rogers's horse "Trigger" all left impressions of their hooves.

The exterior of Grauman's Chinese is supposed to resemble a giant pagoda—one imagined through the eyes of a western showman. It had a huge Chinese dragon draped across its front, two stone "lion dogs" guarding its entrance and the silhouettes of tiny dragons impressed into the sides of its copper roof.

In 1968 Grauman's Chinese Theatre was declared an historic and cultural landmark and has undergone a series of restoration efforts since then. In 1973 the theatre was purchased by Ted Mann, who renamed it *Mann's* Chinese Theatre. In November of 2001 the theatre's original name was returned to its front and it is Grauman's Chinese Theatre that it remains to this day.

MAY 19

1880

Robert Louis Stevenson Gets Married in San Francisco

ON THIS DAY IN CALIFORNIA HISTORY Scottish novelist Robert Louis Stevenson married Fanny Osbourne in the rectory of St. Andrews Presbyterian Church on Post Street in San Francisco. He had met her in France in 1876 and followed her all the way to her native Oakland to await her pending divorce.

Stevenson loved the idea of being out at the very edge of civilization, out where Kit Carson and Mark Twain and "Black Bart" the Napa Valley highwayman had been not all that long before him. This was the kind of life of adventure that Stevenson so clearly loved to write about, and just as clearly would have loved to live.

Stevenson was not well when he arrived in the Bay Area (he had suffered from tuberculosis since childhood), but while there he did find the energy to walk the beaches of Monterey, the streets of San Francisco, and to explore some of the area near the Napa Valley town of Calistoga. This California interlude certainly helped him to feel better, though, and find the strength to set off with his new wife and stepson for his native Scotland.

After spending some time in Scotland with Stevenson's parents, Fanny and R. L. set off for Switzerland, France, and England, and then returned to the United States in the late 1880s to winter in New York. In 1888 they returned to the West Coast and Fanny's native Oakland where they leased a yacht from a prominent local doctor, Samuel Merritt, and set sail for the South Seas. It was here, on the island of Samoa, that they would spend their last years.

It's always hard to tell about these things, but had Stevenson not been so sickly—and in constant search of a suitable place to live in order to protect his heath—he might perhaps have spent the rest of his days in the Bay Area and works like *Treasure Island* (1883) and *Kidnapped* (1886) might have become part of *California's* literary history rather than that of the British Isles.

MAY 20

1873

Levi Strauss Markets Jeans with Copper Rivets

ON THIS DAY IN CALIFORNIA HISTORY businessman Levi Strauss and tailor Jacob Davis received a patent for denim pants made with metal rivets sewn in at the stress points—a pant now commonly called "jeans"—and changed world fashion forever.

Strauss had been born in Germany in 1829 and in 1847, just 18, moved to New York City with his mother and two sisters to join his brothers, Jonas and Louis, in their dry goods business. In 1853, just 24, he moved to San Francisco to open up a dry goods business of his own, and it was here, as a wholesaler of dry goods, that Strauss would make his "big strike."

When he got to California Strauss noticed that the clothes prospectors wore when they went about the business of digging in the earth didn't really hold up to the kind of punishment meted out by that kind of work. Working in mines, digging in the earth, and brushing up against sharp objects generally caused the miners' clothes to wear out at an excessively rapid pace.

To address this problem, Strauss decided to make a pant that could withstand that kind of abuse, a *canvas* pant.

He got the "durable" part right, but in the beginning the pants he made weren't all that comfortable. It was while trying to address this problem, to develop a pant that was durable *and* comfortable, that he discovered *denim*, a fabric that was both at once, and that could be dyed blue to conceal the stains that inevitably ended up covering the pants.

And so it was that Strauss and Davis came to make and market "Levi's," a durable blue denim pant that incorporates copper rivets into its design to strengthen pocket areas. They did a great job of providing miners with pants that could endure the trials of mining, and, as just about everyone now knows, became the pant of choice for people all over the world.

MAY 21

1979

The Case of Dan White

ON THIS DAY IN CALIFORNIA HISTORY San Francisco supervisor Dan White was convicted of murdering San Francisco mayor George Moscone and supervisor Harvey Milk.

Moscone was the son of a San Quentin prison guard and had graduated from the University of the Pacific. He went on to study law at Berkeley and it was there that he met a man named John Burton who would be instrumental in helping him launch his career in politics.

In 1960 Burton's brother Philip persuaded Moscone to run for a seat in the state assembly. He didn't win that race, but three years later did win a seat on the San Francisco Board of Supervisors, on a platform of defending the poor, minorities and small business owners. In 1966 he won a seat in the California State Senate.

Moscone rose quickly through the ranks of the Democratic Party in Sacramento and became associated with a group of progressive San Francisco politicians in the legislature led by the Burton brothers. That association went so well that in 1974 Moscone briefly even considered making a run for governor.

Moscone pursued a liberal agenda during his years as mayor of San Francisco. He appointed large numbers of women, gays and minorities to city commissions and boards, decisions that were popular with his liberal supporters, but very unpopular with his conservative opponents.

One member of Moscone's conservative opposition was supervisor Dan White, who had grown frustrated with his efforts to work with some of the more liberal members of the board, especially gay supervisor Harvey Milk. That frustration led him to resign his post, a decision he later asked the mayor to disregard. Moscone refused, however, and in the aftermath, White went into San Francisco City Hall and gunned down both Moscone and Milk.

155

MAY 22

1899
San Francisco State University Founded

ON THIS DAY IN CALIFORNIA HISTORY San Francisco State University was founded. It was situated in the southwestern part of the city near Lake Merced and today enrolls some 30,000 students.

The university was originally called the "San Francisco Normal School" (a 2-year institution) and opened its doors in 1899. In 1921 it was renamed "San Francisco State Teachers College," and in 1923, granted its first degrees under that name. In 1935 the school's name was simplified to "San Francisco State College," the name it retained until 1974, when it was renamed yet again, this time "San Francisco State *University*."

San Francisco State is often remembered today for the student political activity that went on there during the late 1960s. With ever-irritating native son Richard Nixon in the White House, an unpopular war raging in Southeast Asia, and '60s San Francisco nearby, it was an inspiring time and an ideal launching pad for radical student activity.

As was the case at many American college campuses in those days, the student newspaper was filled with writing about corruption in high places and in a better position than most to create quality journalism. Its editor back then was Ben Fong-Torres, who went on, with Jann Wenner to found *Rolling Stone* magazine.

San Francisco State can claim an impressive alumni list as well. Singer Johnny Mathis went to school there, as did Willie Brown (the flamboyant former mayor of the city), actors David Carradine (star of the 1970s TV hit, *Kung Fu*), Danny Glover (*Lethal Weapon*), Peter Coyote, actress Annette Bening (*American Beauty* and *Being Julia*), and comedian Dana Carvey, best-known for his work on television's *Saturday Night Live*. Writers Ernest J. Gaines (*The Autobiography of Miss Jane Pittman*) and Anne Rice (*Interview with the Vampire*) are also alumni.

MAY 23

1903

First Transcontinental Road Trip

ON THIS DAY IN CALIFORNIA HISTORY two men, Horatio Nelson Jackson and his mechanic, Sewall Crocker, left San Francisco in a 1903 Winton, headed for New York. It was the first attempt ever made to drive a car across the continent.

Jackson and Crocker took on the challenge of driving coast to coast as the result of a bet they had made that a car could handle such a drive. No one knew for sure whether it could or not. There were no gas stations at the time and fewer than 150 miles of paved roadway between the nation's east and west coasts. To refuel their car, they stopped at general stores along the way.

To provision themselves for their long-distance road trip, Jackson and Crocker brought sleeping bags, pistols and rain gear. It was not easy to squeeze everything they thought they might need into the car, so to make additional room, they removed its cloth top.

The trip was slow going. The Winton averaged just four miles per hour and the trip took two months to complete. Three weeks after its departure from San Francisco, another car, a Packard, followed, but took a tougher, riskier route. The drivers of the Packard wanted to beat the Winton to New York, but nevertheless arrived three weeks later. The last car to leave San Francisco for New York that summer was an Oldsmobile, the only car of the three that could still be found on American roads a hundred years later.

Five years later Henry Ford made his "Model T" available to the public for the first time, but it wasn't until the 1920s that cars became cheap enough for large numbers of people to own one. In 1919 U. S. passenger car registrations totaled fewer than 7,000,000, but by the end of the 1920s, they had climbed to more than 23,000,000. Over 2,000,000 of these cars were the property of Californians, giving the state the largest per-capita car count in the nation.

MAY 24

1976

California Wines Outdistance their Competition

ON THIS DAY IN CALIFORNIA HISTORY two California wines made history, for it was on this day that a man named Stephen Spurrier, the owner of a wine shop and wine school in Paris, held a tasting there of French and American wines. All the judges were French.

Just staging a tasting competition wasn't such a big deal, of course. The big deal was the *outcome* of the tasting. The judges said that a 1973 Napa Valley Chardonnay from Chateau Montelena was the "best white" they tasted and a 1973 Cabernet Sauvignon from Stag's Leap Wine Cellars the "best red."

That was something that had never happened before. A California wine had never been ranked higher than a French wine in an international wine-tasting competition, and so by accomplishing that feat here—in France and with French judges—California was suddenly on the international wine map in a very big way.

This new-found celebrity of California wine had a profound effect on its popularity. Vineyards and wineries in California were nothing new, of course. Californians had been growing grapes and making wine since the 1830s.

But the state's wines had struggled to gain distinction and the industry underwent profound changes as it went along. Disease wracked state's vines during the 1870s, '80s and '90s, and poor labeling of cuttings long thwarted efforts to get them planted in the right places. In 1919 Prohibition dealt the industry another blow, forcing winemaking and wine drinking underground.

Wine-drinking "fashions" have undergone a number of changes through the years. French wines were popular in the early 1960s, sweet wines like rosé in the late 1960s, white wine in the 1970s, and red wine in the 1980s. But whatever the fashion, the tasting in 1976 seems to have permanently turned the tide in the "right" direction for California wine.

MAY 25

1977

First of the *Star Wars* Movies Released

ON THIS DAY IN CALIFORNIA HISTORY the first of the now-legendary *Star Wars* movies was released. It was Harrison Ford's most high-profile movie role to date and a movie that would ensure Carrie Fisher a place in the Hollywood pantheon, too.

George Lucas, the moviemaker who dreamed up the *Star Wars* movies, was born in Modesto on May 14, 1944. He wanted to be a racecar driver, but a serious car wreck forced him to reconsider that ambition. Once he got well, he enrolled himself in the local junior college and from there went on to USC, where he made his first moves towards his *Star Wars* movies.

After graduating from USC in 1966, Lucas did a little drifting about, as arts majors often do, and eventually drifted into a partnership with Francis Ford Coppola, with whom he founded American Zoetrope studios in 1969. The idea behind the new studio was to create an environment in which directors could direct along more innovative lines than those available in Hollywood and they certainly managed to achieve that.

Lucas's *American Graffiti* appeared in 1973 and the first of the Star Wars films was released in 1977. The second Star Wars movie, *The Empire Strikes Back*, came out in 1980, the third one, *Return of the Jedi*, in 1983, and the final installments of the series in 1999 (*The Phantom Menace*), 2002 (*Attack of the Clones*), and 2005 (*Revenge of the Sith*).

Lucas's special effects firm, Industrial Light and Magic (ILM), speeded along the development of such things as movie computer graphics, 3D computer character animation, and THX sound. And not only was *Star Wars* one of the most profitable films ever made, it, along with the *Indiana Jones* films and the rest of the *Star Wars* series, made Lucas one of the richest men in film, and the nation's, history.

159

MAY 26

1877

Isadora Duncan Born in San Francisco

ON THIS DAY IN CALIFORNIA HISTORY dancer Isadora Duncan, the woman widely considered to be the "mother of modern dance," was born in San Francisco. She had been born "Dora Angela Duncanon," but later changed her name to "Isadora Duncan."

Never that popular in the United States, she was quite popular in Europe, and in 1900 moved to Paris, where she not only inspired dance artists to take artistic risks, but other kinds of artists, too, including authors, painters, photographers and sculptors.

In Paris Duncan's first home was on the Rue Delambre in Montparnasse, an area that was then developing a substantial artistic community, and she would later tell friends that she had routinely danced before dawn each morning in the Luxembourg Gardens, Paris's most popular park. Whether the story was true or not, it was one that certainly *should* have been.

In any case, in Paris Isadora was able to pursue her art and her unconventional lifestyle to her heart's content.

She broke the rules when it came to dance and she broke the rules when it came to her love life, too. One of her lovers was British actor and set designer Gordon Craig, with whom she had a child, another, Paris Singer, one of the sons of the man who invented the sewing machine, with whom she also had a child. Tragically, her children drowned in a boating accident on the Seine in 1913.

Isadora lived an impulsive and adventurous life and it was her love of the "wild side" that would ultimately prove to be her un-doing. She often wore a long, fringed shawl, and in September of 1927, the shawl pulled tightly around her neck, its long fringes got caught up in the rear wheels of a Bugatti sports car in which she was riding. She was pulled out of the car and to her death, a fittingly dramatic ending for a woman whose entire life had been one long, breathless drama.

MAY 27

1937

Golden Gate Bridge Opens

ON THIS DAY IN CALIFORNIA HISTORY San Francisco's Golden Gate Bridge was completed. The entire structure, including approaches, is 1.7 miles long, and the two towers to which the span is attached each soar 746 feet above the waterline.

In November of 1930 officials of the Golden Gate Bridge and Highway District proposed that voters underwrite the cost of building the Bridge, and on November 4, voters from the District's member counties vote do just that, approving $35,000,000 worth of bonds. Still, the idea was not without its critics.

Some people said bridging "the Gate" would bottle up San Francisco's celebrated harbor and compromise the nation's maritime security. Some said building it would bankrupt the six Bay Area counties that were funding the project. Some said a suspension bridge this long just simply couldn't be built. None of these predictions would turn out to be true, but the fear that some or all of them might be was strong.

Construction on the Bridge began in January of 1933 and took over four years to complete. It spanned an area routinely shrouded in fog and buffeted by 60 mph winds.

It also required a mind-boggling amount of material to complete. Its two great cables alone required 80,000 miles of steel wire and enough concrete was used to make the piers that anchor it to pave a five-foot-wide sidewalk from San Francisco to New York.

Building the Bridge made it possible, for the first time, to *drive* between the city of San Francisco and Marin County without having to drive all the way around San Francisco Bay to get there. But to make that happen, a state-of-the-art engineering marvel had to be constructed, a bridge with its piers sunk in the open sea. It has remained an important part of San Francisco's physical and symbolic identity ever since.

MAY 28

1892

Sierra Club Founded

ON THIS DAY IN CALIFORNIA HISTORY the Sierra Club was organized in San Francisco, with John Muir, the Club's founder, as president. The Club would remain a powerful force in American life in the years ahead.

Muir was the original American environmentalist and one of the most passionate naturalists the nation has ever produced. He championed the protection of "all of nature," but was especially interested in protecting the Yosemite Valley. His passion extended to everything natural, but he felt the Sierra Nevada mountain range was particularly sacred and called it the "Range of Light."

Muir anticipated many principles of modern conservation that were quite radical in his day. He recognized that everything in nature is interconnected and that, consequently, the effort to "protect the environment" needed to be an effort to protect whole living systems, not just isolated "parts" of them. Muir was an ecologist long before the word found its way into the nation's vocabulary and an animal rights activist long before that cause had a name, too.

Muir's concerns as an environmentalist were, naturally enough, the concerns of the Club he founded, which has worked long and hard to promote the protection, exploration and enjoyment of the nation's wilderness areas and to educate people about how best to use the earth's natural resources responsibly.

Many issues on which the Sierra Club takes a stand are more than a little controversial. It thinks the nation's rivers and streams should be allowed to flow pretty much as they do naturally and is no fan of the many dams that have been constructed over many of them. In the early 20th century it fought against the damming and flooding of the Hetch Hetchy Valley in Yosemite National Park and was an opponent of the O'Shaughnessy Dam being built over central California's Tuolumne River.

MAY 29

1973

First Black Mayor of Los Angeles Elected

ON THIS DAY IN CALIFORNIA HISTORY Thomas ("Tom") Bradley became the first black mayor of the city of Los Angeles.

He had been born in Texas to a family of sharecroppers. From Texas the family moved to Arizona to pick cotton (his grandfather had been a slave), and then in 1924, to Los Angeles, where his father worked as a train porter and his mother as a maid. It was here that Bradley would find his future.

He attended Los Angeles Polytechnic High School in the 1930s, where he was a standout athlete in football and track, and won a scholarship to UCLA, where, in addition to being a good student, he was a top quarter-miler. During his junior year he decided to take the entrance exam for the LAPD, scored well, and after graduating from UCLA, joined the department.

In 1940 there were 4,000 officers on the Los Angeles Police Department, and 100 of them were black. The city's black population at the time was only around 75,000, but by 1950 it would grow to 250,000, and by 1960, to almost 500,000. Obviously, more black officers would be needed to police the city and Bradley would play an important role in helping to bring that about.

Bradley retired from the LAPD in 1961 with the rank of lieutenant. During his last years on the force he attended law school at night, and after retiring, began to practice and become active in local politics. In 1963 he made his first run for political office and was elected to the Los Angeles City Council.

In 1969 Bradley ran for mayor of Los Angeles, but was defeated by the incumbent, Sam Yorty. He opposed Yorty again in 1973 and won, and would go on to be elected mayor four more times, finally retiring in 1993. Bradley also ran for governor two times, in 1982 and 1986, but lost both races to George Deukmejian, in 1982 by fewer than 53,000 votes.

MAY 30

1908

Mel Blanc Born in San Francisco

ON THIS DAY IN CALIFORNIA HISTORY Mel Blanc, the voice of Bugs Bunny, Daffy Duck, Tweety Bird, Sylvester the Cat, Porky Pig, Elmer Fudd and Yosemite Sam, was born in San Francisco. During his long and illustrious career, he would work for the two leading studios in the animated cartoon business, Warner Brothers and Hanna-Barbera.

It was while working in radio that Blanc's ability to create different voices for different characters was first noticed. Then radio personality Jack Benny needed someone to "voice" the "characters" on his program, including the Maxwell motorcar he "drove," a violin teacher named Professor LeBlanc, "Polly the Parrot," and Benny's pet polar bear, "Carmichael."

For a time, Blanc also had his own radio show, which aired for a little less than a year, on which he played the luckless owner of a repair shop and several support characters as well.

In addition, he found work on such national radio programs as *Burns and Allen* and *The Great Gildersleeve* (as Floyd the barber) and on Jack Benny's long-running *television* show. On the Benny show he could always be counted on to get a laugh as "Si, the Mexican," a character who spoke only one word at a time, and as the train conductor with just one line: "Train leaving on track five for Anaheim, Azusa, and Cucamonga."

But it was as the voice of animated characters at Warner Brothers and Hanna-Barbera that Blanc would make his lasting mark. In 1936 he joined the Schlesinger Studios, a subsidiary of Warner Brothers and quickly showed just how versatile a voice he had; here he brought Bugs, Daffy, Tweety, Sylvester, Porky and other animated creations to life. In the early 1960s Blanc moved to Hanna-Barbera and became the voice of Barney on *The Flintstones*. He died in 1989.

MAY 31

1996

Timothy Leary Dies in Los Angeles

ON THIS DAY IN CALIFORNIA HISTORY one of the most memorable voices of "the sixties," author, psychologist and psychedelic drug advocate Timothy Leary, died at his home in Los Angeles.

He had been born in Massachusetts in 1920 and did his undergraduate college work at West Point and the University of Alabama, where he graduated with a degree in psychology in 1943. He finished up at the University of California, Berkeley, from which he received a Ph.D. in 1950.

After graduating from Berkeley, Leary secured an assistant professorship there, which he held for five years, followed by a three-year run as director of research for the Kaiser Foundation. From there, it was on to Harvard to lecture in psychology.

It was on a visit to Mexico during his Harvard years that Leary tried psilocybin ("magic mushrooms"). Its effects intrigued him immensely, and when he returned to Harvard, he began researching psychedelic drugs, including both psilocybin *and* LSD, with Harvard colleague Richard Alpert. He believed that, used correctly, these drugs could alter people's personalities in beneficial ways.

In 1963 Leary and Alpert were dismissed from Harvard after some of the parents whose children had experimented with these drugs under Leary and Alpert's direction complained about it to the university. "We saw ourselves," said Leary, "as anthropologists from the twenty-first century inhabiting a time module set somewhere in the dark ages of the 1960s."

Leary wrote prolifically about his extraordinary life "on drugs," much of it intended to persuade readers that he had found "the way". His books included *The Psychedelic Experience* (1964), *The Politics of Ecstasy* (1965), *High Priest* (1968), *Confessions of a Hope Fiend* (1973), *Flashbacks* (1983), *Change Your Brain* (1988), and *Intelligence Agents* (1996).

This Day

in

June

JUNE 1

1888

U. C. Gets Lick Observatory

ON THIS DAY IN CALIFORNIA HISTORY the Lick Observatory on Mount Hamilton near San Jose was transferred to the Regents of University of California.

The Observatory's benefactor and builder, James Lick, had moved to San Francisco from Chile in early 1848 and was already a rich man when he arrived. James Marshall had discovered gold just seventeen days after Lick's arrival in the city, so his timing could hardly have been better. In San Francisco he invested his money in real estate and became even richer.

Once Lick realized that his fortune laid in real estate, not in digging for gold, he began by acquiring lots in what would soon become the *city* of San Francisco. In time he built a flour mill in San Jose (so expensive it was known as "Lick's Folly"), established orchards and a vineyard in the Santa Clara Valley, bought property around Lake Tahoe, and even bought a rancho in Los Angeles that included what is today Griffith Park.

Lick also built the first luxury hotel in San Francisco ("Lick House," destroyed by fire during the 1906 earthquake) and a fine home for himself in the city. For a time, he even owned Catalina Island.

At his death in 1876, Lick left instructions calling for the construction of a state-of-the-art observatory. The decision as to exactly *where* the observatory should be built was left to his trustees, however, and sites on Lake Tahoe, Mt. St. Helena, and several in the San Francisco Bay area were all considered. In the end, Mt. Hamilton east of San Jose was chosen.

The work done here would be distinguished. It was here that eight of Jupiter's twelve satellites were first seen (Galileo spotted the first four in 1610), and here that "the first great successes in photographing comets and the Milky Way" were achieved.

169

JUNE 2

1961

Ricky Nelson's "Travelin' Man" Continues Riding High

ON THIS DAY IN CALIFORNIA HISTORY the song "Travelin' Man" by rock-and-roll heartthrob Ricky Nelson was riding high in America's pop music record charts. He had become a TV star in the late 1950s on *The Adventures of Ozzie & Harriet* and had used that platform to launch his singing career with the song "I'm Walkin'."

At the time that sales of "Travelin' Man" were doing so well, Nelson had been a rock star four years, Elvis Presley was a legend, and American popular music was headed in a variety of new and interesting directions.

The heyday of Nelson's music career was the period between 1957 and 1964. Though he did have a hit with the song "Garden Party" in 1972, one that memorably expressed his frustration with being locked into his teenage image and songs by his fans, he was already well past the high point of his musical career by then. But when he was hot he was hot. During the late 1950s and early 1960s, only Elvis sold better.

The Adventures of Ozzie & Harriet gave up the ghost in 1966, and Nelson's pop-chart success, like that of most of the other teen idols, disappeared with the British Invasion, but neither event forced Nelson from the entertainment business. He put together a new group called the Stone Canyon Band, and continued to hone his craft and tour, even if all his fans really wanted to hear was the Ricky Nelson of old.

Unfortunately, Nelson died in a plane crash in 1985. It happened while he, his fiancée, and the Stone Canyon Band were flying to a performance date in Dallas. The exact cause of the crash continues to be disputed, but one thing is certain: a rock-and-roll giant left us that day, even though he still lives on in the endless rewritings of rock-and-roll history, in the Rock and Roll and Rockabilly Halls of Fame, and in a star on Hollywood Boulevard.

JUNE 3

1770

Mission Carmel Founded

ON THIS DAY IN CALIFORNIA HISTORY Mission Carmel was founded on the shores of Monterey Bay. It was the second of California's twenty-one missions and the one most loved by its founder, Fr. Junipero Serra. It was here that he would make his headquarters and, ultimately, be buried.

The mission was originally established on a site now occupied by the Royal Presidio Chapel in Monterey and was moved, in 1771, to a point further to the south. In Serra's time (he died in August of 1784), the church and surrounding buildings here were made of wood; the stone church and buildings that stand at the mission today were not completed until 1797.

It was a beautiful place for a mission. Here surf, rocks and sand dunes met a dense carpet of coastal forest and green meadows; salt-sea air covered everything in the morning and usually cleared to bright, crisp sunshine as the day wore on. It was all so peaceful, just the place to pursue the "contemplative life."

Because the mission had been Serra's headquarters, and was situated in such an idyllic place, the Catholic Church had once considered developing the property into a summer retreat house for the faithful. It would have served such a purpose admirably, but the Carmel Development Company had other ideas, and chose to promote Carmel as an artists' colony instead.

It is, in many ways, the perfect setting for an artists' colony—beautiful, remote, inspiring and peaceful, an ideal place to "commune with nature" and be "alone with your own thoughts"—and several prominent figures in the American arts community have chosen to live here at one point or another in their lives, including poet Robinson Jeffers, photographer Ansel Adams, actresses Kim Novak and Doris Day, and landscape painters too numerous to even begin to list.

JUNE 4

1930

Pantages Theater Opens

ON THIS DAY IN CALIFORNIA HISTORY the Pantages Theatre opened in Hollywood at 6233 Hollywood Boulevard. It cost over a million dollars to build and was one of the most beautiful theatres in the city. "Talkies" had only been around for three years.

Sid Grauman and his father built the "Million Dollar Theater" at Third and Broadway in 1918, and followed with the "Egyptian" on Hollywood Boulevard in 1922. This was the year that King Tut's tomb was discovered and the Graumans wanted to capitalize on the wave of "Egyptian chic" then sweeping the nation. The theatre's entryway mimicked the interior of an Egyptian temple and inside elaborately-carved columns and sphinxes framed the stage.

The Egyptian was a huge success for the Graumans and so, in 1927, they built their world-famous "Chinese Theatre," taking the "theme theater" in a new direction.

The last of the great Hollywood movie houses to be built on Hollywood Boulevard was the Pantages, and it would be the largest, most original and most ornate of them all. The vaulted grand lobby was the largest one in the city and there were grand stairways leading to the balcony at both ends of it. The theatre's ceiling was an enormously ornate blend of gold- and henna-colored forms and its stage the city's largest, seventy feet wide and one-hundred-and-eighty feet long.

The first movie shown at the Pantages was *Floradora Girl*, starring Marion Davies, and the opening night invitation list was a who's who of contemporary Hollywood. Observing a ritual that would continue for years to come, each star stepped from their limousines onto a red carpet to make their entrance.

During its long and elaborate history, the Pantages would be the site of many movie premieres, and between 1949 and 1959, the Academy Awards were held here.

JUNE 5

1981

First Official Recognition of AIDS

ON THIS DAY IN CALIFORNIA HISTORY the American Center for Disease Control issued a press release describing five cases of AIDS that had been diagnosed in Los Angeles. The following month, some cases of Karposi's sarcoma, a skin cancer, were reported to the CDC by a Dr. Michael Gottlieb of San Francisco.

It would turn out that the cases were related and that the AIDS virus had now officially entered the American population. This disease that's now believed to afflict almost 40,000,000 people worldwide was initially believed to be confined to California's gay community, but as we now know, that's not the case.

Since these first reports were released on this day in 1981, over 136,000 cases of AIDS have been reported in California alone and over 80,000 people there have died from the disease. Of this total, 26,000 cases were reported for people living in San Francisco, as were over 17,000 of the 80,000 deaths reported.

It is believed that somewhere between 108,000 and 124,000 people infected with the AIDS virus are currently living in California, almost 19,000 of them in San Francisco alone, and that new infections in the state are developing at the rate of 6,700 to 9,000 cases a year.

And as large as these numbers are, the cumulative number of cases of the disease reported in the state is second to the number reported in New York and just 15 percent of the total number reported for the nation as a whole.

Because San Francisco had such a large gay community, the rise of AIDS had an enormous effect on life in that city. Some late-eighties estimates put the size of the gay community there at 100,000 people (20 percent of the city's adult population), many of them affluent professionals, and therefore people whose lives had a big impact on the life of the community as a whole.

173

JUNE 6

1978

Proposition 13 Passes

ON THIS DAY IN CALIFORNIA HISTORY the now infamous Proposition 13 was passed by the voters of California. It was the brainchild of antitaxation activist Howard Jarvis and it would have a profound effect on the state for years to come.

In June of 1978 California's voters approved this measure by a margin of 65 to 35 percent. The immediate effect of this new legislation was to reduce the state's property tax revenues by 57 percent, a whopping $6.1 billion. First of all, the state property tax rate was capped at one percent—one percent, that is, of the state's total assessed real-estate value. Secondly, the values themselves were rolled back to their 1975-1976 levels.

Potential future growth in property tax revenues would be controlled by capping annual increases in tax bills at 2% and values could be reassessed only when property changed hands. Proposition 13 also made it harder for the state legislature to raise taxes, by requiring that any such change in the tax rate be approved by two-thirds of the state legislature, and that increases in local taxes also be approved by a vote of the people.

At the time of its passage, Proposition 13 was extremely popular with property owners, but it was at best a mixed blessing. As the state budget grew tighter, efforts were made to push the cost of financing public services down to *local* government, but local budgets had grown tighter, too. It turned out that no level of government had adequate funds to do the job.

Naturally, with less money available for education, California's educational system became something less than what it once was, and with less money available to spend on roads and bridges, roads and bridges fell into disrepair, too. The same thing happened with police and fire services and with virtually all services that depended on property-tax money for their support.

JUNE 7

1968

Sirhan Sirhan Indicted for Shooting Bobby Kennedy

ON THIS DAY IN CALIFORNIA HISTORY Jordanian national Sirhan Sirhan was indicted for shooting presidential candidate Robert F. Kennedy at the Ambassador Hotel in Los Angeles. He disagreed with Kennedy's pro-Israeli politics, and for that reason, shot him just minutes after Kennedy had won the California primary.

Sirhan believed himself betrayed by Kennedy's support of Israel's "Six Day War" against its Arab neighbors and that is believed to have been what motivated him to do what he did. In any case, shortly after Kennedy finished addressing his supporters in the main ballroom of the Ambassador Hotel, Sirhan discharged a .22-caliber pistol eight times into the crowd that was gathered around Kennedy in the hotel's kitchen, hitting the senator three times, and grazing his jacket with a fourth round.

In March of 1969 he admitted that he had deliberately shot Kennedy, though he also maintained that he did not remember doing so. Whether he "remembered" it or not, personal journals and diaries discovered in the aftermath of his arrest attest to the fact that he had long obsessed over killing the senator.

Sirhan's lawyer tried to get the venue for the case changed from Los Angeles to Fresno, but was unable to do so. Sirhan was convicted following his trial in L. A. and subsequently sentenced to death. In 1972 that sentence was commuted to "life," however, when the California Supreme Court decided to commute all death sentences that had been imposed in the state prior to that date.

Despite the "softening" of Sirhan's sentence, there has been little support for releasing him from prison. Each time he has become eligible for parole, his request has been denied (12 consecutive times as of 2003), and he continues to remain confined at the state penitentiary at Corcoran in Kings County, where he is likely to spend the remainder of his days.

JUNE 8

1864

Mark Twain Moves to San Francisco

ON THIS DAY IN CALIFORNIA HISTORY Mark Twain moved into the Occidental Hotel in San Francisco to begin an 18-month stay in town as a reporter for the *Daily Morning Call.*

Twain originally came West with his brother Orion when Orion took a job as secretary for the territorial governor of Nevada. Going west with his brother provided Twain with an opportunity to see more of the mid-19th-century American frontier, to escape service in the Civil War, and to try his hand at mining and writing.

The mining didn't pan out, but Twain did land a job at Virginia City's *Territorial Enterprise* in 1862, after that paper published a couple of pieces he had written. For the next two years he reported the local news.

In 1863 he made a visit to San Francisco and stayed at the Lick House there. While he was in the city he managed to sell some articles to the *Golden Era* literary journal and that success gave him the "in" he needed to move from Virginia City to San Francisco in 1864 to accept a job as a reporter with the *Call.*

It was while living in San Francisco that Twain met the city's leading writers, a group that regularly met at the offices of the *Golden Era* on Montgomery Street, and that included Bret Harte, author of "The Luck of Roaring Camp," who worked next door to the *Era* at the U. S. Mint. Twain credited Harte with helping him perfect his writing style during the time they knew one another here, and coming from Twain, that is high praise indeed.

During the time he lived in San Francisco, Twain put his pen to work on a variety of subjects. He wrote "Jim Smiley and his Jumping Frog" while he lived here, the story that would make his name when it appeared in the *New York Saturday Press*, and it was here that he met a man named "Tom Sawyer," destined to become much more famous in literature than in life.

JUNE 9

1980

Ansel Adams Receives Presidential Medal of Freedom

ON THIS DAY IN CALIFORNIA HISTORY President Jimmy Carter presented legendary California photographer Ansel Adams with the Presidential Medal of Freedom, the highest honor the government can bestow upon a civilian. A San Francisco native, Adams spent his entire professional life making luminous black-and-white photographs of some of the nation's most memorable wild places.

He founded "Group f/64" with fellow photographers Edward Weston, Willard Van Dyke, and Imogen Cunningham in 1932 ("f/64" was the smallest aperture that a camera could then be set to) and invented what is known as the "zone system," a technique that permits photographers to exert greater control over the finished result when developing their film.

Adams first became interested in photography as a child, after reading a book entitled *In the Heart of the Sierras*, by a man named George Fiske, then a well-known American landscape photographer and one of the Yosemite Valley's earliest photographers. The Fiske photographs captured his imagination and in 1916 he persuaded his parents to take him to Yosemite, where he first photographed it. From that time on, a camera was never far from him.

Adams joined California's Sierra Club and remained a member throughout his life. He was an avid mountain climber and climbed mountains all over California and in other places, too.

It can be said without exaggeration that Adams's photographs of the western American landscape are like no others. They are unmistakably vivid, unmistakably bold, unmistakably "Adams." And not only are they great art (some, like his ones of Death Valley, moving from realism into something like abstract art), they often had very practical effects, too. His photographs of the Sierra Nevada mountains are said to have helped get both the Sequoia and Kings Canyon areas designated as national parks.

JUNE 10

Dividing Up the Golden State

ON THIS DAY IN CALIFORNIA HISTORY the California State Assembly voted 46 to 26 in favor of putting a measure on the state ballot that would allow voters to decide if they wanted to break up the state into multiple states. Whatever else it was, it was nothing new.

The first effort to divide California up was mounted in 1850. A group of prominent Californians introduced a bill in the California legislature proposing that California be split into *two* "territories"— the "Territory of Colorado" (the northern half), and the "Territory of Southern California" (the southern half). It didn't pass.

Four years later, in 1854, the California legislature proposed a *trisection* of the state into the "State of Shasta" (California's northernmost counties), the "State of Colorado" (the "middle" counties), and the "State of California" (the southern counties). This proposal *almost* passed.

In 1859 a third effort to divide up the state was initiated. Andrés Pico, the brother of California's last Mexican governor, introduced a bill into the California legislature proposing that the state be divided at the thirty-sixth parallel (near Big Sur). The counties below this line would become the "Territory of Colorado," the counties above it, the "State of California."

Pico's proposal was put to a legislative and popular vote and *passed overwhelmingly*. For it to take effect, however, the President and the Congress had to approve it, and before that could be brought about, the imminent threat of Civil War became the exclusive focus of the nation's leaders.

In 1881 sectional sentiment flared up again. This time the ignition source was a proposal put forth in the *Los Angeles Herald* that Los Angeles, San Diego and San Bernardino counties be combined with what was then the Arizona Territory to create a new state called "Calizonia."

JUNE 11

1859

Comstock Lode Discovered

ON THIS DAY IN CALIFORNIA HISTORY the fabled Comstock Lode of silver was uncovered in Nevada near California's eastern border. There are probably those who think that such an event should properly be considered part of Nevada's history, and so it is, but it is also a big part of the history of California.

During the early 1860s two thousand new buildings a year were going up in San Francisco and this torrent of new construction was financed largely by the wealth extracted from Nevada's silver-rich mines, and the Comstock Lode in particular (all exploited primarily by San Franciscans). By the end of the century, in fact, silver would be responsible for bringing more than $500,000,000 of new wealth into the city, and for creating private fortunes that would dwarf those that had been created by the Gold Rush.

The western Nevada mines made George Hearst (William Randolph's father) a millionaire, as they did a man named Adolph Sutro. The money Sutro made actually came from building an elaborate tunnel into the Comstock Lode and gave him the capital he needed to invest in San Francisco real estate, his ultimate holdings, some say, growing to between one-twelfth and *one-sixth* of all the land in the city.

But no one got richer from the Nevada silver mines than the men who came to be known as the "Silver Kings"—James G. Fair, James C. Flood, William S. O'Brien and John W. Mackay.

Flood and O'Brien made their money accumulating mining *stocks* (getting tips on which ones to buy from the patrons of the saloons they kept), Mackay had been a miner himself and had owned a silver mine, and Fair was an experienced mine superintendent. These men became spectacular examples of a type that would surface again and again in the wide-open frontier economy of late-19th-century San Francisco—the "sudden millionaire."

179

JUNE 12

Bonds to Build the L. A. Aqueduct Approved

ON THIS DAY IN CALIFORNIA HISTORY L. A. voters approved the bonds that would let the city's chief water engineer, William Mulholland, build the Los Angeles Aqueduct. The bonds were approved by a margin of 9 to 1.

What L. A. had to have to grow to anything more than a dusty village was water. From the time that the first colonists arrived here in 1769, the only source of water was the modest Los Angeles River. The eleven families that made up this small first group of Angelenos dammed the river to secure drinking water and water to irrigate, but as the city grew, it was clear that the river could not handle the water needs of a large city.

William Mulholland, an immigrant from Ireland, had come to L. A. in 1877 when it truly was still nothing more than a dusty cow town and had gone to work for the Los Angeles Water Company as a "ditch tender," a person who maintained the ditches that distributed water from the Los Angeles River to city residents. By 1886 he had risen from that position to the position of Chief Engineer for the company.

In 1902 the city of Los Angeles took over the water company, retaining Mulholland as Chief Engineer. One of his key responsibilities was identifying new sources of water for the city and he played an important role in the decision to build an aqueduct from the Owens Valley at the southern end of the Sierra Nevada Mountains to the San Fernando Valley just north of downtown Los Angeles, a distance of nearly 250 miles.

Building the aqueduct cost over $20,000,000, took five years to complete, and by 1923, had drained all of the water out of Owens Lake. Once a beautiful blue mountain lake, and periodic resting stop for millions of birds, Owens Lake is now just a salt flat where the wind routinely stirs up dust storms.

JUNE 13

1852

Wells, Fargo & Company Opens for Business

ON THIS DAY IN CALIFORNIA HISTORY Wells, Fargo & Company opened for business in San Francisco and Sacramento. The company had been founded less than three months before in New York City by Henry Wells and William G. Fargo.

At the beginning, Wells Fargo was heavily involved in financial activity related to the Gold Rush, which was the leading financial venture of the day, but it was also involved early on in the delivery of gold, mail and valuables, a business it remained in from 1852 to 1918. The company used a variety of different methods to do its delivery work, including stagecoaches, steamships, Pony Express riders and, once they were available, cars.

Wells Fargo started out as a local venture, running freight and passenger coaches between San Francisco, Sacramento and Marysville. Services soon extended to other California towns, however, and in 1866, to towns outside of California.

Forty years into its history I. W. Hellman took over as president of the company. Hellman had made a lot of money investing in Southern California real estate and had also founded the Farmers & Merchants Bank of Los Angeles and was interested in expanding the Wells Fargo franchise, making it a significantly bigger bank than it already was.

In 1905 the express and banking halves of Wells Fargo were formally separated, the banking side of the business merging with the Nevada Bank, which had been founded by the "Silver Kings," Fair, Flood, Mackay and O'Brien.

Like the Bank of America, Wells Fargo grew with the West. It financed ventures in agriculture, aerospace and film, among others, and grew increasingly larger as the 20th century wore on. It is today the fourth largest bank in the United States and the fourteenth largest bank in the world.

JUNE 14

1888

Charles Crocker Dies

ON THIS DAY IN CALIFORNIA HISTORY Charles Crocker, one of California's 19th-century master builders, died from injuries sustained two years earlier in a carriage accident in New York City.

Crocker had been born to modest circumstances in upstate New York and moved with his family to Iowa at the age of fourteen. He was ambitious from the beginning, and worked hard not only on the family farm, but on neighboring farms, at a sawmill, and at an iron forge, too. In 1845 he established an iron forge of his own.

Like everyone else in mid-19th-century America, Crocker heard that there were people making big money in the California gold fields, and always eager to improve his lot in life, decided to head out West to make big money, too.

But two years of working in the mines persuaded him that digging for gold wasn't *his* road to riches, so he decided to open a retail goods store in Sacramento instead. By 1854 he was one of the wealthiest men in town. In 1855 he was elected to the Sacramento city council, and in 1860, got himself elected to the California state legislature.

In the early 1860s Crocker went into partnership with Huntington, Stanford and Hopkins to build the Central Pacific Railroad. The far-western side of this venture, *their* side, was the hardest leg to build, because it required tunneling through the Sierra Nevada mountains. The hard-driving Crocker got it done, however, *seven years* ahead of schedule, using teams of Chinese laborers.

In the years to come, Crocker became president of the Southern Pacific Railroad, got involved in banking ("Crocker Bank" is now gone, but its offices were once a common sight in California), built the luxurious Del Monte Hotel in Monterey and made another fortune speculating in real estate. He even foresaw the role that massive irrigation would play in the state's economic future.

JUNE 15

1958

"Yakety-Yak" by the Coasters is a Hit

ON THIS DAY IN CALIFORNIA HISTORY the song "Yakety-Yak" by the Coasters was in the first week of its 15-week run in the Billboard "Top 40." The Coasters were an L. A. "doo wop" group that sang clever "story" songs that had evolved out of a group called the Robins. Carl Gardner and Bobby Nunn of the Robins had formed the group and it quickly became a big success.

The songwriters for the Robins had been the legendary Mike Leiber and Jerry Stoller, who were both originally from the East Coast, but who met at Los Angeles City College and there began a collaboration that would in time turn them into two of the most important songwriters and producers of the 20th century. They both loved rhythm and blues and combining that music with witty pop lyrics proved to be their ticket to fortune and fame.

Gardner and Nunn recruited bass singer Billy Guy, tenor Leon Hughes, and guitar player Adolph Jacobs to complete their original lineup and released their first single, "Down in Mexico," in 1956. In 1957 they released "Young Blood" and "Searchin'," and not too long after that, relocated to New York City, where additional personnel changes were made. Nunn and Hughes left, Dubb Jones and Obie Bessie were added, then Bessie left and was replaced by Cornell Gunter.

It was this last lineup—Gardner, Guy, Jones and Gunter, with King Curtis on tenor saxophone—who recorded "Yakety-Yak."

They followed it up with "Charlie Brown," "Along Came Jones," "Poison Ivy," and "Little Egypt," and found the sound and the lyrics that would make them rock-and-roll legends. The group's last hit was "Love Potion No. 9" in 1971. All but Gardner have now passed away. Still, they were one of the most memorable sounds to come out of the West Coast and remain a joy to listen to whenever their songs are played.

JUNE 16

"Monterey Pop" Opens at Monterey Fairgrounds

ON THIS DAY IN CALIFORNIA HISTORY the Monterey Pop Festival, the world's first rock music festival, opened in Monterey.

The Monterey Pop Festival was the first rock music festival ever and the bands that appeared there would go on to become household words in the years just ahead. They included Jefferson Airplane, Big Brother and the Holding Company, the Grateful Dead, the Jimi Hendrix Experience, the Mamas and the Papas, Eric Burdon and the Animals, Booker T and the MGs, the Paul Butterfield Blues Band, the Byrds, Country Joe and the Fish, the Steve Miller Band, Simon and Garfunkel, and the Association.

During the course of this three-day musical event over 200,000 young people came to participate in what was to have been the *First* Annual Monterey International Pop Music Festival. It would turn out to be first *and last* Monterey International Pop Music Festival, however, a one-of-a-kind "happening" that would live on in rock music lore ever after.

The bands that came to Monterey played music 24 hours a day for three straight days, played for free, and played to celebrate what promoters of the festival called "Music, Love, and Flowers." For these three days everyone at least *seemed* to set the world's troubles aside—the Cold War, Vietnam, racial tensions and poverty—and instead just lose themselves in the music that filled the crisp, clear air and beautiful physical space in which they had been lucky enough to find themselves.

"Monterey Pop" opened doors that few realized were available to be opened. One minute American youth culture was merely the last few gasps of the fifties—short hair, sock hops, and all—the next minute it was the dawning of the Age of Aquarius, drugs, long hair, free love and flower power, something completely unlike what had come before.

JUNE 17

1579

Sir Francis Drake's Sails into "Drake's Bay"

ON THIS DAY IN CALIFORNIA HISTORY English naval officer, privateer and adventurer Sir Francis Drake landed his ship, the *Golden Hind*, on the shores of a tiny inlet on the Marin County coastline north of San Francisco Bay. The ship had developed some problems that required immediate attention and Drake landed just long enough to give it the attention it needed and again be on his way.

Drake was an important figure in English naval history. He first went to sea on a cargo ship at about age 13, and at 23, set sail with his cousin Sir John Hawkins for the New World, intending to seize some of 16th-century Spain's mineral wealth there.

In a famous incident in 1573 Drake allied himself with some French privateers and African slaves to attack a group of Spanish ships near Panama (the "Spanish Silver Train") and made off with a fortune in gold. He would also have made off with a fortune in silver, but it was just too heavy to carry in addition to the gold and had to be left behind.

In 1577 England's Queen Elizabeth commissioned Drake to move against Spanish ships and ports along the Pacific Coast of North America. Drake left England with five ships and a crew of 150, but by the time he made it to the western coast of South America, only his flagship and its crew were left. He pushed forward anyway, attacking ships and ports as he went, and may have gotten as far north as today's U. S. border with Canada.

On this day in 1579 Drake sailed into the waters of an inlet on the northern California coast known today as "Drake's Bay." Though there is still some controversy as to the exact point on the coast where Drake landed, the character of the coastline that surrounds Drake's Bay appears to be a good fit for Drake's description of where he was. Drake christened the area "New Albion" (New England) before sailing away.

JUNE 18

ON THIS DAY IN CALIFORNIA HISTORY California girl Sally Ride became the first American woman to fly in outer space, on the space shuttle *Challenger*.

She had been born in the San Fernando Valley town of Encino in 1951 and attended high school at the exclusive Westlake School for Girls. She began her college career at Swarthmore College in Pennsylvania but finished up at Stanford. She graduated with degrees in English and physics and would go on to Stanford to earn a master's and a Ph.D. in physics.

Ride made her space flights while working for NASA, but left in 1987 to work for the Stanford University Center for International Security and Arms Control. She stayed just two years, however. In 1989 she took a position as a professor of physics at the University of California, San Diego.

Once in the university community, Sally Ride's long-standing interest in increasing science literacy among young women blossomed in a big way. Statistics had shown for years that up through the early elementary grades, boys and girls showed about equal interest in science, but by grade eight, twice as many boys as girls continued to show that interest.

Ride believed that this probably had a lot to do with the relative lack of encouragement young girls typically received in the traditional educational system when it came to subjects like science and math and not with any "inherent" intellectual differences between the sexes.

In an effort to remedy this imbalance, her company, "Sally Ride Science," offers "science camps" for middle-school-age girls, "science festivals," where young girls can conduct experiments, meet scientists, and just generally have fun "doing science," and publishes books about science and about *careers* in science for girls.

JUNE 19

1878

Eadweard Muybridge Helps Settle a Question

ON THIS DAY IN CALIFORNIA HISTORY photographer Eadweard Muybridge took a photograph of one of Leland Stanford's horses at full gallop, proving that that there are indeed times when horses have all four feet off the ground. Most people thought otherwise, but Muybridge proved that Stanford had it right.

Muybridge had been born "Edward James Muggeridge" in Kingston-on-Thames, England, in 1830, but changed his name to "Eadweard Muybridge" as an adult, because he believed that that was the proper *Anglo-Saxon* way to spell it. He no doubt also wanted to link his identity to that of his homeland's first people and felt that spelling his name that way did the trick.

In any case, Muybridge migrated from England to America and in time found his way to frontier California where he became an assistant to California photographer Carleton Watkins. In 1867 he began to build his own reputation by making photographs of San Francisco and Yosemite, photographs for which he quickly became famous. These images, like those made by Watkins, showed how grand and glorious California's natural landscape truly was.

In 1872 former governor Stanford hired Muybridge to help him determine if a galloping horse's four hooves all ever left the ground at once. Six years later, in 1878, he set up a series of fifty cameras to capture the movement of one of Stanford's horses at full gallop. The shutter of each camera was connected to a trip wire that the horse set off as it galloped by.

These photographs do, indeed, show that all four of a horse's hooves leave the ground at various points during the course of a full gallop. Muybridge later invented a machine called the "Zoopraxiscope," a device that could make a series of still images appear to be in motion and that was a precursor to the modern motion picture projector.

JUNE 20

1947

"Bugsy" Siegel Gunned Down in Beverly Hills

ON THIS DAY IN CALIFORNIA HISTORY gangster Benjamin "Bugsy" Siegel was assassinated by a mob hit man in Beverly Hills.

He had been born in Brooklyn, forty-one years before, to a poor Russian Jewish family. "Poor" wasn't something that Siegel wanted to be and he began to work at putting that behind him early on. As a kid, he joined a street gang on the Lower East Side, and later, in partnership with another kid named Moe Sedway, set up his own "protection racket."

As a teenager, Siegel became a friend of gangster legend Meyer Lansky and, with him, formed a small gang. He is reputed to have worked as a hit man for the gang and even to have hired himself out to other gangs "as needed." He was heavily involved in bootlegging during the '30s and in the formation of "Murder, Inc.," too.

In 1937 Siegel was sent to California by his East Coast mob associates to develop gambling rackets on the West Coast. Working closely with a Los Angeles mobster named Jack Dragna and a gang boss named Mickey Cohen, Siegel set up a wire service that permitted his bosses in the East to get their cut on West Coast gambling activity faster than they otherwise would.

With the help of friends like actor George Raft and Hollywood socialite Dorothy DiFrasso, Siegel found his way into Hollywood's inner circle. Once there, he began to live in the extravagant Hollywood fashion of the times and to extort, some allege, money from Hollywood studios, in addition to his other activities.

Siegel is often said to have had an important role in the development of Las Vegas into the gambling playground that it is today. Just how crucial his personal role was is a matter of some dispute, but what is certain is that the Mob was involved in Las Vegas gambling from the beginning and that Siegel was instrumental in launching the Strip's first big hotel and casino, the Flamingo.

JUNE 21

1940

Dick & Pat Nixon Get Married at the Mission Inn

ON THIS DAY IN CALIFORNIA HISTORY Richard M. Nixon and his wife, Pat (Ryan), got married at the historic Mission Inn in Riverside.

Nixon was a local boy, born in Yorba Linda in 1913 and raised in nearby Whittier. He graduated from Whittier College, studied law at Duke, and later became a United States Congressman from California, Vice President of the United States, and then President (the only man to have ever been elected twice to these two offices).

Pat had been raised in Southern California, too. She was actually born in Nevada but her family moved to the Los Angeles area when she was very young and it was there that she would grow up and meet the future President.

The Mission Inn where the Nixons got married was a somewhat whimsical and bizarre place located in downtown Riverside. The property had originally been a two-story, twelve-room adobe boarding house built in 1876 by a man named Christopher Columbus Miller, and predated the city of Riverside itself. Miller's son Frank began expanding the structure in 1902 and continued to build on it until his death in 1935.

His method of construction was eclectic and the Inn he created a mélange of architectural styles, all of them efforts to celebrate California's mythical Spanish past. Section after section took the structure in new directions, yielding an enormously complex whole that would in time evolve into something more like a medieval city than anything properly understood as a "building."

The Inn was closed in 1985 so that it could be restored and reopened again for business in 1992. Today it remains alive and well, regularly accommodating guests in its 250-some rooms and suites. It has been the cultural and literal center of Riverside for almost 130 years now, and is also where Ron and Nancy Reagan spent their first honeymoon night in 1952.

JUNE 22

1964

Ban on Henry Miller's *Tropic of Cancer* Lifted

ON THIS DAY IN CALIFORNIA HISTORY the United States Supreme Court lifted what had been a thirty-year ban on Henry Miller's celebrated first book, *Tropic of Cancer*. When it first came out in 1934 the book broke an enormous amount of new ground on the question of what was obscenity and what was "art." The U. S. Supreme Court decided, in a 5-4 decision, that it was "art."

Miller had been born in Brooklyn, and had lived in Paris for a long time, too, but in 1944 he chose to move to the splendid Big Sur area of the California coast to live, paint, and write. It was during this period that he would publish many of the books for which he is still best remembered, including *The Air-Conditioned Nightmare* (1945), *Remember to Remember* (1947), *The Books in My Life* (1952), *Big Sur and the Oranges of Hieronymus Bosch* (1957), and *Stand Still Like the Hummingbird* (1962).

Miller was one of the great American nonconformists and he translated virtually everything that happened to him into his books. Big Sur was no exception. He loved the wild beauty of the place and in his book, *Big Sur and the Oranges of Hieronymus Bosch*, he gives us a vivid sense of the California paradise that he then called home. He would remain here until 1963.

Tropic of Cancer, though it had been published in Paris in 1934, only made it into print in the United States in 1961, and immediately provoked a series of obscenity trials that became testing grounds of the nation's antipornography laws.

The U. S. Supreme Court decision handed down on this day in 1964 set aside the rulings of some state courts that had pronounced Miller's book "obscene" and declared that it was "literature." It was one of the first important shots to be fired in the nation's "sexual revolution" and a milestone in the effort to protect First Amendment rights.

JUNE 23

1921

Oil Strike on Signal Hill

ON THIS DAY IN CALIFORNIA HISTORY Royal Dutch Shell brought in the first well on "Signal Hill" in southern Los Angeles County. Over time, it would prove to be one of the most productive oil fields ever brought in in the United States.

Signal Hill rises 365 feet above the community of Long Beach, and Long Beach sits about twenty miles directly south of downtown Los Angeles. Because the hill is so much higher than the ground that surrounds it, it was used long ago by the Tongva Indians as a place to make signal fires, fires which could be seen as for off as Catalina Island, twenty-six miles off the coast.

Between the years 1913 and 1923, the Balboa Amusement Producing Company ("Balboa Studios") used an eleven-acre patch of ground on Signal Hill to shoot the outdoor scenes of their movies, including those of two of their more high-profile actors, comedians Buster Keaton and Fatty Arbuckle. Other parts of the hill were devoted to private residences, as well as to fruit, vegetable and flower gardens.

But then Shell Oil brought in the Signal Hill field, beginning with their "Alamitos #1" well, in which the pressure was so great that when it finally erupted, crude oil shot 114 feet in the air. Soon Signal Hill was covered with derricks, so many that it was nicknamed "*Porcupine* Hill."

The discovery of oilfields like Signal Hill had a lot to do with turning L. A. and the rest of Southern California into a very big place. It turned out that L. A.-area crude was rich in gasoline, and an ample supply of low-price fuel was exactly what the many thousands of cars that had begun to fill up the Greater Los Angeles basin needed. It also provided much of the capital needed to build new homes and streets and such things as the port facilities at San Pedro and Long Beach.

191

JUNE 24

1842

Ambrose Bierce Born

ON THIS DAY IN CALIFORNIA HISTORY Ambrose Bierce, a man who would come to loom large in the state's 19th-century literary history, was born in Horse Cave Creek, Ohio.

When the American Civil War began, Bierce was almost twenty years old and, like many young men of the day, enlisted in the army—in his case, the *Union* Army. He fought in several of the most important battles of the war and in 1864 received a serious head wound at the Battle of Kennesaw Mountain that ultimately led to his discharge from the military in January of 1865.

He returned to the service during the summer of 1866, however, and got involved in inspecting military outposts out West, a task that in time brought him to San Francisco.

In San Francisco Bierce resigned from the Army and took up journalism. He wrote for several San Francisco periodicals, including both *The Argonaut* and *The Wasp*, and in 1887 became one of the first regular columnists to be employed by the *San Francisco Examiner*. He eventually became one of the most influential journalists on the West Coast.

As a writer, Bierce was noted for his clear and economical use of English, as well as for his realistic style, qualities that have kept his work fresh and readable, while that of many of his contemporaries has long gone unread. His views are also notable for their "dark" side, so much so, in fact, that they earned him the nickname "Bitter Bierce."

Bierce wrote with distinction across a variety of genres and his much-quoted *The Devil's Dictionary* sells well to this day. In October of 1913 the 70-year-old author began a tour of the old battlefields on which he had fought as a young man, which ended with his joining up with Pancho Villa's Mexican army and disappearing into the mists of history.

JUNE 25

1835

First House in "San Francisco" Built

ON THIS DAY IN CALIFORNIA HISTORY William A. Richardson abandoned his post as a crewman on a whaler that had docked at Yerba Buena Cove, apparently believing that he had a brighter future on shore than by continuing with his life at sea.

With that thought in mind, he erected a "structure" comprised of four wooden poles with a ship's sail stretched over them that was, along with the Presidio and mission that the Spanish had built here in the 18th century, one of the very first buildings in what would soon become the city of San Francisco.

At about the same time that Richardson raised up his wood-and-canvas home in the southeastern part of the "city," a man named Jacob Leese also built a home nearby. Leese had been in partnership with Los Angeles merchant Hugo Reid in the hide and tallow trade, but had now moved his base of operations to Yerba Buena.

San Francisco's "start-up" European population had numbered just 244: colonists who left northern Mexico in late 1775 and arrived in the Bay Area in the spring of 1776.

By 1848 the population of the city had only grown to nine hundred and the city itself amounted to little more than "two hotels, twelve stores, a billiard hall, a bowling alley and two newspapers." Not much to show for its first seventy-two years of life, but that was about to change in a big way.

When news arrived in May 1848 that gold had been discovered on the American River, San Francisco's already small population suddenly shrunk to just seven.

Once the wealth from mining gold began to roll in, however, that short-term bust turned back into a boom, and the city really began to grow with a vengeance. By the end of the fifties the city's population had reached 56,800, and by 1900, had swollen to 400,000, making it the ninth largest city in the nation.

JUNE 26

1945

U. N. Charter Signed in San Francisco

ON THIS DAY IN CALIFORNIA HISTORY representatives of 50 nations meeting in Francisco signed the document that would create the United Nations.

World War II was a watershed event in human history. The war drew most of the planet into the conflict, and by its end, 100,000,000 had been wounded, disabled, or killed, counting both military personnel and civilians.

Beginning with conferences in Teheran (1943) and Washington, D. C. (1944), and concluding with a meeting at Yalta in the Crimea in 1945, the idea of how the world should go about handling international conflicts going forward was discussed in detail. The Yalta Conference included the three leaders of the world's great powers at that time—England's Winston Churchill, Russia's Joseph Stalin, and Franklin Delano Roosevelt, President of the United States.

At Yalta they agreed that a "United Nations" council needed to be set up that would mediate conflicts between nations in the future. Once the Germans surrendered in 1945, the Allies moved rapidly to convene a conference to get this done and chose San Francisco as their meeting place. Representatives of fifty-one countries signed the document that created the revolutionary new body.

President Woodrow Wilson had tried to create such a body at the conclusion of World War I called the League of Nations. The goals of the League were equally lofty and far-reaching, but the world wasn't yet ready for such a radically civilized approach to conflict, and it wasn't a success.

The efforts of the world's leaders to create such an organization at the conference in San Francisco *were* successful, however, even though those of the city to have that body permanently housed there were not. New York City was chosen to be the U. N.'s permanent home.

194

JUNE 27

2001

Actor Jack Lemmon Dies in Los Angeles

ON THIS DAY IN CALIFORNIA HISTORY actor Jack Lemmon died at his home in Los Angeles. He was born in Boston seventy-six years earlier and had been educated at Boston prep schools and Harvard University, where he had been a member of the university's theatrical group, "Hasty Pudding."

Lemmon worked in radio, theater *and* film throughout his long career in the entertainment business. He made his movie debut in the 1954 film *It Should Happen to You* and was a mainstay of the silver screen from then on, playing everything from the serious roles he played in *Days of Wine and Roses* (1962), *Save the Tiger* (1973), *The China Syndrome* (1979), and *Missing* (1982), to the comedic ones for which he is perhaps best remembered, in such films as *Some Like It Hot* (1959) and *Grumpy Old Men* (1993).

Lemmon remains best known today for the eight films he did with actor Walter Matthau, which included *The Fortune Cookie* (1966), *The Odd Couple* (1968), *The Front Page* (1974), *Buddy, Buddy* (1981), *Grumpy Old Men*, *Grumpier Old Men* (1995), *Out to Sea* (1997) and *The Odd Couple II* (1998).

The big-screen magic between these two was generated by their skill at being constantly at odds with one another on-screen, even though they were the best of friends offscreen. Walter always played the "mean" and "difficult" one, Jack the "nice guy," sweet and lovable whatever the situation.

But Lemmon never "fell into type" or let himself lapse into just playing himself on screen *or* stage. He played the lead in an ambitious television production of Eugene O'Neill's *Long Day's Journey into Night* (1987), made an interesting cameo appearance in Oliver Stone's *JFK* (1991), and garnered several fine reviews for his portrayal of a washed-up real-estate salesman in the movie *Glengarry Glen Ross* (1992).

JUNE 28

1978

U. S. Supreme Court Decides the Bakke Case

ON THIS DAY IN CALIFORNIA HISTORY the United States Supreme Court voted 5-4 to force the medical school at the University of California at Davis to admit Allan Bakke, a white man, who argued he had been a victim of reverse racial discrimination.

The case, styled the "Regents of the University of California v. Bakke," was a landmark in the area of affirmative action in the United States. It barred the use of quotas in the college admissions process, but nonetheless affirmed the idea that race could be used as a "factor" in that process.

Bakke, a white male, had applied for admission to the University of California, Davis, medical school in 1973 and had been denied admission, despite the fact that he was *more* qualified than some applicants who had actually been let in. He applied for admission again in 1974 and was again denied.

There were two kinds of admission at Davis: "regular" admission and "special" admission. The process involved a rating system that assigned numerical values to each applicant's application materials, which were then summed and the applicants ranked accordingly. Applicants admitted through the "special" admissions process were not compared with, and did not compete with, those admitted under the "regular" admissions process.

In both of the years that Bakke applied to the school, applicants were admitted under the "special" admissions process with credentials that were inferior to his.

When he learned of this, Bakke filed suit in California Superior Court, arguing that he had been discriminated against on the basis of race and thereby denied his rights under the "equal protection" of the law. The California Supreme Court agreed with him, and the University of California then appealed the ruling to the United States Supreme Court, which upheld the California court's decision.

JUNE 29

1925

Earthquake Hits Santa Barbara

ON THIS DAY IN CALIFORNIA HISTORY, at 6:42 a.m., an earthquake shook almost all of Victorian Santa Barbara to the ground. It was a fairly powerful quake, 6.3 on the Richter scale, and began beneath the Santa Barbara Channel. When the earth stopped moving, thirteen people were dead and sixty-four injured.

It was a Monday, but mercifully the quake struck early in the morning, when most of the city's downtown buildings were still empty. G. Allan Hancock and his son Bertram (members of the prominent Hancock family of Los Angeles) were killed when a sixty-thousand-gallon water tank crashed through the roof of the hotel in which they were staying.

Most of the city's more recent construction—the Lobero Theater, the *Daily News* building on De la Guerra Plaza, and the El Paseo complex—survived the shaking, as did many of the more recently-built homes. The older buildings, however, didn't fare so well. Most of the ones that had been built in the 19th or early 20th centuries, which was most of them, including Mission Santa Barbara itself, sustained serious damage from the shaking.

Suddenly the opportunity to create a "new" city, shaped from top to bottom by a dominant architectural theme, presented itself. Henceforth all new design and construction had to have a "Spanish flavor" to it, which gave the city a remarkably attractive and coherent look, making it a showpiece of California living by the sea.

In the years since the 1925 earthquake, Santa Barbara's city fathers have rigorously maintained this red-tile-roof, white-stucco-wall theme, and made their city one of the finest examples of aesthetically-appealing urban design in America. The late Thomas More Storke, a Santa Barbara newspaperman and philanthropist once called his city "the ideal home of man" (that was back in 1901), and it would certainly be hard to imagine a better one.

JUNE 30

1864

Yosemite Made a State Park

ON THIS DAY IN CALIFORNIA HISTORY the Yosemite ("yo-'sem-et-ee") Valley—and the "Mariposa Big Trees" near it—were made into a state park. President Lincoln signed the legislation permanently putting this area under the protection of the state.

The Valley itself is not a big place—just seven miles long and less than a mile wide—but it is a place full to bursting with natural wonders: thousand-foot waterfalls (Niagara is just 164), towering granite cliffs, and trees far older than any other living things.

Originally it was inhabited by a tribe of Indians who lived there and was first entered by white men in 1849. In the mid-1850s a man named "Grizzly" Adams lived there and made a name for himself by taming local grizzly bears and later appearing with them in public— even in the streets of San Francisco.

English immigrant James M. Hutchings, the Valley's first "Mr. Yosemite" and the creator of *Hutchings' California Magazine*, a popular illustrated periodical of the day, came here in 1855 and spent the rest of his life promoting the Valley's wonders. Horace ("Go west, young man") Greeley came in the summer of 1859, Ralph Waldo Emerson in 1871, and Presidents Grant, Garfield and Hayes before the century was out.

John Muir, the illustrious founder of California's Sierra Club and a man whose name would in time become synonymous with the state's natural environment, Yosemite in particular, first came to the Valley in 1868.

An amateur but avid student of geology, he would ultimately succeed Hutchings as Yosemite's foremost guardian angel and also be among the first people to argue that it was the movement of glaciers, long, long ago, that had given the Valley its shape. The commonly accepted view today, it is one that many "authorities" in Muir's time thought preposterous.

198

This Day

in

July

JULY 1

1839

Sutter Sails into San Francisco Bay

ON THIS DAY IN CALIFORNIA HISTORY "Captain" John Sutter, the man who would go on to build the fort that would in time grow into the city of Sacramento, was on board the brig *Clementine* as it sailed into Yerba Buena Cove.

He had traveled across North American and throughout the Far West, looking for the right place to make a new start, and that search had finally taken him to California.

Sutter had first read about the American West in a book by the Swiss writer, Gottfried Duden, a countryman of his. He reached the Missouri Territory late in 1834 and spent the next five years working as a trader in Santa Fe, hobnobbing with missionaries and mountain men on the Oregon Trail, and sailing the inland waterways of the Pacific Northwest. He visited Fort Vancouver in western Canada, Sitka, Alaska, and Honolulu, too.

Once in California, Sutter was quick to make his way to the Sacramento Valley, where he soon began building his fort.

When he arrived in California there were only about 5,000 Europeans living there, almost all of them Spanish, and about 30,000 Indians. In order to secure the land he needed to build his settlement, he became a Mexican citizen, and in June of 1841, took title to 48,827 acres of land in the Sacramento Valley. He named this place "Nueva Helvetia," or "New Switzerland," to honor his homeland, and farmed wheat, planted vineyards and cut timber.

For a time, Sutter prospered, but the coming of the Gold Rush (ironically, triggered by the discovery of gold near his property) proved to be his undoing. When miners rushed in to extract the gold from northern California's rivers and streams, they overran his lands, stealing or destroying nearly everything he had worked to build, and left him a poor man in the process. He would end his life penniless, still trying to redress these wrongs.

JULY 2

California Tennis Stars Set Records

ON THIS DAY IN CALIFORNIA HISTORY two of the state's many famous tennis players reached important milestones. In 1938 Helen Wills won her eighth and final Wimbledon singles championship. In 1966 Billie Jean King won the first of what would ultimately be six Wimbledon single titles.

Berkeley native Wills was the U. S. girls' singles champion for 1921 and 1922 and won two gold medals at the Paris Olympics in 1924. She won thirty-one major titles during her career, including seven U. S. singles championships, eight Wimbledon singles titles, and four French singles titles.

When she won the women's singles title in 1923 at age 17, Wills was the youngest player to ever do that, and went on to win the finals rounds of her first sixteen major-title matches in straight sets. Between 1919 and 1938 she put together an astonishing 398-35 match record, including a winning streak between 1927 and 1932 in which she did not lose a single set.

Long Beach native King won twelve Grand Slam singles titles and twenty-five Grand Slam doubles titles over the course of her career. In 1966 she won the first of six singles titles at Wimbledon and was ranked number one in the world for the first time.

In 1973 she accepted a challenge from former great Bobby Riggs, then 55, who boasted that the woman's game was so inferior to the men's that *even he* could beat the top female players in the world. King had been reluctant to accept the challenge, but eventually relented and beat him 6-4, 6-3, 6-3.

Wills and King were part of what would turn out to be a steady stream of female tennis talent to emerge in California throughout the 20th century. From May Sutton and Hazel Hotchkiss early in the century to Venus and Serena Williams late, California women were a major force in the sport.

202

JULY 3

1937

Del Mar Racetrack Opens

ON THIS DAY IN CALIFORNIA HISTORY the beautiful Del Mar Racetrack, twenty miles north of San Diego, opened for betting.

It was the idea of three men who were big names in the world of entertainment at the time—Bing Crosby, Jimmy Durante and Pat O'Brien—and their intention was simply to have a track available for their use when they and their buddies were time at the beach. This way they could enjoy the sun and play the ponies, too.

But the Del Mar Racetrack quickly grew beyond the modest expectations that Crosby, Durante and O'Brien had originally had for it, becoming another chic hangout for the headliners of the day and therefore a very "in" place in its own right. Ava Gardner, Dorothy Lamour and Paulette Goddard came to the track, as did W. C. Fields, Red Skelton, and Edgar Bergen. Don Ameche played the ponies here, and so did Desi Arnaz, Lucille Ball and many other celebrities, too.

And not only did high-profile folks in the entertainment industry come to what was then still a very fresh and "away-from-it-all" spot on the Southern California coast, the biggest names in horse racing also beat a path to Del Mar's door. Johnny Longden, long the winningest jockey in the sport, rode mounts here, as did Willie Shoemaker, who broke Longden's win record, Laffit Pincay, Jr., who broke Shoemaker's, Eddie Delahoussaye, and, in more recent times, Chris McCarron.

In 1938, after being open just one year, the legendary racehorse "Seabiscuit" graced the Del Mar track. Another track legend, jockey George "Iceman" Woolf, was in the saddle that day, and Seabiscuit won his race against a horse named "Ligaroti" by a nose. Woolf was a very big name in horse-racing circles back then and the cup recognizing the nation's best jockey each year would eventually be named in his honor.

JULY 4

"Venice of America" Established

ON THIS DAY IN CALIFORNIA HISTORY the city of Venice ("Venice of America") was officially established.

In 1892 a man named Abbot Kinney and his partner, Francis G. Ryan, bought a sizable stretch of land south of Santa Monica that they subdivided and named "Ocean Park." In 1900 the area was linked to downtown L. A. by Henry Huntington's "Big Red Cars," making it easy for Angelenos to get to.

Kinney's new city came complete with canals, gondolas, a "St. Mark's" Hotel and pigeons. Concessions were introduced the year after its official "founding," brought down from the Lewis and Clark Exposition held in Portland, Oregon, in 1905, the same year construction of the city was complete.

But just fifteen years later, the city that Kinney hoped would be the center of art and culture on the West Coast was little more than a seaside eyesore, and by 1925, almost all of its once-grand canals had been filled in and forgotten. Around 1970, however, this charming seaside community that had held so much promise back in the early years of the 20th century started coming back to life.

During the 1970s Venice's art galleries hung works by Robert Motherwell, Andy Warhol and Robert Rauschenberg, and its restaurants fed the likes of Bob Dylan and Muhammed Ali. Brightly-colored murals were a common sight, street musicians played everywhere and local actors regularly improvised "beach theater" for anyone who cared to watch.

Bodybuilders continued to build their bodies here, too, and what is perhaps the world's largest army of roller skaters continued to roll along the sidewalks that run between Venice Beach and the Santa Monica pier. Inevitably, real estate developers fell in love with Venice, too, and have done their best to make it as dearly-priced as California's other chic seaside sanctuaries.

JULY 5

1938

Herb Caen Starts Writing for the *Chronicle*

ON THIS DAY IN CALIFORNIA HISTORY journalist Herb Caen (pronounced "Kane") started writing a daily column for the *San Francisco Chronicle* that soon became "essential reading" for "with-it" San Franciscans. Just 22 when he started, it was a job he would hold down (with an interruption from 1950 to 1958, when he worked for the *San Francisco Examiner*) until his death in 1997.

Caen originally attracted the attention of San Francisco's reading public with a column entitled "It's News to Me." It was filled with witty writing, the work of a man very much in-the-know about San Francisco and the place where the words "Beatnik" and "hippie" first found their way into the English language, two words that Caen invented.

Caen wrote a number of books about life in San Francisco life, too, including *Baghdad-by-the-Bay* (1949), *Don't Call It Frisco* (1953), *Only in San Francisco* (1960), and *One Man's San Francisco* (1976). In 1996 he received a special award from the Pulitzer Prize committee for his many years of work as "the voice of San Francisco," capturing, but just as often *creating*, the city's universally-acknowledged "magic."

This was also the year that Caen was quoted comparing San Francisco—unfavorably—with heaven. He said, "One day if I do go to heaven . . . I'll look around and say, 'It ain't bad, but it ain't San Francisco.'" Now, that's a fan!

For many years there was a double-decker freeway that ran along the San Francisco waterfront that drew the ire of many locals, Caen included. He bad-mouthed it frequently in his column, calling it the *Dam*barcadero, not the *Em*barcadero, Freeway. In 1989 the Loma Prieta earthquake severely damaged it, ultimately resulting in its demolition. It was replaced, appropriately enough, with a boulevard christened "Herb Caen Way."

JULY 6

1925

Merv Griffin Born in San Mateo

ON THIS DAY IN CALIFORNIA HISTORY entertainer, executive and talk-show host Merv Griffin was born in the San Francisco suburb of San Mateo. He would become a fabulously successful figure in the entertainment business.

Griffin began his show-business career as a singer, working with the Freddy Martin Orchestra, but it was when he became a solo performer in nightclubs that his popularity really began to soar. He even had a number one hit with a song with the unlikely title of "I've Got a Lovely Bunch of Coconuts" (1950). Amazingly, the song sold three million copies.

It was during one of these nightclub performances that he was "discovered" by Doris Day, which led to his being screen-tested by Warner Brothers for a part in a movie they were making. But it would not be as a big-screen star that he was destined to make his mark. That would happen on the "little screen," TV.

Griffin had begun to make regular appearances on such TV programs as *The Arthur Murray Show* and *The Jack Paar Show*, while he was still involved with movies, but it was his sub-in for Paar on *The Tonight Show* that led to his really big break in the business. After that appearance NBC offered him a daytime talk show of his own and it was as a daytime talk-show host that he would be remembered best by the public.

In 1969 he even tried to make it as a late-night talk show host, but that only proved he had it right the first time.

Griffin created the hugely successful TV game shows *Jeopardy!* and *Wheel of Fortune*, and when he sold his production company to Columbia Pictures in 1986, was paid $250 million for it, continuing as executive producer of both shows. Not all of his business ventures turned out this well, of course, but these two played big parts in making him a billionaire.

JULY 7

1846

United States "Officially" Annexes California

ON THIS DAY IN CALIFORNIA HISTORY Commodore John D. Sloat, Commander-in-Chief of U. S. Naval Forces in the Pacific, publicly announced that a state of war existed between the United States and Mexico and that the United States intended to occupy California and make it part of itself.

The proclamation was addressed to people of California and said that since the government of Mexico had "commenced hostilities against the United States," the two countries were at war and he would be hoisting the American flag throughout the province.

Sloat went on to state that the Americans had come to the Californians "as their best friend" and that the province would henceforward be part of the United States, that its citizens would enjoy the freedoms and rights enjoyed by other Americans, and that their religious freedoms would be protected, too.

It also stated that the Californians could look forward to a more prosperous economy, a dramatic reduction in the duties paid on goods imported from foreign countries and "a great increase in the value of real estate and the products of California." In fact, said Sloat, "the country cannot but improve more rapidly than any other on the continent of America."

However, Sloat continued, should any Californians feel that this was not a state of affairs that they could live with, they were free to sell their property and find a place more to their liking, and were free to do so, provided they remained neutral regarding the hostilities currently underway.

Of course, the things said by American officials in the heat of relieving nations of their territory don't always turn out quite the way they are presented, but the picture the Commodore painted appeared to be a promising one and, whatever else might be said of it, certainly sounded the right note.

JULY 8

1910
Detention Center Built on Angel Island

ON THIS DAY IN CALIFORNIA HISTORY construction was completed on the Angel Island immigrant detention center. The Spanish explorer Juan de Ayala had "discovered" the island in 1775, naming it "Isla de Los Angeles," a name later anglicized and shortened to "Angel Island." During the Civil War it served as a military post when Fort Reynolds was built there.

Between 1910 and 1940 Angel Island served as a port of entry for Chinese immigrants on the West Coast, and during this period, some 175,000 Chinese spent various lengths of time there, awaiting official permission to enter the United States. Though it was publicly billed as nothing more than an official entry and processing point for newly-arrived Chinese immigrants in the U. S., its real purpose was to *control* the flow of Asian immigrants into the country.

The first Chinese immigrants had arrived in California in 1848, and as word got out about the discovery of gold in California, thousands more came shortly thereafter. They had come to work on what they called "Gam Sann" or "Gold Mountain," and get rich like everyone else who had headed here from the four corners of the earth in the mid 19th century. But they were soon forced out of the gold fields by discriminatory laws and relegated to menial, low-paying jobs instead.

Beginning with the Chinese Exclusion Act of 1882, a series of laws was passed to restrict the entry of Chinese into the United States and the building of the facility on Angel Island simply made the process more formal and better organized. (The U. S. Immigration Service called it "The Guardian of the Western Gate.") This official anti-Chinese sentiment in American law endured until World War II, when China was an American ally, and really until the mid-1960s, when the nation's immigration laws were completely rewritten.

JULY 9

1956

Tom Hanks Born in Concord

ON THIS DAY IN CALIFORNIA HISTORY actor Tom Hanks was born in Concord, northeast of Oakland. The family eventually moved from Concord to Oakland, where Hanks attended Skyline High School, and then Chabot College in Hayward, ultimately finishing up at Cal State Sacramento.

Ironically, Hanks had no luck getting cast in a college play, even though theatre arts was his major, and found his first opportunity to act with a community theatre company instead.

But it was not going to be on stage, but rather in movies, that Hanks would find his real opportunity as an actor. In New York he struck up a friendship with a couple of theatre directors who liked him so much that they helped finance his move back to the West Coast, this time to L. A., where he was soon cast as one of the two leads in the TV sitcom, *Bosom Buddies.*

The work in *Bosom Buddies* received favorable notices and led to roles in Ron Howard's *Splash* in 1984, *The Money Pit* in 1986, and *Big* in 1988, which was his break-out film, the one that made him into a truly big star.

Hanks played an unforgettable women's-league baseball coach in the film *A League of their Own* in 1992, the kindly bookstore magnate in *Sleepless in Seattle* (1993), a courageous Philadelphia lawyer fighting AIDS in the movie *Philadelphia* (also 1993), and Forrest Gump in the movie of the same name (1994). He won back-to-back best actor Oscars for these last two roles.

More big-screen success followed with *Apollo 13* in 1995, *Saving Private Ryan* and *You've Got Mail* in 1998, and *Road to Perdition* in 2002. On June 12, 2002, Hanks became the youngest recipient ever of the American Film Institute's Life Achievement Award and in August 2005 became a vice president of the Academy of Motion Picture Arts & Sciences.

JULY 10

1852

Tulare County Established

ON THIS DAY IN CALIFORNIA HISTORY Tulare County was established at the southern end of the Great Central Valley.

It was initially formed in 1852 from parts of adjacent Mariposa County, but through the years has ceded parts of itself to other counties nearby. It's still about the size of Connecticut, however, and remains one of the larger counties—geographically speaking—in the state. Its eastern half is mountainous and includes all of Sequoia National Park and most of Mt. Whitney. A large lake could once be found in the western half of the county and it was the reeds in that lake, or "tules," that gave the county its name.

Like its neighbors, Tulare County is a predominantly agricultural area, but the majority of its citizens remain among the most impoverished in the state. Despite the fact that its agricultural wealth now makes it the state's most prosperous agricultural economy (Fresno County long held this distinction, but in 2001 Tulare surpassed it), its tax base is so spare that it can only keep its libraries open two days a week.

Most of the county's permanent population is involved in one aspect or another of front-line rank-and-file agricultural labor and so they are not the ones getting rich from all the wealth that is generated here, and half of this population is Hispanic, much of it relatively new to the United States.

Over a quarter of Tulare County's residents live in its principal city, Visalia. Although it is the oldest city in California between Stockton and Los Angeles, it did not experience significant population growth until around 1980. Other cities in the Central Valley grew large when the railroad came in the late 19th and early 20th centuries, but the railroad passed Visalia by, and it has only been since 1980 that it has grown from a population of around 25,000 to what is today a population of over 100,000.

JULY 11

1922

First Concert Held in the Hollywood Bowl

ON THIS DAY IN CALIFORNIA HISTORY the first concert was held in the Hollywood Bowl. It was built on the site of a natural amphitheatre that had been known as the "Daisy Dell."

In the beginning, the Bowl wasn't all that much different from its natural state, outfitted only with some wooden benches and, in time, a simple awning to cover the stage. In 1926 an architectural firm was hired to regrade the area where the audience sat and add permanent seating. They also built a "shell" to cover the stage.

These improvements did improve seating *capacity* and protect performers from the elements, but added nothing to the quality of the performances themselves. The reshaping of what had been a natural amphitheatre actually made sound carry less effectively than it had before and the new shell didn't help things, either.

For the 1927 season architect Lloyd Wright designed a wooden shell in the shape of a pyramid. The listening experience at the Bowl improved dramatically with the new shell, but the structure's futuristic shape found few fans. Wright was given the opportunity to take a second shot at the shell's design, however, the only restriction being that he come up with an *arched* shape.

His shell design for the 1928 season was again a wooden structure, but this time one formed into concentric, 120-degree arches, each with movable panels that could be adjusted to improve the quality of the sound they transmitted. It was even designed so that it could be taken apart and stored, but this wasn't done, so after one winter in the open air, it too had to be demolished.

For the 1929 season the Bowl's shell was rebuilt by the architectural firm that had made the original improvements to the Bowl site back in 1926. The shell they built "took," and though its acoustics were deemed inferior to those of the Lloyd Wright shells, it covered the stage until 2003.

211

JULY 12

1946

The Adventures of Sam Spade Airs on ABC Radio

ON THIS DAY IN CALIFORNIA HISTORY *The Adventures of Sam Spade* aired on ABC radio for the first time. The Dashiell Hammett novel from which the character had been taken had already been made into a movie three times, most memorably by Humphrey Bogart in *The Maltese Falcon* in 1941.

Sam Spade had a life on radio, too. Edward G. Robinson first brought him to life there in a *Lux Radio Theater* production in 1943, and Bogart had a go with him on radio as well, in an *Academy Award Theater* production in 1946. For the ABC Production, Howard Duff took a shot at bringing Spade to life, this time with a much more tongue-in-cheek interpretation.

In the late 1920s and early '30s Hammett lived and wrote in San Francisco and published the books that would constitute his claim to literary fame, as well as make him the father of the modern, "hardboiled" American detective novel.

He lived an interesting life, one well-suited to a man who would eventually write detective fiction. He left school at age 13 and worked at a variety of different jobs, ultimately becoming an operative for the Pinkerton Detective Agency, where he worked from 1915 to 1921. It was this experience that would decisively shape the direction his writing would take.

And his work would exert a strong influence on most of the writers of detective fiction who would follow him, including the great Raymond Chandler.

Chandler imitated the fast-paced, hardboiled style that made Hammett's books such page-turners, but Chandler took the art of writing "detective stories" to a new level of sophistication, lacing his prose with vivid and memorable similes and turns of phrase that were thoroughly his own and unlike anything that can be found in Hammett's books.

JULY 13

1898

San Francisco Ferry Building Opens

ON THIS DAY IN CALIFORNIA HISTORY the "Ferry Building," once the official gateway to the city of San Francisco, opened its doors.

Before there were bridges spanning the Golden Gate and the Bay, and before passenger airplanes were a common sight in the nation's skies, the only direct way to get to San Francisco from Marin or the East Bay was by ferryboat. It was here on this day in 1898 that the first of those boats docked.

A young San Francisco architect named A. Page Brown designed the building. His original design called for a building 840 feet long, but the cost of building the foundation alone was so high, its length had to be reduced to 660 feet. Expensive or not, the building's foundation saved it from damage during the great earthquake of 1906 *and* the Loma Prieta earthquake of 1989.

Another distinctive feature of the Ferry Building is its clock tower, 240 feet high and modeled after the 12th century bell tower of the cathedral of Seville in Spain. It was long the city's "front door" and one of its best-known landmarks, too.

When they exited the ferryboats, passengers walked down a peach-colored terrazzo floor trimmed in dark red marble. This color scheme continued up the walls for twelve feet and then changed to terra-cotta. The entire area was illuminated by the natural light that streamed in through 14-foot-wide skylights situated 42 feet above the floor. When passengers exited the building, they were greeted by a view of the city straight up Market Street.

During the 1920s and '30s, as many as 50,000 people a day commuted to their jobs in San Francisco by ferryboat, gliding to and from work over the waters of San Francisco Bay. People made friends, played cards, read their newspapers, paced the decks, or just whiled away the time during their leisurely ride to work. It must have been a great way to start the day.

213

JULY 14

1903
Author Irving Stone Born in North Beach

ON THIS DAY IN CALIFORNIA HISTORY best-selling author Irving Stone, whose real name was Irving Tenenbaum, was born in the North Beach neighborhood of San Francisco.

Stone had strong academic leanings from the beginning. After completing an undergraduate degree in economics at Berkeley, he enrolled at USC to complete a master's. After that, he planned to head back to Berkeley to pursue a Ph.D., but it was at that point that he had a change of heart. He decided to head off to Paris instead, hoping to make his mark there.

As it does with all writers worth reading, it took Stone a while to get his bearings. His first novel, *Pageant of Youth* (1933), was set in Berkeley and was rejected nineteen times before it found its way into print. During these years Stone also got interested in the life, paintings and letters of Vincent Van Gogh, who was not well-known in the United States at the time. His book *Lust for Life*, published in 1934, did much to change that.

And what also changed was the direction in which Stone began to take his writing. *Lust for Life* was a huge success (though it was rejected sixteen times before it was finally published), and during the course of creating it, Stone found his true vocation as a writer: creating large and compelling treatments of famous people's lives.

There was *Sailor on Horseback* (1938), based on the life of Jack London, and *Clarence Darrow for the Defense* (1941), a treatment of that famous lawyer's life. These were followed by *Adversary in the House* (1947), based on the life of Eugene Debs, and *The Agony and the Ecstasy* (1961), based on the life of Michelangelo. Stone also did books on John Adams (*Those Who Love*, 1965), Sigmund Freud (*The Passions of the Mind*, 1971), Heinrich Schliemann, the man who discovered the ruins of ancient Troy (*The Greek Treasure*, 1975), Charles Darwin (*The Origin*, 1980), and others.

July 15

1976

Twenty-Six Schoolchildren Kidnapped in Chowchilla

ON THIS DAY IN CALIFORNIA HISTORY twenty-six children were kidnapped from a school bus in the tiny Central Valley town of Chowchilla.

The bus driver, Ed Ray, had stopped the bus to see if he could render aid to the occupants of what appeared to be a broken-down white van. He immediately realized that he had made a mistake, however, for when he looked through the glass of his automatic front doors, what he saw was a man holding guns and wearing a nylon stocking over his head.

The masked man mounted the bus's steps, ordered Ray to the back of the bus, and sat down in the driver's seat. Before Ed had even made to the back, however, two more masked men emerged from where the van was parked and got on the bus, too. The Chowchilla kidnapping had begun.

One of the men drove the bus, one stayed up front to keep an eye on Ed and the kids, and one followed in the white van. A few minutes later, the bus pulled into a drainage slough and the engine was turned off. The van pulled up alongside and half of the twenty-six kids were loaded into it. Then a second van pulled up and the remaining children were loaded into it.

The vans then headed off to what would turn out to be a hidden moving van in Livermore where the children and the driver were unloaded and locked in.

Once the kidnappers drove off, Ed Ray and some of the older children began trying to dig themselves out. Sixteen hours later, they succeeded, and walked to a nearby guard shack where they explained their situation to the guard there. A short time later, the kidnappers, including the son of the quarry's owner, were apprehended while attempting to escape to Canada. All three were later sentenced to life in prison.

JULY 16

1769

California's First Church Established in San Diego

ON THIS DAY IN CALIFORNIA HISTORY Franciscan missionary Junipero Serra erected a brush shelter in what is today downtown San Diego that would become California's first church and the state's first mission, San Diego de Alcala. From this tiny seed would grow the immense modern-day city of San Diego.

Tribes of California Indians had lived in this area for thousands of years prior to the coming of the Spanish, but the arrival of Serra and his countrymen marked the first permanent presence of Europeans in this area. The explorer Juan Cabrillo sailed into San Diego Bay in 1542, as did Sebastian Vizcaino sixty years later, in 1602, but California was so remote from the centers of civilization of the day, no one saw any need to settle it.

Russian fisherman had been coming down from the eastern reaches of that vast country for years to fish the Pacific all the way down to what is today northern California, and by the 1760s were a worrisome enough presence to the Spanish for Spain to make its first serious efforts at establishing settlements here. The official story was that they were bringing Christianity to the Indians, but the real story was that they were concerned about another European power getting a foothold here.

Serra came to California as part of one of these first parties, the one led by Captain Gaspar de Portola, who had arrived in the area twenty days before, two days before Serra himself.

The first site Serra selected for a mission overlooked beautiful San Diego Bay, but the soil was not as fertile as it was hoped it would be, the water supply not adequate to support irrigation efforts, and the Spanish soldiers, garrisoned nearby, scared off the natives. Given these drawbacks, it was decided to move the mission six miles inland, to a site near the San Diego River and nearer to the area's Indian villages, and it was here that it would remain.

JULY 17

1955

Disneyland Opens in Anaheim

ON THIS DAY IN CALIFORNIA HISTORY Disneyland opened its doors in Anaheim. Nothing like it had ever existed before, and it quickly made a place for itself in American popular culture.

To create the "entertainments" that went into the making of his "park" Disney drew on stories he himself had made famous as an animator and cartoonist, and periods and "places" he was fascinated by personally—frontier and "turn-of-the-century" America (the turn before last), the wilds of Africa, the future.

Disney's original idea was to create a *permanent* family fun park, one without the negative elements so often associated with the traditional traveling carnival. There were none to speak of at the time and certainly none with activities that parents and children could enjoy together.

During his years as a studio head, many people had written Disney to ask if they could visit the studio's lot and meet their favorite Disney character. Walt quickly realized that just coming out to the lot wouldn't be all that much fun, but what if a place were built that was specifically designed for tourists to visit, a place where, say, they could take pictures of themselves or family members with statues of Disney characters?

It was from these modest beginnings that Disney's ideas grew. Next came a small play park with a boat ride. Other "themed areas" came next, and the entire concept grew bigger and bigger, until it finally grew into the idea of "Disneyland."

Obviously, a park this big couldn't be built on a studio lot and so another place had to be found. On the advice of the Stanford Research Institute, Disney acquired 160 acres in nearby Anaheim and cleared them for construction. Construction began on July 18, 1954, and took exactly one year to complete. Over 500,000,000 people have now visited this amazing place.

JULY 18

1968

Intel Incorporates

ON THIS DAY IN CALIFORNIA HISTORY the company Intel ("INTegrated ELectronics") was incorporated in Santa Clara.

Its founders were Gordon E. Moore, a chemist and physicist, and Robert Noyce, a physicist *and* coinventor of the integrated circuit. In partnership with a man named Andy Grove they would make Intel into one of the most successful companies in the world.

The company's first creation, the 4004 microcomputer, came out in 1971. It was smaller than a thumbnail, contained 2,300 transistors and could execute 60,000 operations in a second, an extraordinary feat at the time; it was followed by the 8008 microcomputer, which could process data twice that fast.

But the real making of the Intel microprocessor was not just its speed; it was the fact that IBM chose it to operate their first personal computer. It was all up, up, and away from there.

In 1982 the company introduced the first 286 chip, which contained 134,000 transistors and could perform three times as fast as other microprocessors available at the time. The "486" appeared just seven years later and contained 1.2 million transistors, plus the first built-in math coprocessor. This chip could perform at the same level as a mainframe computer.

In 1993 Intel introduced its first "Pentium" processor, a device that could operate five times faster than the 486 processor and which contained *3.1 million transistors.*

The Pentium processor could execute 90 million instructions in a second, fifteen hundred times the speed of the company's original microcomputer and represented a true quantum leap in processing capacity. In the years since, Intel has developed chips that are so fast it's hard to even comprehend the speeds at which they operate, and that make possible the complex technological world that now surrounds us.

JULY 19

1926

Zane Grey Catches Record-Size Swordfish

ON THIS DAY IN CALIFORNIA HISTORY author Zane Grey caught a record-size swordfish just off Catalina Island. He had been fishing for a long time and had finally reeled in "a big one."

Big-game sportfishing has long drawn sportsmen to this area. It was here that big-game sportfishing got its start in 1898 and here that the "rules" of sportsmanlike saltwater angling were originally formulated. Though their populations have now thinned dramatically, tuna, swordfish, marlin, "yellowtail" and barracuda once teemed in these waters and big-game fishermen came from all over the world to fish for them. Among them was Zane Grey.

A man of means, Grey chartered his own boat with a captain when he went out fishing off the Southern California coast and on one such outing in 1914, he and his captain trolled the waters off San Clemente Island just south of Catalina for twenty-one days, searching for swordfish. They sighted nineteen of them during this outing, but didn't catch any. On the twenty-fifth day, Grey finally hooked into one, but was unable to reel it in.

Grey may have ended this outing empty-handed, but he vowed that he would return the very next year and resume the task of catching a giant swordfish right where he had left off. In the summer of 1915 he did so, and within just a few days, managed to hook and land three of them, the largest of which weighed 145 pounds. Just a few days later, his hook was taken by a truly enormous fish, a fish he had to play for hours before he could get him into the boat.

The fish was estimated at three hundred and sixty pounds, but when it was finally unloaded at Avalon two days later, it weighed just a little more than three hundred pounds. He later hooked into a swordfish estimated to be twice the size of this one, but that one, as they say, got away. But on this day in 1926 Grey's "ship," a 582-pound swordfish, finally did come in.

JULY 20

1938

Natalie Wood Born in San Francisco

ON THIS DAY IN CALIFORNIA HISTORY actress Natalie Wood was born in San Francisco. Her parents were Russian Orthodox immigrants, and her given name, Natalia Nikolaevna Zakharenko.

Natalie had shown a talent for acting from a very early age, and since her name was obviously way too much of a mouthful for the average American to say, let alone remember, her parents changed it to something much easier, "Gurdin." By the age of five she was already beginning to appear in films as "Natalie Gurdin" and well on her way to becoming a well-known actress.

At the age of 16 Natalie got her first big break in the movies when she got the role of "Judy" in the Nicholas Ray classic, *Rebel without a Cause* (1955). James Dean, Sal Mineo and Dennis Hopper also starred in the movie, and though it earned Wood her first Oscar nomination and will always be remembered as one of the classic American films about alienated youth, it will also be remembered as the movie whose three headliners—Dean, Mineo, and herself— would all die young and all under tragic circumstances.

By the time she was 28 Wood had already been nominated for an Oscar three times: for her portrayal of "Judy" in *Rebel without a Cause*, for her role as a jilted small-town girl in *Splendor in the Grass* (1961), and for her role as the pregnant salesgirl in *Love with the Proper Stranger* (1963). She had also made a name for herself in Leonard Bernstein's *West Side Story*.

Wood was as much in demand off the screen as on it, and over the course of her career dated everyone from Elvis Presley to Robert Wagner. She was married to Wagner twice, marriages that were, like the rest of her life, highly publicized and stormy. She was on board the family yacht, *The Splendor*, in 1981, when she apparently fell overboard and drowned, the last of the *Rebel without a Cause* stars to die under tragic circumstances.

JULY 21

1952
Town of Tehachapi Destroyed by Earthquake

ON THIS DAY IN CALIFORNIA HISTORY the tiny town of Tehachapi near Bakersfield was destroyed by a 7.7 magnitude earthquake. It struck just before 5 a.m. and was triggered by a sudden movement in the "White Wolf Fault" at the southern end of the San Joaquin Valley. It would turn out to be the largest earthquake to hit Southern California during the 20th century.

The quake rattled the earth over a 160,000-square-mile area, affecting the alignment of steel beams in buildings under construction in Las Vegas and breaking a pipeline and disturbing the lake beds at Owens Lake, 125 miles to the northeast. There was even damage to buildings in Los Angeles, 80 miles to the south, and to a building in San Diego, 180 miles to the south.

Twelve people lost their lives and at least eighteen were injured, and not only was there $48,000,000 of property damage in the immediate area of the shaking, twenty aftershocks measuring 5.0 or more damaged hundreds of buildings across Kern County, 100 of them to such an extent that they had to be demolished. The quake bent railroad rails and crushed tunnels and disturbed the flows of subsurface water and oil wells, too.

The behavior of the Kern County earthquake came as a surprise to experts. The White Wolf fault was not previously thought to be a danger and the size of the quake itself seemed to be out of all proportion to the stretch of earth that gave way.

The answer had to be that the quake commenced far below the earth's surface, and that much of the area that moved, moved far below ground level, betraying little of its presence at the surface. Though an enormous amount of energy was released, it had to have radiated outward in a horizontal direction and not taken the vertical path that would have left significant evidence at the earth's surface that a major earthquake had rumbled through here.

JULY 22

1916
Bombing in San Francisco

ON THIS DAY IN CALIFORNIA HISTORY a bomb went off during a "Preparedness Day" parade in downtown San Francisco, killing 10 people and injuring 40 more.

The parade was organized by business and patriotic groups in the city to promote America's readiness to enter World War I and no labor groups chose to participate. This lack of participation by labor groups was branded by the parade's organizers as unpatriotic and when the time came to decide who should be blamed for the bombing, it was their names that rose to the top of the list.

There had been no love lost between business and labor groups here for years, as was the case in other parts of the state, but various considerations, most of them related to business, had kept the powers that be from pushing the issue into open warfare.

The city's labor groups were also known to be unsympathetic to the idea of preparing for the coming war in Europe, largely, no doubt, because it would be they, more so than most other groups in the nation, who would be called upon to fight it.

And so it wasn't that big a stretch to assume that labor agitators were the ones behind the bombing at Steuart and Market Streets on this day in 1916, and that in particular it might be a local labor leader by the name of Thomas J. Mooney who was the brains and principal agitating force behind it all.

Mooney was well-known for his past efforts to organize labor strikes in the Bay Area. He had been involved in a long strike against Pacific Gas & Electric a few years before, and just eight days before this Preparedness Day parade, had tried to organize a wildcat strike among employees of the United Railroads in San Francisco. There was no solid evidence directly linking him to the crime, but he was arrested, tried and sentenced to hang. In 1918, however, his sentence was commuted to life in prison.

JULY 23

1850

City of Stockton Incorporated

ON THIS DAY IN CALIFORNIA HISTORY the city of Stockton was officially incorporated. Located sixty miles east of San Francisco and forty-five miles south of Sacramento, it is California's fourth largest inland city and the thirteenth largest city in the state.

Stockton was originally founded in 1847 by a man named Charles M. Weber on the site of an old Hudson's Bay Company settlement called "Rancho del Campo de los Franceses."

The first name Weber gave the community was "Tuleberg," but he later thought better of that choice and changed it to "Stockton," in honor of Commodore Robert Stockton, the American naval officer who served as California's second military governor and who first declared California to be a U. S. territory and himself to be its commander in chief.

Stockton's location made it an important communications and trade center for the men working the southern mines during the Gold Rush, but once mining activity died down, its excellent position as the easternmost inland port on the California coast, and location in the midst of so much top-grade agricultural land, made it a natural conduit for the harvest of the Great Central Valley.

Stockton is also the home of the University of the Pacific, which originally opened its doors in Santa Clara in 1851, then moved to San Jose and began admitting women, making it the first *independent* coeducational college in the state (in 1871). In 1925 it moved back to Stockton.

Some of the town's more notable citizens have included Benjamin Holt, the inventor of the caterpillar tractor, governor James H. Budd (1895-1899), jazz pianist Dave Brubeck, legendary coach Amos Alonzo Stagg, who coached at the University (then "College") of the Pacific in the 1930s and '40s, actress Janet Leigh and Chinese-American author Maxine Hong Kingston.

July 24

Barry Bonds Born in Riverside

ON THIS DAY IN CALIFORNIA HISTORY baseball great Barry Bonds was born in Riverside; he would grow up in the north, however, and graduate from Junipero Serra High School in San Mateo. His father was baseball great Bobby Bonds, who played for seven different teams during his 14-year career in the majors, two of them California teams—the California Angels and the San Francisco Giants.

Bonds was drafted by the San Francisco Giants straight out of high school, but he chose to attend college first and earn a degree before commencing his career in the majors. When he graduated, he signed with the Pittsburgh Pirates, with whom he stayed for seven years, before signing with the San Francisco Giants, his father's old team.

Bobby Bonds was the first player in major-league baseball to hit 300 home runs *and* steal 400 bases and the only other player to accomplish that feat to date is his son, Barry. Bonds actually went on to surpass his dad's record by becoming the only player in major-league history to hit *400* home runs *and* steal 400 bases.

Bonds holds some other very impressive records, too. He's the only player to hit 73 home runs in a single season and on August 7, 2007, became the game's all-time home-run hitter with 756. He has won league MVP honors seven times (no other player has won it more than three), "Golden Glove" honors for excellent defensive play eight times, and is considered one of the greatest players to have ever played the game.

But Barry Bonds has also been the center of a heated debate in the world of baseball about the use of performance-enhancing drugs and whether his own use of them accounts for the success he has had in the sport, especially in recent years. It's a subject still being debated today and one that has cast a dark shadow over many of this player's very real accomplishments.

JULY 25

1797

Mission San Miguel Arcangel Founded

ON THIS DAY IN CALIFORNIA HISTORY Mission San Miguel Arcangel was founded by Franciscan cleric Fermin Lasuen, Junipero Serra's successor as head of the California missions. It was named for the Archangel Michael, one of the principal angels according to Catholic theology and a "leader" of God's "heavenly hosts."

Fr. Buenaventura Sitjar, a cleric from Mission San Antonio, and a contingent of Spanish soldiers surveyed the area where the mission was to be built. They needed a place with good water resources, fertile land and adequate timber to build with. The area they chose was located near the Salinas River and not far from the coastline, about halfway between Monterey and Santa Barbara.

San Miguel Arcangel was the eighteenth of California's twenty-one missions and one of four that Fermin Lasuen established during 1797. Its first church burned down in 1806 and ten years were devoted to making and storing new bricks before building a new one. The new church was completed in 1819.

On the afternoon of December 4, 1848, five white men and an Indian visited the mission. One of the white men was a murderer who had recently escaped from jail, one was a deserter from the U. S. Army, two were deserters from a U. S. warship, and the fifth and last man, was a newly-arrived Irishmen. The people then living at the mission were a Mr. William Reed and his family. (The church had sold its missions to private parties in the 1830s.)

At the mission the vistors sold the Reeds some gold, spent the night, and the following morning proceeded on their way. Not long after leaving, however, they returned, murdered the occupants, and took back their gold, leaving eleven dead, including an unborn child. As soon as the evil that had been done here was discovered, a posse was formed and the deaths at the mission avenged. One perpetrator was shot; one drowned in the ocean; three faced a firing squad.

JULY 26

1943

Air Pollution Comes to L. A.

ON THIS DAY IN CALIFORNIA HISTORY Los Angeles suffered its first serious bout of air pollution.

Normally, the view here seemed to go on forever in what were then typically clear and sun-filled skies, but on this particular morning, visibility was reduced to just three blocks. And so began an atmospheric phenomenon destined to play a big role in the city's future: "smog."

Whatever it was that filled the city's air that morning—"smoke" or "fog," no one yet knew what to call it—a few things about it were clear enough. It made people cough, made their lungs hurt, and caused their eyes to water.

But almost as quickly and mysteriously as it had appeared, the haze in the air vanished, dispersing by noon that same day. Nevertheless, the city council insisted that the cause of the haze be found and the city's health department launched an investigation.

What this was, it turned out, was L. A.'s first big bout of *smog*. Cars had been filling the city's streets since the 1920s, and as they multiplied, so too did the amount of exhaust that they emitted into the air. On this summer morning in 1943 noxious fumes in L. A.'s atmosphere had finally built up to the point where the city's air quality "went critical."

It was not an unprecedented event, however. Episodes of diminished air quality had surfaced in the city prior to this, but they seemed to disperse fairly quickly, and for the most part, passed without much comment.

Some thought they were caused by the fumes emitted from a rubber plant in East Los Angeles (not true, it would turn out) and city officials promised to clear up the matter in four months (not true either). Finally, a professor at Caltech confirmed that the cause of the haze in the air was *car exhaust*.

JULY 27

1948

Figure Skater Peggy Fleming Born in San Jose

ON THIS DAY IN CALIFORNIA HISTORY world-champion figure skater Peggy Fleming was born in San Jose. Her passion for figure skating surfaced early and before her career was over, she would make herself not just into one of the great figures in California sports history, but in world sports history.

Her career as a big-time skater began in tragedy, however. In 1961, when she was just 12 years old, her coach William Kipp and the entire United States skating team were killed in a plane crash while en route to the 1961 World Figure Skating Championships in Prague. Her coach and all of her teammates gone, Peggy had to dig deep to find the motivation to go on with her skating.

Which she did. Under the influence of her new coach, Carl Fassi, she would go on to win five U. S. figure-skating titles, three world titles, and a gold medal at the 1968 Winter Olympics at Grenoble. Six months after the games at Grenoble, she starred in her first television special, the first of five that would showcase her grace and skill as a skater.

Peggy has skated for four Presidents and has also spent over twenty years as a figure-skating commentator for ABC sports, sharing her considerable knowledge of the sport with the television-viewing public. In 1994 *Sports Illustrated* magazine named her one of "40 for the Ages," one of 40 competitive athletes who had significantly "altered" or "elevated" the world of sports during the preceding 40 years.

In 1999 *Sports Illustrated* again honored Peggy at its "20th Century Awards" by naming her one of a group of seven athletes who had had a profound effect on their sport, a group that included Arnold Palmer, Billie Jean King, and Jackie Robinson. Her days as a competitive figure skater are over now, but her influence on figure skating is likely to endure for a long time to come.

JULY 28

1984
Twenty-Third Summer Olympics Begin

ON THIS DAY IN CALIFORNIA HISTORY the opening ceremonies for the twenty-third Summer Olympics were held in Los Angeles.

The city had been selected on May 18, 1978, without a vote; it had been the only city to bid to host the 1984 games. The U. S. had led the boycott of the 1980 Games in Moscow and now it was time for payback. Fourteen members of the "Eastern Bloc," including the Soviet Union and East Germany, countries that normally dominated many summer games events, simply did not participate.

The games were nonetheless memorable for a variety of reasons. For one thing, the absence of most of the "Eastern Bloc" nations helped one member of that bloc, Romania, enormously. It decided that it *would* participate in the games and its athletes won 53 medals, a national record for a Romanian team.

For another, several important records were set at this particular playing of the Games.

American sprinter Carl Lewis equaled the success that legendary American sprinter Jesse Owens had had at the Berlin Games in 1936 by winning four gold medals. A female hurdler from Morocco became not only the first *female* athlete from an Islamic country to win an Olympic event, but the first athlete from Morocco, male or female, to win one. These Games were the first ones to hold a women's marathon event, too.

These Games introduced synchronized swimming and wind surfing to the menu of Olympic events and at them American gymnast Mary Lou Retton became the first gymnast outside Eastern Europe to win the all-around gymnastics competition. Part of composer John Willams's composition "Olympic Fanfare and Theme" became the soundtrack for the Games and he would go on to write the scores for future games as well. The 1984 Games were also the first ones ever to make a profit, $200 million.

JULY 29

1905

Times Announces "River Coming to Town"

ON THIS DAY IN CALIFORNIA HISTORY the following headline appeared in the *Los Angeles Times*: "Titanic Project to Give City a River."

It would seem to be good news. Los Angeles was growing and additional sources of water were certainly something the city needed. The only message that Angelenos might have been guilty of reading into the headline was that the new water was going to be for *their* benefit. Well, it was—and it wasn't.

A titanic project to "give the city a river" was certainly in the works, but the people standing to benefit most from this arrangement were the city's main power brokers.

Men like Henry E. Huntington, who owned the Pacific Electric Railway, E. H. Harriman, president of the Southern Pacific Railroad, Harrison Gray Otis, owner and publisher of the *Los Angeles Times*, Harry Chandler, Otis's son-in-law, and other movers and shakers who had bought land in the San Fernando Valley that would skyrocket in value once more water was piped in.

When they arrived at Owens Lake, former mayor Fred Eaton and William Mulholland met with J. B. Lippincott of the recently-formed U. S. Reclamation Service and he gave them access to public land office records that identified exactly which parcels of land and which water rights they needed to buy to run their giant aqueduct from Owens Lake to Los Angeles.

In any case, the *Times* article revealed why Eaton, Mulholland and Lippincott had been poking around in the Owens Valley. And though it was silent about the San Fernando Valley end of the deal (the owner of the *Times*, after all, was a major player), it did begin the process of encouraging voters to approve the bonds needed to build the massive aqueduct from the Owens to the San Fernando Valley and make them nervous about what might happen to their own land values if they didn't.

JULY 30

1932

Tenth Olympiad Held in Los Angeles

ON THIS DAY IN CALIFORNIA HISTORY the opening ceremonies for the Tenth Olympiad were held in Los Angeles. It was the culmination of a process that had begun in 1920 when the city's leaders set their sights on bringing the games to the city and was part of a larger effort to transform the not-so-long-ago cow town into a city worthy of the world's attention.

The Los Angeles Coliseum, a structure that could seat 75,000 people, was complete and ready for use in 1923, and because it was, L. A. real estate developer William May Garland, one of the two U. S. representatives to the International Olympic Committee at the time, was able to persuade the committee that L. A. was ready to handle such a big event and become only the second American city to do so since the Games were revived in 1896.

L. A.'s decade-long effort to prepare to host the 1932 Games was shaped at every turn by the knowledge that this was going to be the city's big chance to showcase itself on an international stage, and despite the fact that the Crash of October 1929 had taken the wind out of most sails in the American economy, it didn't take the wind out of this event. When the athletes arrived in mid-July, the nation was in a full-scale depression, but you couldn't tell it from the flags and banners flying in L. A.

Seating in the Coliseum was expanded to 105,000, which made it the largest sports arena in the world. An auditorium to hold indoor events had been open on Grand Avenue since 1924, and the Rose Bowl in Pasadena, as well as the then-new UCLA campus in West-wood, was used to stage many of the track and field events. Crew and sculling events were held in the Long Beach Marine Stadium, pistol and rifle competitions at the LAPD's shooting range in Elysian Park, and the equestrian events at the then nearly-new Riviera Country Club.

JULY 31

1846

Mormons Sail into San Francisco Bay

ON THIS DAY IN CALIFORNIA HISTORY the first party of Mormons to come to California sailed into San Francisco Bay. There were more than 200 people on board and they had completed a difficult six-month voyage from Brooklyn to the tiny Spanish village of Yerba Buena.

The group was led by a man named Sam Brannan, who, in 1847, had met with Brigham Young, then leading a group of Mormons to the Great Salt Lake Basin, and tried to persuade him to establish his Mormon colony in California, instead of at Salt Lake. He was not successful.

About twelve families from this "founding" group moved inland and established what would turn out to be the short-lived farming community of "New Hope" on the Stanislaus River, the first "English-speaking" community established in the state. Another member of the group, John M. Horner, became wealthy farming in the Bay Area and helped found eight towns there.

There were Mormons at Sutter's Mill when James Marshall discovered gold in the American River on January 24, 1848, and it is the journal of one of these early Mormon immigrants named Henry W. Bigler that historians have relied on to establish the exact date that gold was first discovered here.

Members of the Mormon community were involved in digging for gold in the California gold fields, too, and one of the richer regions of the "gold country" was known as "Mormon Diggings."

In fact, the success of some of the Mormon miners in the California diggings was a boon to Salt Lake City in its early years. They brought an estimated $25,000-$30,000 in gold there to help the newly-established community find its feet and Brigham Young even sent some of the faithful in Salt Lake on gold-mining "missions" for the church.

This Day
in
August

AUGUST 1

1873
Andrew Hallidie Drives the First Cable Car

ON THIS DAY IN CALIFORNIA HISTORY the first cable car made its way down a San Francisco street. The car's inventor, Andrew Hallidie, was at the controls.

Legend has it that what inspired Hallidie to invent the cable car in the first place was some experiences he'd had watching a couple of horses literally kill themselves attempting to drag heavy loads up San Francisco streets.

That may be true, but it is also true that Hallidie was uniquely positioned to do something about the situation, because he also held the patent on something called wire rope (used to move heavy loads in areas where gold was mined) and saw how it could be used to propel street cars up and down San Francisco's steep streets.

In any case, he got his patent for a cable car approved in 1871, and in 1873, on August 1 or 2, depending on whose account you choose to believe, the first cable car made its way down Clay Street, from Jackson to Kearny.

One thing cable cars did was make it possible to live on some of the higher hills in the downtown area, which is what the "Big Four" railroad barons, Collis P. Huntington, Mark Hopkins, Charles Crocker, and Leland Stanford, did. Because of the cable car, they were able to build their homes on "Nob Hill," and from there, look down upon the city they'd played such a big part in building.

Cable cars stayed in continuous service in San Francisco from their advent in the early 1870s until 1982, when they were all pulled from the streets to be reconditioned.

Two years and $60,000,000 later, they were reintroduced (they would have just three routes this time, not eight), to the delight of just about everyone. More than just a way of getting around town, they are one of the city's principal symbols, and are likely, as a consequence, to keep rolling for a long time to come.

August 2

1769

Portola and Serra Reach the Site of Los Angeles

ON THIS DAY IN CALIFORNIA HISTORY a Spanish expedition led by Captain Gaspar de Portola and Father Junipero Serra first reached the site of present-day Los Angeles. They were actually en route to Monterey Bay to establish a presidio and mission there, but noted in passing—well, Fr. Crespi, the chaplain and diarist of the group, did —that this area would be an excellent spot for a settlement.

Portola was governor of *both* Californias at this point—Alta ("Upper") and Baja ("Lower")—and had undertaken this expedition for the Spanish crown in order to help consolidate its holdings in *Alta* California.

Rumors had reached Madrid that the English and the Russians might both be trying to get a foothold here and the Spanish were eager to prevent that from happening. England had colonies on the east coast of North America, after all, and had recently conquered Canada. Russian fishermen routinely sailed down into the waters off the northern California coast to hunt fur seals.

In any case, it was clear enough to Spain that potential threats to its westernmost North American territories existed and the time had come to do something about it. What is decided to do was place a series of presidios along the coast of Alta California, beginning in San Diego and extending all the way up to Monterey.

On this day in 1769 it was but a small fraction of the group that had originally started out from Baja California who were making their way north to Monterey Bay.

The expedition began with three hundred members, but half lost their lives en route and many of those who survived fell ill from scurvy and were unable to travel further for months. But on this day in 1769 those healthy enough to travel crossed the river that their captain named "El Rio de Nuestra Senora La Reina de Los Angeles de Porciuncula," the *Los Angeles* River.

236

August 3

Ellen Browning Scripps Dies in La Jolla

ON THIS DAY IN CALIFORNIA HISTORY newspaperwoman and philanthropist Ellen Browning Scripps died in the peaceful Southern California seaside resort of La Jolla. She had been born in London 95 years before and had come to the United States, along with five brothers and sisters, with her father in 1844.

When Ellen's family arrived in the U. S., they first moved to Illinois, where other members of the family had migrated before them. Ellen's father had been a prominent bookbinder in the city of London and Ellen had read "good books" from an early age. She started her working life as a teacher, but later got involved in the business of journalism instead.

Her first experience with journalism came with the *Detroit Evening News*. Her brother, James, had founded the paper in August of 1873, and when he did so, Ellen joined him, investing some of her modest savings in the project, too. She started out as a proofreader and also wrote some "filler" about people and events that the paper used to "fill out" its pages when it needed to.

In the years that followed, Ellen joined her brothers in other newspaper ventures, including the founding of the *Cleveland Press*, investing her savings in each one as it came along and becoming, in time, a very wealthy woman. Her wealth would get an additional boost in 1900 when her brother, George, would leave part of his estate to her, too.

In 1896 Scripps retired to La Jolla, where she became an active philanthropist contributing to the support of local schools, churches and parks, and the city's women's club, public library and hospital. She was an important backer of the Scripps Institution of Oceanography, the San Diego Natural History Museum and the San Diego Zoo, and in her late eighties, helped fund the Claremont colleges, one of which, Scripps College, bears her name.

August 4

1834

Governor Figueroa Secularizes the Missions

ON THIS DAY IN CALIFORNIA HISTORY Governor José Figueroa took charge of secularizing the state's twenty-one missions.

It was intended from the beginning that the missions would revert from religious to secular institutions, as the Indians were converted and taught trades with which they could support themselves. But as the missions thrived, and the church accumulated ever-greater land holdings and influence through them, the padres grew increasingly reluctant to simply let it all go and set their charges free.

Governor Figueroa saw things differently, however. On August 4, 1834, he issued a proclamation officially granting half of all mission properties to their Indian residents and even proposed a schedule for rolling out the proposed changes: the first ten missions would be transferred from the control of the church to the control of the Indians in 1834, the next six in 1835, and the last five in 1836. Unfortunately, Figueroa died in 1837 and the equitable process laid out in his proclamation was ignored.

Instead of being transferred to the Mission Indians who had spent so much of their lives living on and working them, mission lands were distributed by the Mexican government to citizens as a reward for government service. Religious services continued to be held in the mission churches, but the mission's material wealth— real estate, livestock, orchards and vineyards—simply fell into a new set of privileged hands.

The mission buildings themselves began to fall into disrepair once the secularization process began, many collapsing in on themselves before efforts to restore them were begun 1903. Today, however, most of the original missions have been restored and are a popular destination for tourists from around the world, vivid reminders that a very different kind of California once thrived here before the Americans came.

AUGUST 5

1962

Actress Marilyn Monroe Found Dead

ON THIS DAY IN CALIFORNIA HISTORY actress Marilyn Monroe was found dead from a drug overdose in her Brentwood home. Her life had been hard from the start. Her mother abandoned her to foster care at birth and later married her off as an underage teen.

A native Angeleno, Marilyn had been born in the charity ward of Los Angeles County Hospital on June 1, 1926. Her birth certificate identified her as "Norma Jean Mortenson," but she was baptized as "Norma Jean Baker." It was only later, when she began working in movies, that she would become "Marilyn Monroe."

Marilyn's mother was a strange woman. She released her daughter to foster care, but eventually bought a home in which to raise her. Just a few months after moving in, however, Marilyn's mother suffered a mental breakdown and was taken to the California State Mental Hospital in Norwalk, where her grandmother, Della, had also once been confined.

Despite the tough circumstances of her upbringing, Marilyn was smart and ambitious and determined to make her way in the world. A photographer named David Conover spotted her while she was working in a factory in Los Angeles and immediately saw her potential. She eventually signed up with the Blue Book Modeling Agency and soon her unforgettable face and form were appearing on the covers of literally hundreds of magazines.

What Marilyn really wanted to do was act, however, and in 1946 she got that chance at 20th Century-Fox. Here she officially became "Marilyn Monroe," but because her first two films did so poorly, Fox dropped her after a year on their payroll. A brief tour at Columbia Pictures didn't work out, either, but in 1948, she returned to Fox, and with the release of *Gentlemen Prefer Blondes* and *How to Marry a Millionaire* in 1953, her rise to fame and fortune was in full swing.

August 6

1880
Actor Leo Carrillo Born in L. A.

ON THIS DAY IN CALIFORNIA HISTORY long-time character actor Leo Carrillo was born in Los Angeles.

He had been born into an old and respected Southern California family that could trace its roots all the way back to the conquistadors. His great grandfather had been California's first provisional governor, his grandmother a member of the wealthy Bandini family of San Diego, and his father, the first mayor of Santa Monica.

Carrillo worked for a time as a newspaper cartoonist and even tried his hand at acting on stage, but it was as a character actor in movies that he really hit his stride, playing supporting or character roles in more than ninety films. And it is for his work in one of these roles, that of "Pancho," the sidekick of the "Cisco Kid," that he is best remembered today.

But Carrillo is remembered for much more than his work in Hollywood. In addition to working as an actor, he was also interested in efforts to preserve California's natural and "historical" environment and he worked hard to make that happen.

Governor Earl Warren appointed him to the state's "Beach and Parks" commission, where he served for eighteen years, and he also played key roles in the efforts to preserve the Olvera Street area in downtown Los Angeles, acquire "Hearst's Castle" and make it into a state historic monument, purchase the land needed to save the Los Angeles Arboretum from the blades of bulldozers and turn the Anza-Borrego Desert into a state park.

To honor his involvement in these preservation efforts, the state of California named a park in his honor, Leo Carrillo State Park west of Malibu, and made his ranch in Carlsbad a registered state historical site. Governor Pat Brown frequently referred to him as "Mr. California," and in 1961, the year he died, he even published a book he'd written about this state he loved so much.

AUGUST 7

Alma de Bretteville Spreckels Dies

ON THIS DAY IN CALIFORNIA HISTORY San Francisco socialite and patron of the arts, Alma de Bretteville Spreckels, died. She had been one of the city's more interesting and colorful figures and was fondly known as "the great grandmother of San Francisco." She was also a rags-to-riches story of the first order.

Alma had been born on a sandy farm in the Sunset District of San Francisco in 1881 where the family made its living running a laundry, bakery and massage parlor on Francisco Street. She left school at 14 to help her mother with the business, and it was then that she first came into contact with the city's social elite.

Alma was ambitious from the beginning. She read biographies of the rich and famous and the society columns of the city's newspapers. In her late teens she enrolled herself at the Mark Hopkins Institute of Art, where she got her first work as a model.

But her break-out assignment as an model occurred in the late 1890s when she posed for sculptor Robert Aitken, then creating an entry for a competition to choose a monument to be erected in Union Square. The chairman of the selection committee was sugar magnate Adolph Spreckels, one of the richest men in the city, and Aitken's entry certainly allowed him to get a good look at Alma.

In any case, Aitken's entry was the committee's choice, which led to young Alma's beautiful form being permanently immortalized atop the Dewey Monument and, after a five-year courtship, marriage to Adoph Spreckels.

From what was soon to be her lofty position atop San Francisco society, Alma became an important patron of the arts, a tireless supporter of charities during World World I, the Great Depression, and World War II, and the driving force behind one of San Francisco's most recognizable landmarks, the California Palace of the Legion of Honor.

August 8

1937

Dustin Hoffman Born in L. A.

ON THIS DAY IN CALIFORNIA HISTORY actor Dustin Hoffman was born in Los Angeles. When he graduated from Los Angeles High School, he was voted "least likely to succeed," but his ambition was to become a concert pianist, and with a view to doing that, he enrolled in the Los Angeles Conservatory of Music.

He soon decided that a change of direction was in order and that what he really needed to do was become a doctor. He enrolled in Santa Monica College, but poor grades soon forced him to reconsider his options once again. To boost his GPA, he took an acting class (he was assured that "nobody flunks acting"), and it was that decision that proved to be his turning point.

Obviously, Hoffman found acting very much to his liking and something for which he most definitely had a talent. He did his first work on the stage at the Pasadena Playhouse, but to really get his career off the ground, he knew he had to move to New York.

In 1960 Hoffman landed a role an off-Broadway production and the following year snatched a walk-on role in a Broadway show. His acting career was still far from taking off, however, and so he decided that more training was what was needed. He enrolled himself at the Actors Studio to learn how to become a "method actor" and in 1967 made his film debut in *The Tiger Makes Out*.

But Hoffman's "real history" as an actor began with his portrayal of Benjamin Braddock in *The Graduate* (also 1967), for which he was nominated for a "Best Actor" Academy Award.

Two years later, he was nominated for "Best Actor" again for his portrayal of Ratzo Rizzo in *Midnight Cowboy*, and in the years that followed, his range and versatility as an actor became legendary. *Little Big Man* (1970), *Straw Dogs* (1971), *All the President's Men* (1976), *Kramer vs. Kramer* (1979), *Tootsie* (1982), and *Rain Man* (1988), proved that he was one for the ages.

242

AUGUST 9

1916

Lassen Volcanic National Park Established

ON THIS DAY IN CALIFORNIA HISTORY Lassen Volcanic National Park in the northeastern corner of California was established.

The park is about fifty miles east of Redding and one of the world's few remaining volcanic landscapes. In 1914 Lassen Peak, the southernmost tip of the Cascades and the world's largest plug dome volcano, began to rumble and spew lava across this remote California landscape. This activity continued throughout 1915, and in 1916, the area was officially set aside as national park land.

The volcanic activity of this area of California was well-known to the Indians who had long lived here. In fact, they believed that Lassen Peak was "full of fire and water" (which, of course, it was) and believed that it would one day blow apart. They were hardly scientists, but they certainly sensed the direction in which the forces at work here were headed.

In any case, Lassen Peak rises up on the northeast side of what was once a mountain a thousand feet higher and some eleven to fifteen miles wider at its base than it is today. It was once a volcano, is composed of previously erupted rock and ashes, and is still given to periodic lava flows. It was during one of these fiery eruptions, between 2,000,000 and 10,000 years ago, that the mountain collapsed in on itself and Lassen Peak was formed.

This eruption was also responsible for the creation of the other intriguing geological formations that characterize this landscape, including "Brokeoff Mountain" on the other side of the two-mile-wide crater that Lassen Peak rises up from and the park's second highest peak (9,235 feet), Mount Conrad, Mount Diller and Pilot Pinnacle, all of which are remnants of the huge volcanic disturbance that occurred here during the late Pleistocene. The "Cinder Cone" volcano and "Chaos Crags" are the result of later volcanic activity in this area.

243

August 10

1969

First of the Manson Murders Discovered

ON THIS DAY IN CALIFORNIA HISTORY the first of the "Manson murders" was discovered by Los Angeles police. Actress Sharon Tate, eight months pregnant and the wife of director Roman Polanski, Jay Sebring, a leading Hollywood hair stylist, coffee heiress Abigail Folger and her boyfriend, Polish writer Wojciech Frykowski, all lay dead at Polanski's Benedict Canyon estate.

Manson was the self-appointed leader of a group of disaffected middle-class kids collectively known as "the Family," who were, like many kids in the the late 1960s, estranged from their families, hungry for affection and searching for a leader to follow.

Charlie had charisma, and through that charisma, coupled with ample doses of sexual manipulation, drugs, and quasi-religious rituals, got control of his "Family's" collective mind, allowing him to get them to do whatever he wanted them to. And what he wanted them to do was slaughter some rich white people in the hope of triggering a race war that would ultimately leave him and his "Family" at the top of the heap in a new world order.

Charlie didn't do the murders himself. He was much too crafty for that. He had three members of his "Family" do the actual killing. In the case of Sharon Tate and her houseguests, the killers were Charles "Tex" Watson, Patricia Krenwinkel and Susan Atkins. The murder site was literally saturated in blood. Mercifully, Tate's husband Roman Polanski wasn't home this fateful night.

The following night businessman Leno LaBianca and his wife Rosemary were murdered in their home in the tony Los Feliz district of Los Angeles. The members of the Family involved this night were Watson and Krenwinkel (again), but this time a girl named Leslie Van Houten was part of the group. On this occasion Charlie went into the home to tie up the victims himself before sending in members of the Family to do the actual murders.

AUGUST 11

1965

Watts Riots Break out in Los Angeles

ON THIS DAY IN CALIFORNIA HISTORY rioting broke out in the Watts area of south central Los Angeles. Before it ended on August 16, at least 34 people had been killed, 1,100 injured, 4,000 arrested. In addition, 600 buildings were either damaged or destroyed. The final estimate of damage to property was $100 million, making these riots one of the costliest disasters in the nation's history.

The specific event that triggered the riots was the pulling over in Watts of an African-American driver named Marquette Frye by a white California Highway Patrol officer named Lee Minikus. During the course of questioning Frye a crowd began to gather, and it was not long before the boy's mother, Rena Frye, was on the scene, too. A struggle ensued and the Fryes were taken into custody.

Shortly after this incident, the rioting began, but the confrontation with the Fryes was only the match for a fuse that had been a long time in the making. Poverty and unemployment had been commonplace for years, drugs were everywhere, and the police routinely busted residents for minor crimes.

The population of the area was almost completely black and the officers assigned to patrol the area almost all white. (Only 5 of the 205 officers then assigned to this part of the city were black.) It was a recipe for violence and on this summer day in 1965 the community's frustrations with the situation finally boiled over into the streets of their long-suffering neighborhood.

As the damage and violence escalated, Governor Reagan called in the National Guard to bring the situation under control. Afterward, he appointed a commission to investigate its causes, and to absolutely no one's surprise, they were the obvious: high unemployment, poor schools and living conditions, ill treatment at the hands of the police, and all of the social fallout that typically befalls a community consumed by drugs.

AUGUST 12

1885

Helen Hunt Jackson Dies in San Francisco

ON THIS DAY IN CALIFORNIA HISTORY Helen Hunt Jackson died in San Francisco. She had been born in Amherst, Massachusetts, where her father was a minister and professor of Latin, Greek and philosophy at Amherst College. Her mother was a writer, too.

Helen's father was determined to have an educated daughter and sent her to a private school for girls in Massachusetts, the Ipswich Female Seminary, as well as to the Abbott Institute in New York City, where Emily Dickinson, another girl from Amherst, was a classmate. The two women would be friends for life.

Under the pseudonym "H. H.," Jackson became a poet of note, as well as a writer of essays, children's stories and novels. In 1879, however, her interests turned to the plight of the Indians. She investigated their situation in depth and worked hard to bring attention to the injustices these people had suffered. She raised money, circulated petitions, and even wrote letters to the *New York Times* on their behalf.

She also turned her hand to writing a book about U. S. Indian policy and the nation's long history of broken treaties with the Indians. It called for dramatic changes in government policy and Hunt sent a copy of it to every member of the United States Congress. The nation's legislators were in no mood to listen, however, and so the book fell on deaf ears.

Hunt subsequently went to Southern California for some rest and relaxation, and while she was there, worked for the Department of the Interior, documenting the pitiful condition in which she found the state's Indians. She would draw upon this experience, along with some stories about California's Indians she had been told, to create her novel *Ramona* (1884), a book inspired by *Uncle Tom's Cabin* and one that would play a big role in shaping the nation's idea of California's allegedly romantic past.

246

AUGUST 13

1913

Wheatland Riot Occurs in Yuba County

ON THIS DAY IN CALIFORNIA HISTORY a riot broke out on the Yuba County hops ranch of farmer Ralph Durst, then the state's largest employer of migrant farm labor. It happened near Wheatland and was a watershed event in the history of the state, because it galvanized the state's farm workers to organize.

Durst had advertised throughout California and even in southern Oregon for almost twice as many workers as he actually needed— 1,500 versus the 2,700 advertised for and the 2,800 who actually showed up. When those who had responded to Durst's ad got to his property, what they found was low pay, few toilets and no housing. This obviously didn't sit well with those who had come expecting to work for reasonable pay under reasonable conditions, and one of them, "Blackie" Ford, got into a confrontation with Durst.

The confrontation led to the calling in of the local sheriff and his deputies, one of whom fired the shot that was responsible for starting the riot.

Before it was over, the Yuba County district attorney, a deputy and two of the workers present were killed, the sheriff beaten into unconsciousness, and many others injured. The state militia ultimately had to be sent in to restore order, but things didn't end there. The following year there was a march on Sacramento to protest the conditions under which California's farm workers worked.

After the riot Governor Hiram Johnson established a Commission on Immigration and Housing to look into the working conditions of California's migrant farm workers. The results were written up in a report that provided the first detailed look at what it meant to be a migratory farm worker in California and were consequently a significant step in the process that would lead to the rise of Cesar Chavez's United Farm Workers and the effort to improve conditions for those who made their living this way.

247

AUGUST 14

1924

Pasadena Art Institute Incorporates

ON THIS DAY IN CALIFORNIA HISTORY the Pasadena Art Institute was officially incorporated. Pasadena was, in many ways, the perfect place to establish such an institute, for it is the kind of place that requires the support of an affluent, educated, art-loving citizenry and Pasadena certainly had that.

The Institute secured some property on the corner of Orange Grove and Colorado Blvds. ("Carmelita Park"), which included a 22-room Victorian mansion. Here it staged its first exhibits of 19th-century American and European art, as well as the work of California artists and artists from other parts of the world.

Carmelita Park had been given to the city of Pasadena in 1941 with the proviso that "adequate" land be set aside for the Institute. The city agreed to lease this site to the Institute without cost for twenty years, provided that a new permanent museum was constructed to replace the facilities then there.

In April 1942 the Institute merged with the Pasadena Museum of Art. The newly-merged entity retained the name "Pasadena Art Institute" and relocated its headquarters to a gallery in the Grace Nicholson Studios at 46 North Los Robles Avenue.

In 1953 the Institute received a bequest of almost 500 pieces of art from the estate of a woman who had represented such modern masters as Kandinsky, Klee and Feininger, and in 1954, changed its name to the "Pasadena Art Museum." From that point on it concentrated its collecting and exhibiting efforts on *modern* art.

November 1969 saw the opening of the Institute's long-promised new facilities in Carmelita Park. Over the course of the next twenty years it would exhibit works by such artists as Richard Diebenkorn, Roy Lichtenstein, Claes Oldenburg, Frank Stella and Andy Warhol and develop an international reputation for the quality of the exhibitions of modern art held there.

AUGUST 15

1846

First Newspaper in California Begins Publication

ON THIS DAY IN CALIFORNIA HISTORY the first newspaper in California, *The Californian*, began publication in Monterey. Its founders were Walter Colton, then Monterey's *alcalde* or mayor, and a man who had had experience as an editor, and Robert Semple, a former printer. It would be the first of many more to come.

The paper made its appearance just two months after the "Bear Flag Revolt" in which a group of Americans first tried to take California from Mexico, their purpose being, as Semple said, to "conciliate the Natives and unite the foreigners residing in California." In May of 1847 Semple moved the paper to San Francisco and new issues stopped appearing altogether in 1848 when the paper was merged with *The California Star*.

In 1849 *The California Star* was absorbed by *The Alta California*, the paper that became California's first *daily* newspaper and one that was continuously published from 1850 until 1891. *The Alta California* didn't have much competition from other papers at the beginning, but some like the *Pacific News* and the *Sacramento Union*, were, in fact, significant.

The Gold Rush attracted a truly international community of miners to mid-19th-century California and one of the things this diverse population needed was newspapers. To answer this need, French and German newspapers appeared in San Francisco (*L'Echo du Pacifique*, *California Staats-Zeitung* and *California Demokrat*) and a Chinese-language newspaper in Sacramento.

As California's population grew, so too did the number, variety, and sophistication of its newspapers. The earliest major daily to appear in the state was the *San Francisco Bulletin*, which began publishing in 1855, and the following year the *San Francisco Call* made its debut. The *San Francisco Chronicle* started publishing in 1865 and remains to this day that city's principal newspaper.

AUGUST 16

1853
John D. Spreckels Born

ON THIS DAY IN CALIFORNIA HISTORY San Diego founding father John D. Spreckels was born in Charleston, South Carolina. The family soon moved on to New York, however, and from there to San Francisco, where Spreckels grew up and was educated.

Spreckels studied at Oakland College and in Hanover, Germany, and after that, returned to San Francisco, where he went to work in the family's sugar business. In 1876 he went to Hawaii to work in the family business, and four years later, established the shipping business that would make him a rich man in his own right.

In 1887 Spreckels had the opportunity to visit San Diego. Impressed by the real-estate boom then underway there, he decided that it would be a good idea to invest some money in the city, starting with the construction of a wharf at the foot of Broadway Street. The boom ended, but Spreckels's interest in San Diego didn't. It would be a love affair that would last the rest of his life.

In time Spreckels acquired control of the Coronado Beach Company, the Hotel del Coronado and San Diego's street railway system. For a time he owned the *San Francisco Call* newspaper and later bought the *San Diego Union* (in 1890) and the *San Diego Tribune* (in 1901). After the great Francisco earthquake and fire, Spreckels moved his family to San Diego permanently and built a mansion for his family on Coronado Island.

During his years in San Diego, Spreckels became the wealthiest man in the city. At one time or another, he owned all of North Island, the San Diego-Coronado Ferry System, the Union-Tribune Publishing Company, the San Diego Electric Railway, the San Diego & Arizona Railway, and Belmont Park in Mission Beach. He built several office buildings and hotels in downtown San Diego and there was a time when he personally paid 10% of all the property taxes collected in the county.

AUGUST 17

1892 · 1920
Actresses Mae West and Maureen O'Hara Born

ON THIS DAY IN CALIFORNIA HISTORY two women who would play big roles in the early history of Hollywood were born. The first was the endlessly provocative and witty Mae West, born on this day in Brooklyn in 1892, the other, red-headed beauty Maureen O'Hara, born on this day in Dublin in 1920.

Mae West was forty years old when she came to Hollywood. She had played on Broadway, written plays (risqué ones), and generally made a living making a spectacle of herself. In 1932 Paramount Studios offered her a contract, giving her the chance to show the whole world what Mae West was all about.

Her best work was done in the '30s and early '40s, work that sailed right through the censor's nets with an amazing stream of double entendres, snappy one-liners that could in theory be taken two ways, but that were in fact intended only one. The censors were no match for this woman's wit.

She maintained an apartment at 570 North Rossmore Avenue in Hollywood during her entire 48 years in the city; it was where she lived when she got here and where she was living when she died.

Maureen O'Hara began her acting career on the stage of the Abbey Theatre in Dublin. She was offered a screen test in London when she was just 17, and though no one thought much of her acting, actor Charles Laughton thought she "had that certain something"— in her case, "unforgettable eyes," that might make her a star.

Relying on that hunch, Laughton brought O'Hara to Hollywood in 1939, where she starred opposite him in *The Hunchback of Notre Dame*. She would go on to a full career in the movies, including a starring role in *How Green Was My Valley* (1941), *Miracle on 34th Street* (1947), and *Rio Grande* (1950) with John Wayne. It was with Wayne that she would be paired in the moviegoing public's mind from then on.

251

August 18

1873

First Ascent of Mount Whitney

ON THIS DAY IN CALIFORNIA HISTORY the summit of Mt. Whitney, the highest point in the lower 48 states, was reached by three local fishermen: Charley Begole, Johnny Lucas and Al Johnson. They had scaled all 14,494 feet of it.

The mountain had been named "Mount Whitney" nine years before when it was "discovered" by a California Geological Survey team and named for the team's leader, Josiah Whitney. But many local residents favored calling it "Fisherman's Peak" to honor three local fisherman who had scaled its heights, and some, unsatisfied even with that choice, proposed "Dome of Inyo" instead.

The issue was argued back and forth in the local newspaper for two years and finally a bill proposing that the name of the peak be officially changed to "Fisherman's Peak" was introduced into the state legislature.

As fate would have it, however, the bill found its way to the floor of the California state senate on April Fool's Day of 1881 where the proposed name for the mountain was "amended," as a joke, to *"Fowler's* Peak." To end the horsing around with the bill's language, Governor Perkins vetoed the bill, leaving the name of the mountain "Whitney," which it remains to this day.

Future president of the Sierra Club and author of *The Mountains of California*, John Muir, made his first ascent of Mount Whitney on October 21, 1873, becoming the first known person to scale the mountain using the "eastern" approach, the route that is today referred to as the "Mountaineers Route."

He had attempted to climb the mountain by approaching it from the southwest, as the climbers that had preceded him had, but that approach didn't work out for him and he retreated to the town of Independence after spending a cold night on the mountain, returning later to make his second attempt from "the east."

AUGUST 19

1937

First Klystron Tube Put into Operation

ON THIS DAY IN CALIFORNIA HISTORY the klystron tube, an important milestone in the march toward the high-tech world we all now live in, was first put in operation at Stanford University.

Its creators, Russell and Sigurd Varian, were then graduate students there, studying under Professor Frederick Terman, a man fascinated by the commercial possibilities of vacuum tubes. Terman knew that these devices would play a big role in the high-tech world then beginning to unfold and he wanted Stanford to play a big role in their development.

Just ten years before, in a lab on Russian Hill in San Francisco, a man named Philo T. Farnsworth had worked out the basic principles of television and transmitted a simple black-and-white image onto a screen by electronic means. His invention utilized vacuum tubes, those tubes that Professor Terman thought would have such an important part to play in the development of future technology. Terman wondered else those tubes might be able to do.

And so he set a couple of Stanford graduates loose to research those possibilities, providing them with a lab to work in, supplies to work with, and ready access to his own considerable knowledge of the subject.

These students, Russell and Sigurd Varian (Russell had actually once worked for Farnsworth), set to work on developing a vacuum tube device that could amplify ultra-high-frequency currents and convert them into microwaves. They called their creation the "klystron tube."

It would quite literally revolutionize the world of high-energy physics and lead to the creation of the kind of radar systems used in today's aircraft, as well as play an important role in airplane and missile guidance systems, satellite communications and in television and telephone transmission systems, too.

AUGUST 20

1992
"Friz" Freleng Gets a Star

ON THIS DAY IN CALIFORNIA HISTORY animator, cartoonist and cartoon director and producer "Friz" Freleng got his star on Hollywood Boulevard. He had begun his career at Walt Disney Pictures in Kansas City, working with some of the early masters of animation, including Hugh Harman and Rudy Ising (who later cofounded the animation studios at Warner Brothers and MGM).

When Disney moved to Hollywood in 1924, Freleng followed, but he soon partnered up with Harman and Ising instead to establish an animation studio of their own. They produced a pilot and successfully sold it to producer Leon Schlesinger, who brought the three over to Warner Brothers to work on the "Looney Tunes" series he was then producing.

When Harman and Ising left Warner Brothers over budget disputes in 1933, Freleng was promoted from animator to director. His first big creation on his own was *I Haven't Got a Hat* (1935), starring Porky Pig, one of the earliest examples of an animated character being given a distinct and memorable personality.

In 1940 Freleng directed the Daffy Duck animated short, *You Oughta Be in Pictures*, and went on to personally originate or help develop a number of animated headliners, including Yosemite Sam (1945), Tweety and Sylvester (1947) and Speedy Gonzales (1955). His work would continue to focus on this group, plus Bugs Bunny, until the Warner studios closed in 1963, and before he was done, would garner four Oscars for his animation work there.

After Warner Brothers, Freleng went on to work with fellow cartoon director Dave DePatie and together they created the "Pink Panther" character for the opening shots of the film of that name (1963). The character proved so popular with audiences that Freleng used him in a short he made for United Artists studios, for which he won his fourth Academy Award.

254

AUGUST 21

1938

Site Work for Shasta Dam Begins

ON THIS DAY IN CALIFORNIA HISTORY site work for what would be Shasta Dam began. The dam was built across the Sacramento River, twelve miles above the city of Redding, and five miles downstream from where the Pit and Sacramento Rivers come together. Work on the dam went on for a full seven years, from 1938 to 1945.

When it was completed, it stood over 600 feet high, was 3,460 feet wide at the top, 543 feet wide at the base and contained over 6,000,000 cubic yards of concrete. The 46-square-mile body of water the dam held back came to be known as Shasta Lake, the principal northern reservoir of the Central Valley Project.

Shasta Dam was built to control flooding in this far northern part of the state and even out the unequal distribution of irrigation water in the Great Central Valley. It was also intended to be an important source of *hydro*electric power and is, in fact, the fourth largest power generation plant of this type in the state.

Shasta Dam started out as a state project, but since it was the 1930s and the state was strapped for cash, the federal government had to step in to move the project forward.

Congress had passed the Rivers and Harbors Act in August of 1935, which provided $12,000,000 for the dam's building, and later that year, President Roosevelt stepped in and contributed an additional $4,200,000 from the Emergency Relief Appropriation funds under his control. Altogether the Bureau of Reclamation budgeted $36,000,000 for this project, making Shasta Dam one of the costliest dams ever built.

And, of course, it was not meant to exist in a vacuum, sufficient unto itself. Shasta Dam was intended to be part—the first part—of a vast web of dams, canals and aqueducts running the entire length of the Great Central Valley, one of the most ambitious water redistribution projects ever undertaken.

255

AUGUST 22

1913
Jack London's "Wolf House" Burns to the Ground

ON THIS DAY IN CALIFORNIA HISTORY Jack London's "Wolf House" in Sonoma County burned to the ground. He had boasted it would stand a thousand years and be his home for the rest of his days, but it was not destined to be so.

London was born in San Francisco in 1876 and was largely self-educated. After finishing grammar school, he started working long hours in a local cannery and soon found he wanted no part of that. To escape this drudgery, he borrowed money from his foster mother to buy a sloop and become an "oyster pirate" instead.

("Oyster pirates" did just what it sounds like: pirate oysters from those who "raised" them, in this case, San Francisco Bay oyster farmers, and then sell their "catches" to fish markets that sold them retail, in this case, in Oakland.)

London made his living in a variety of different ways before he found success as a writer. He crewed on a sealing schooner, worked in mills and factories, and spent some time on the road as a tramp. He later attended Oakland High School and the University of California at Berkeley, but did not stay at the University of California long enough to earn a degree. In 1897 he joined in the Klondike Gold Rush.

London returned to Oakland in 1898, convinced that the only way he was going to escape the meaningless workaday world was by becoming a writer.

Like most writers, he came within a hair's breadth of abandoning the effort altogether, but in 1900 he managed to make $2,500 writing, the equivalent of about $75,000 today. In any case, London continued to write and wrote some fifty books before it was all said and done, including *The Call of the Wild* (1903), *Sea-Wolf* (1904), *White Fang* (1906), *The Iron Heel* (1908), *Martin Eden* (1909), and *John Barleycorn* (1913).

August 23

1869

"Sunny Jim" Rolph, Jr., Born in San Francisco

ON THIS DAY IN CALIFORNIA HISTORY long-time mayor of San Francisco and later governor of the state, "Sunny Jim" Rolph, was born in San Francisco. The completion of the transcontinental railroad was the year's big news and it hadn't been that long since Mark Twain had lived in the city.

James Rolph, Jr., was educated in the Mission District of San Francisco and found his first success working in the financial district. He started out as an office boy at Kittle & Company and by 1900 was in a position to go into business for himself.

In 1903 Rolph was part of a group that founded the Mission Bank in San Francisco and would, in time, become its president. He also founded a shipbuilding company there.

Having made a go of it in business, Rolph was soon seen as a man who could make a go of it in politics, too. There was an attempt to draft him into the San Francisco mayoral race in 1909, but he decided to wait and run in 1911 instead. He did and won and would serve as mayor of the city for nearly twenty years, from 1912 to early 1931.

Rolph cut a very high-profile figure in early-20th-century San Francisco. He was a director of the San Francisco Chamber of Commerce and of the Ship Owners & Merchants Tugboat Company. He was president of the Merchants' Exchange and served as vice president of the 1915 Panama-Pacific International Exposition.

Rolph stopped being mayor the same day he started being governor, January 6, 1931, but his days as governor of the state were not happy ones for him. For one thing, it was the Depression and not a good time to be in charge of much of anything. For another, there was the much-publicized incident involving department store heir, Brooke Hart, the son of a wealthy San Jose merchant who was kidnapped and murdered on his watch.

AUGUST 24

1967

"Monkees" Song Continues Its Run on the Charts

ON THIS DAY IN CALIFORNIA HISTORY the song "Pleasant Valley Sunday" by the Monkees was in the middle of its run on the nation's pop record charts. It first entered the charts on July 29, 1967, and remained there nine weeks, getting as high as number 3.

The members of the band were Davy Jones, a British-born singer and percussionist; Mickey Dolenz, a native of Tarzana, who starred in a fifties TV show called *Circus Boy*, and who played drums and sang; Mike Nesmith, a guitarist and singer; and Peter Tork, who played bass and keyboards and also sang.

The Monkees, the television series in which the band starred, ran on NBC from 1966 to 1968 (58 episodes), the first show running on September 12, 1966, the last one on September 9, 1968. Each episode was built around the adventures and music of an artificially-created rock group (which they were) that enjoyed huge record sales (which they did), and which, due to public demand, became a *real* rock group (which they did).

In addition to their successful run on TV, the original Monkees produced six albums, four of which went to number one, and also made a series of successful concert tours. Tork left the group in December 1968 and Nesmith in March 1970, but the group still managed to release three more albums and pushed on until first Jones and finally Dolenz departed, too. The group officially disbanded in 1970.

The Monkees were one of the most popular pop music acts of their time. Most critics dismissed them as the "pre-fab Fab Four," but with the advent of MTV and the reshowing of their TV show in syndication, they came back to life, attracting the interest of a new generation altogether. Their 20th-anniversary tour in 1986 was a big hit, too, helped them to sell millions of records (again), and successfully resurrected "Monkee-mania."

AUGUST 25

1836
Author Bret Harte Born

ON THIS DAY IN CALIFORNIA HISTORY Gold-Rush-era author Bret Harte was born in Albany, New York.

He moved with his mother to California in 1854, just a few years after the first big rush of miners had made their way into the state. They lived in Oakland and Harte worked at a variety of different jobs during his time here: for a pharmacist, as a teacher, as a miner, as a messenger, and as a journalist.

In 1860 Harte moved to San Francisco, where he worked for the literary weekly, *Golden Era*, starting out as a typesetter and later becoming one of its authors. He didn't make much, however, so he supported himself working at the U. S. Mint here.

In 1863 Harte became a contributor to the *Atlantic Monthly*, his first submission an amusing sketch of Spanish California entitled the "Legend of Monte del Diablo." He also contributed work to *The Californian*, a San Francisco weekly that he also edited from time to time. Other writers whose work found its way into print in *The Californian* were Mark Twain, Ambrose Bierce, Ina Coolbrith, Henry George, Prentice Mulford and Charles Warren Stoddard.

Harte was named editor of a new magazine in California in 1868 called the *Overland Monthly* and it was in this role that his abilities as an editor *and* as an author really blossomed. In the August 1868 issue of the magazine he published his still-celebrated short story, "The Luck of Roaring Camp," and in January 1869 an equally celebrated piece, "The Outcasts of Poker Flat."

Harte moved to Boston in 1871 to work for the *Atlantic Monthly* magazine. He never returned to California, but for the rest of his writing life, he set his stories and poems here, and though he did a great deal of writing in the many years after he left the state, it would be for the writing that he did here, as a young man, that he would be best remembered by generations to come.

AUGUST 26

1875
Bank of California Fails

ON THIS DAY IN CALIFORNIA HISTORY the Bank of California failed. It was the first commercial bank in the western United States, had at one time been the second-richest bank in the nation and was a major player in financing the development of the West.

The Bank's founder, William C. Ralston, arrived in San Francisco in 1854, at the age of 28, and began his working life here as a clerk. He eventually got involved in banking, however, and it was in banking, particularly in the financing of companies that mined silver, that he would make his fortune.

Ralston typically collateralized the loans he made with stock in the silver-mining companies he lent money to. If a company was unable to make its payments to the bank, he took direct control of its assets and ended up owning the company itself. As silver mining flourished, and made the men mining it rich, it made Ralston and the Bank of California rich, too.

Ralston also had a flair for living large. He bought a place known as the "old Cipriani house" in Belmont and turned it into a showplace. When he was done with it, it had 4 stories and 100 rooms and was a place where Ralston was said to have held many splendid parties, the home of a man who had definitely "arrived."

But all was not well in Ralston's world. It came out that he had secretly drained the bank's deposits to invest in his some of own ventures and that some of its holdings in Nevada mining companies weren't nearly as profitable as had been claimed.

On August 26, 1875, there was a run on the bank, and the next day, its principal investors demanded that Ralston resign. He did, and during the course of a swim near the Larkin Street pier that day, he drowned. The Bank's failure caused several other banks to fail, too, and limited the availability of investment capital in San Francisco for the rest of the decade.

AUGUST 27

1958

Berkeley Physicist Ernest O. Lawrence Dies

ON THIS DAY IN CALIFORNIA HISTORY eminent U. C., Berkeley physicist Ernest O. Lawrence died. He had been born in South Dakota in 1901 and graduated from the University of South Dakota in 1922. Just three years later, he completed a Ph.D. in physics at Yale and became an assistant professor there.

In 1928 the University of California at Berkeley lured Lawrence to its campus, and two years later, elevated him to the rank of full professor, the youngest one they'd ever had. He would spend the rest of his life at U. C. Berkeley and achieve international fame as the man who invented the cyclotron or "atom smasher," a machine capable of releasing the powerful force of atomic energy.

The story goes that Lawrence got his idea for the cyclotron while sitting in a library one evening, looking over the diagrams that accompanied a journal article he was reading. The author was discussing the production of the high energy particles needed to cause atoms to disintegrate by creating a chain reaction of very small "pushes." The key thing about the process was that it could be done without using any high-voltage source of energy.

Lawrence's first working model of his device was made of little more than sealing wax and wire. In the years that followed, he built larger and larger machines to generate high-energy particles, and around this amazing device, built his Radiation Laboratory, a place that would become one of the most important places for doing high-energy physics research in the world.

In 1939 Lawrence received the Nobel Prize in physics for his work with the cyclotron, and during World War II, his Radiation Lab became one of the major centers in the world for atomic research. After his death in 1958, the Radiation Lab and the U. C. research lab in Livermore were named in his honor, as was element 103, "lawrencium," in 1961.

AUGUST 28

1883

First Recorded Glider Flight Anywhere

ON THIS DAY IN CALIFORNIA HISTORY brothers John and James Montgomery made the first recorded glider flight. They assembled their wood-and-fabric aircraft on the edge of the Otay Mesa, just south of San Diego, and it was there on this summer morning in 1883 that they first got their glider off the ground.

Talk of human flight literally filled the air when the brothers were growing up and both were fascinated by aviation. John was a tinkerer, too, and, like most inventors, tried out a variety of designs before he hit upon one he liked.

During the 1850s there had been speculation about the possibility of flying from the East Coast to California in a balloon, and during the 1860s, experimentation with different forms of lighter-than-air flight had begun. In 1870, young John Montgomery watched a man fly a steam-powered hydrogen balloon above an Emeryville park on the eastern shore of San Francisco Bay.

From that moment, John decided that he wanted to fly, too, and would continue to conduct experiments with lighter-than-air aircraft throughout his college years. St. Ignatius College in San Francisco was a particularly good place for a boy interested in science to be educated at this time. The Jesuits who ran the college were interested in science, too, and made its study an integral part of the school's curriculum.

This was the background that John Montgomery brought with him to his first efforts at glider design in the early 1880s and the fruit of all of this preparation was the 38-pound glider that John's brother James pulled aloft this August morning on the Otay Mesa. The glider ascended to a "height" of fifteen feet, remained airborne for six hundred feet, and then floated safely back to earth. The Montgomerys had staged the first recorded glider flight in human history and the first of many more to come.

AUGUST 29

1911
"Ishi" Discovered near Oroville

ON THIS DAY IN CALIFORNIA HISTORY "Ishi," the last member of a tribe of Yahi Indians who had lived "from time immemorial" in the foothills of Mount Lassen in far northern California, wandered out of the wild and onto a ranch just outside the town of Oroville.

Prior to the arrival of European settlers in this part of California, it is believed that the Yahi population stood at about 3,000. The first big toll these settlers inflicted on the Yahi was the "Three Knolls Massacre" of 1865, which left just thirty members to carry on the life of the tribe. About half of these thirty were hunted down and killed by local cattlemen, forcing the handful remaining into hiding.

Hiding out is no permanent solution, however, and, in time, every remaining member of the Yahi tribe died—everyone except Ishi and three others, that is. Ishi, his mother and sister, and an old Yahi man endured for decades on their own and when at long last white men stirred them from their cliffside retreat, it would finally come down to him. Had he not come out in search of food, his entire tribe could quite easily have vanished without a trace.

But Ishi *did* wander out of the wild, and because he did, and because a sheriff in Oroville had the good sense to lock him up for his own protection, this is not the case. The efforts of a couple of gifted anthropologists from the University of California at Berkeley who were interested in learning everything about him that they possibly could helped save him, too.

Living among "civilized" people is not a particularly healthy way for a wild man to live, however, and though the men into whose hands Ishi fell couldn't have been any better, even if he'd had some say in the matter himself, he ultimately fell victim, as did most Native American peoples who came into contact with Europeans, to a disease against which he had no immunity—tuberculosis. He died from the disease on March 25, 1916.

AUGUST 30

1938

Max Factor Dies in Los Angeles

ON THIS DAY IN CALIFORNIA HISTORY makeup guru Max Factor died in Los Angeles. He had arrived in the city in 1908 and the following year founded the company that would make just about every important early "breakthrough" in makeup technology.

It was Max Factor & Company that developed the first false eyelashes (originally for actress Phyllis Haver), "Pan-Cake" makeup (the forerunner of all modern cake makeups), lip gloss, and "Erace" (the original cover-up cosmetic). They also developed the first "waterproof" make-up and a variety of other "long-lasting" cosmetic products, including lipsticks, nail enamels and eye shadows.

Business was brisk. Everybody who was anybody in early Hollywood was a customer of the Max Factor Hollywood Makeup Studio on Highland Avenue. Factor made himself so much a part of the movie community that his name became a familiar part of the credits at the end of many films. He even made some cameo appearances in films himself.

Factor even coined the word "make-up" and insisted that the best makeup was the makeup that no one knew you were wearing. "No make-up is good make-up," said Max, "unless the other fellow doesn't know you have it on." That might be stretching things a bit, but something approaching "invisibility" was certainly the goal, and no one did it better than Max.

Factor's makeup studio was not just a place where makeup was "put on" or sold to customers, either. It had its own lab, research department and manufacturing facilities, too, and the unspoken message to entrepreneurs and makeup artists alike was that makeup could be very big business. Many of his protégés became skillful makeup artists and successful cosmetics entrepreneurs in their own right and turned the magic they could do with makeup into very successful careers of their own.

August 31

1908
Author William Saroyan Born in Fresno

ON THIS DAY IN CALIFORNIA HISTORY author William Saroyan was born in Fresno. He was the son of Armenian immigrants and grew up poor, his father a farm laborer, his mother busy with keeping the family together.

Saroyan came of age just as the Great Depression began to take hold, and his writing, much of it drawn from personal experience, celebrated optimism in the midst of life's adversity. Though he would lose his father when he was very young and be put, along with his brother, in an orphanage, he would later be reunited with his brother and mother to become a family once again.

Saroyan discontinued his formal education at the age of 15 and decided to become a writer. He supported himself doing odd jobs. He managed to get some of his early articles published in the *Overland Monthly*, and in the early 1930s, some collections of his stories began to appear. His breakthrough as a writer came with the publication of "The Daring Young Man on the Flying Trapeze" (1934), the tale of a starving young writer trying to make it through the hard years of the Depression.

Much of Saroyan's writing deals with "the immigrant experience" in America, particularly the experience of the *Armenian* immigrant. His collection of short stories built around this subject, *My Name is Aram* (1940), struck a chord with a large audience and became an international bestseller. Saroyan wrote plays, too, one of which, *The Time of Your Life* (1939), won a Pulitzer prize.

Though his work was popular before World War II, Saroyan lost much of his audience once the war was over. Times weren't as hard and the reading public turned to other kinds of writing. He lived long past his popularity, however, finally succumbing to cancer in 1981. "Everybody has got to die," he once said, "but I have always believed an exception would be made in my case."

This Day

in

September

SEPTEMBER 1

1933
Upton Sinclair Registers as a Democrat

ON THIS DAY IN CALIFORNIA HISTORY author and socialist politician Upton Sinclair registered as a Democrat in Beverly Hills. He had made a name for himself as an author during the preceding thirty years, writing about socially- and politically-sensitive issues, and had decided to try to put those views into action by running for governor of the state.

Sinclair made his first big splash as a writer with a book called *The Jungle* (1906), which vividly exposed the sordid conditions then prevailing at the nation's meat-packing plants. It caused such an uproar that it resulted in the passage that same year of the Meat Inspection Act and the Pure Food and Drug Act.

After *The Jungle* Sinclair went on to write about a host of other social injustices in 20th-century America. In *The Money-Changers* (1908), he took on bankers and banking; in *The Profits of Religion* (1918), religion. The press was taken to task in *The Brass Check* (1919) and higher education in *The Goose-Step* (1922).

In the early 1930s Sinclair decided to put some of this thinking into action with his "EPIC" ("End Poverty in California") proposals. The Great Depression was making life hard for all Americans and Sinclair decided that he could at least take up the cause of California's down and out, proposing a guaranteed monthly income for those who needed it and state-owned industries to keep the unemployed off the relief rolls.

Though not too practical in its details, EPIC had enormous appeal for thousands of unemployed Californians in the 1930s and nearly put Sinclair in the governor's mansion. He even wrote a self-promotional book to support his candidacy called *I, Governor of California, and How I Ended Poverty: A True Story of the Future.* He attracted almost 38% of the vote and might well have done better than that.

SEPTEMBER 2

1866

Hiram Johnson Born in Sacramento

ON THIS DAY IN CALIFORNIA HISTORY long-time California politician Hiram W. Johnson was born in Sacramento. His father had been a leading politician in the state, too, and a man famous for championing individual rights. Both father and son served in the California state legislature and in the United States Congress.

Johnson was educated in the private schools of Sacramento and after completing his education there, went on to study law at U. C., Berkeley. He was admitted to the California Bar in 1888 and returned to Sacramento to set up his practice. In 1902, at age 36, Johnson moved to San Francisco.

It was here that he really got his political career off the ground. He was elected Assistant D. A. and became known as a hard-liner on political corruption. His predecessor had been gunned down in a local courtroom, so going up against San Francisco's bad guys was clearly not something to be taken lightly.

Johnson was elected governor of California in 1910 and was reform-minded from the beginning, supporting the popular election of U. S. Senators, women's right to vote, and cross-filing for political candidates, allowing them to run for more than one party in primary elections.

It wasn't long before he was making his presence felt on the national scene. In 1912 he teamed up with former President Theodore Roosevelt to found the "Progressive Party" and ran with him in that year's presidential election.

In 1914 Johnson was reelected governor of California, and in 1916, was elected to the United States Senate, where he began what would be a 28-year stay in that office. In 1920 he made a bid for the Presidency, but the Republicans decided to go with Warren G. Harding instead. He ran again in 1924, but that year the party went with Calvin Coolidge.

SEPTEMBER 3

1991

Director Frank Capra Dies

ON THIS DAY IN CALIFORNIA HISTORY film director Frank Capra died at his home in La Quinta. Once quoted as saying that "There are no rules in filmmaking, only sins, and the cardinal sin is dullness," he had led a long and productive life and become one of the true Olympians of American moviemaking.

Capra had been born in Sicily in 1897 and moved to Los Angeles with his parents as a child. He attended Manual Arts High School and worked his way through Caltech (then Throop Institute), graduating in 1918 with a degree in chemical engineering. The year Capra graduated from college, the U. S. entered World War I, and Frank joined the Army, where he was assigned the job of teaching math to artillery officers.

After the war Capra worked at a variety of different jobs, but by 1922 had found his first work in films, making "shorts" in San Francisco. He later moved to Hollywood, where he found work with comedy-makers Hal Roach (*Our Gang* and "Laurel and Hardy") and Mack Sennett (the "Keystone Cops").

In 1933 Capra made *Lady for a Day*, which received 4 Academy Award nominations, and the following year, *It Happened One Night*, a romantic comedy that would win 5 Academy Awards. During the remainder of the 1930s, he made one fine film after another, including *Mr. Deeds Goes to Town* (1936), *Lost Horizon* (1937), *You Can't Take It With You* (1938), and *Mr. Smith Goes to Washington* (1939).

But the film for which he is perhaps best remembered today, *It's a Wonderful Life* (1946), is one which was a financial flop when it was initially released, but one that has nonetheless become an enduring movie classic and one that is now as much a part of the modern American Christmas season as *Miracle on 34th Street* or *How the Grinch Stole Christmas*.

271

SEPTEMBER 4

1781

Los Angeles Founded

ON THIS DAY IN CALIFORNIA HISTORY the city of Los Angeles was officially established. A party of 11 men, 11 women, and 22 children (almost half of them under the age of five) made the journey from northern Mexico to a site near the present-day downtown in order to found the fledgling settlement.

The group was diverse. Among the men, there were four Indians, one mestizo, three Spaniards, two blacks, and two mulattoes; all the women were either mulattoes or Indians. There were no Spanish women among them, for few were willing to leave behind the security of their lives in the Old World for the uncertain fortunes of life in the New One. Going to California in the middle of the 18th century was literally going to the ends of the earth.

During the next one hundred years growth was slow. By 1791 the non-Indian population of L. A. stood at just 139, and after a full forty years of Spanish rule, the whole of Los Angeles amounted to just two missions and a still very primitive pueblo. There were no paved roads, no trash collections, and no sewers.

Things changed little under Mexican rule and L. A. remained a rough-and-tumble town during the 1820s, '30s and '40s. The non-Indian population of the area never exceeded 1,600 during this period, and was mostly comprised of Mexican rancheros, mountain men in from the "wilds," local soldiers, miners (gold had been discovered north of Mission San Fernando in 1842), gamblers, drifters, outlaws, runaways and prostitutes.

On August 13, 1846, the American military marched into town to claim California for the United States and set in motion changes that would alter Los Angeles—and California itself—forever. It is from this date that L. A.'s real history as a city can be traced, for it was in the hands of the Americans that Los Angeles was transformed into the amazing place it is today.

SEPTEMBER 5

1922

Construction on the Winchester House Finally Ends

ON THIS DAY IN CALIFORNIA HISTORY construction on the Winchester House in San Jose finally came to an end. It was the creation of Sarah Winchester, heiress of inventor of the Winchester rifle, who oversaw its construction for over thirty-eight years.

Sarah Winchester was driven by some very demanding demons. She lost her only child when the child was just nine days old, and her husband, William, when she was in her early 50s. A friend suggested that she try to make contact with the spirit of her dead husband through a medium and the medium claimed that she had successfully done so.

The medium brought Sarah no comfort, however. The spirit allegedly told the medium that there was a curse on the Winchester family because of the thousands of people who had been killed by Winchester weapons, and that if Sarah didn't get out of town, the curse would claim her life, too.

Some say the medium told Sarah to go out West and build a new home for herself—and for the spirits of those who had been dispatched by Winchester rifles—and keep building the house for the rest of her life. "You can never stop building the house," the medium reputedly told Sarah. "Stop and you will die."

And so Sarah went out West and began building on the house that would occupy her every waking moment for the rest of her life. She kept crews hard at work twenty-four hours a day, seven days a week, 365 days a year—from the time that construction began in 1884 until the day of her death in 1922.

Still standing, it has 160 rooms, 47 fireplaces, 10,000 window panes, 40 staircases, two ballrooms, and three working elevators. It also has secret passages and stairways, as well as doors and hallways that lead nowhere, and cost $5.5 million to build, a truly enormous amount of money at the time.

273

September 6

1869

First Westbound Train Arrives in San Francisco

ON THIS DAY IN CALIFORNIA HISTORY the first transcontinental westbound train ever to make its way across the United States arrived in San Francisco. The city had only been in American hands for twenty years at this point and had jumped in population from a mere 900 residents in 1848 to approximately 50,000.

During its first ten years in American hands, San Francisco was one of the truly rip-roaring places on earth. It was populated mostly by single men, who were young, for the most part heavily-armed, and drank and gambled at a furious pace at the 500 bars and 1,000 gambling halls that then filled the city. Citizens typically witnessed two murders and one fire every day.

Many other kinds of merchants did well in the early days of the city, too. The money that the bar and gambling-house owners didn't mop up was promptly gathered up by the men who sold eggs for $6.00 a dozen and landlords who rented everything from canvas shanties to ship's hulls (from Gold-Rush-bound ships abandoned in San Francisco Bay) as "housing."

Then the train arrived, bringing somewhat more traditional immigrants and visitors to San Francisco. Many were taken by its obvious charms and consequently made plans to move here. Just as many saw its business possibilities and for that reason chose to marry their fortunes with those of the city.

In the decade that followed, construction on Golden Gate Park would begin, cable cars would become a common sight on the streets of the city and the Grand and Palace Hotels would open their doors. The great mansions of the city's richest citizens would be raised on "Nob Hill," I. Magnin would get his start in retail merchandising, and a variety of social and sporting clubs would be created, including the still-famous Bohemian Club. By 1880 the city's population would swell to 234,000.

September 7

1927

TV Born on Green Street

ON THIS DAY IN CALIFORNIA HISTORY television was "born" in a lab on Green Street in San Francisco. For it was on this day that Philo T. Farnsworth and his team of technicians conducted what they called "Experiment Number Twelve," the experiment that would take them to the day, this day, when their entire "image-relaying apparatus" could be tried out.

To conduct this twelfth experiment, Farnsworth and his team had partitioned the room they'd been using as their "lab" into two parts. In one part a technician placed a slide that had the image of a triangle engraved on it in front of a device called an "Image Dissector" (a *transmitting* vacuum tube). In the other part, technicians manned a *receiving* vacuum tube.

An amplifier and wires ran between the two tubes and the idea was to transmit a moving image from one tube to the other.

A couple of seconds after the experiment began, a line appeared across a small, "bluish" square of light at one end of the receiving tube (the "screen"). It wasn't too clear at first, but after some adjustments to the focus, its fuzzy edges took on some definition. Farnsworth next directed one of his technicians to "turn the slide," and when he did, the line on the receiving tube also turned.

What they had accomplished on this historic day was nothing less than laying the foundations for modern television, showing that an image could be scanned, transmitted and "reassembled" electronically.

It was still a long way to the day when these first experiments would evolve into the TV sets we find in our homes today, but the first big step in that journey had been taken. Other inventors had also been working on TV at this time, but all of them were working on mechanical solutions, and nothing mechanical could scan, transmit and reassemble images fast enough.

275

SEPTEMBER 8

1771 · 1798

Missions San Gabriel and San Fernando Founded

ON THIS DAY IN CALIFORNIA HISTORY Mission San Gabriel Arcangel was founded near the present-day Los Angeles suburb of Montebello and Mission San Fernando Rey de Espana at the southern end of today's San Fernando Valley. Though they shared a "founding *day*," they were founded twenty-seven years apart, Mission San Gabriel in 1771 and Mission San Fernando in 1798.

Mission San Gabriel was the fourth of California's twenty-one missions and was the work of the legendary Fr. Junipero Serra. The original site on which Serra wanted to build the mission was on the banks of the Santa Ana River, but he later decided that the San Gabriel River would be a better choice, though that decision would later change, too.

In 1776 Mission San Gabriel was moved to its present site, five miles closer to the San Gabriel Mountains, and it was here that it remains to this day.

Mission San Fernando was the seventeenth of California's twenty-one missions. It also became one of the wealthier missions and was surrounded by land on which the padres who oversaw its care grew olives, dates, wheat, barley, corn and other foods and maintained sizable herds of livestock. Unfortunately, the original mission church was damaged beyond repair in the 1971 Sylmar earthquake and had to be demolished. It is a replica you see when you visit the mission grounds today.

Missions San Gabriel and San Fernando came near the beginning and the end of California's "mission era." Fr. Serra had built the first nine missions, beginning with Mission San Diego in 1769 and ending with Mission San Buenaventura in 1782. Fr. Lasuen picked up where Serra left off and established the next nine, beginning with Mission Santa Barbara (the "Queen of the Missions") in 1786 and ending with Mission San Luis Rey in 1798.

276

SEPTEMBER 9

1850

California Admitted as Thirty-First State

ON THIS DAY IN CALIFORNIA HISTORY California was admitted as the thirty-first state. The Treaty of Guadalupe-Hidalgo had ceded all of modern-day California, Nevada, Arizona, Utah, New Mexico, and parts of modern-day Colorado and Wyoming, to the United States three years earlier, and the question now was whether California should be admitted as a "free" state or a "slave" state.

Congress didn't want to disturb the "balance" of power at the time, the "count" of states that permitted slave-holding versus those that didn't. Before taking California into account, the balance was even: 15 states permitted the practice; 15 states didn't. Admitting California as a "free state" *or* a "slave state" would disturb this balance and no one wanted to do that.

What was proposed to get past the problem was a measure known as the "Compromise of 1850," which was not one measure but several, and the point of which was to maintain the balance of power between free and slave states in the aftermath of the War with Mexico. This is how it worked.

California would be admitted as a "free" state, the thirty-first state in the union. Slavery would not be banned from the territories of Utah and New Mexico; that determination would be deferred to a later date. And finally, what were called the "fugitive slave laws" would be strengthened, an accommodation that the Southern states had insisted on vigorously.

Word that President Millard Fillmore had signed the bill granting California statehood would not reach the state until October 18, 1850, and the official announcement was more of a ceremonial act than anything else anyway, because the state's government had been in operation for almost a year at this point. But it was on this day that President James K. Polk actually *signed* the bill that made California part of the United States.

September 10

1976

Dalton Trumbo Dies

ON THIS DAY IN CALIFORNIA HISTORY controversial author and screen-writer Dalton Trumbo died in Los Angeles. He had been born and raised in Colorado, but where he would make his name was in Los Angeles, the city to which he moved with his mother and two sisters just after his father died in 1925.

Like most writers, Trumbo struggled hard to get to a place where his writing could actually be a source of financial support. In L. A. he worked for nine years on the night shift at a bakery. He used his days to write and do coursework at UCLA and the University of Southern California.

Finally, he got some stories and essays published in *Vanity Fair* magazine, and, in 1932, his contributions to a film magazine called the *Hollywood Spectator* were published. When he was offered the position of managing editor at the *Hollywood Spectator*, his nights as a baker came to an end. "I never considered the working class anything other than something to get out of," he once said.

In 1935 Trumbo began working as a reader and screenwriter at Warner Brothers and in the years that followed, wrote the screen-plays for a number of classic American movies, including *Thirty Seconds over Tokyo* (1944), *The Brave One* (1956), *Spartacus* and *Exodus* (both 1960), *Lonely Are the Brave* (1962), *The Sandpiper* (1965) and *Papillon* (1973).

But the creation for which Trumbo will most likely be remembered longest is his 1939 novel, *Johnny Got His Gun*.

Inspired by the story of a World War I soldier whose body had been horribly disfigured in combat, "Johnny" has lost his legs, arms, eyes, ears, nose and tongue, in a word, his "access" to the outside world. What he has left is his mind and it is through "Johnny's" mind that we experience his world. It is one of the most compelling antiwar novels ever written.

SEPTEMBER 11

1894

Pio Pico Dies

ON THIS DAY IN CALIFORNIA HISTORY Pio Pico, the last Mexican governor of *Alta* California, died in Los Angeles. During his life he signed the treaty that ceded Alta California to the United States, survived the takeover of the region by the Americans and even got himself elected to the Los Angeles City Council.

He was born at Mission San Gabriel in 1801, the son of a Spanish soldier. His grandfather had actually come to California from Mexico as part of the famous Anza expedition of 1776 and his ethnic roots were as diverse as 19th-century California itself, including African, Indian, Hispanic and European elements.

Pico had been a revolutionary in his youth and became governor in 1845 following a bloodless revolt that drove Manuel Micheltorena from office.

But he knew that he was presiding over the twilight years of Mexican California. The American presence in the province increased with each passing day, and though he would actually have preferred that California be taken over by some European power, like England or France, that was not to be.

In 1846, with American troops in San Diego and Los Angeles, Pico escaped to Mexico. Two years later he returned as a private citizen and made his home in L. A. Though he had once been rich, he lost his fortune to gambling and ended his days depending on family and friends for support.

Pico was the last of California's Mexican governors, his term in office the shortest of them all. The first governor, Pablo de Sola, was in office when Alta California passed from Spain to Mexico. Luis Arguello, his successor, was a native-born Californian, and José Maria de Echeandia, Arguello's successor, actually held the position for six years (1825-1831). Most of California's Mexican governors, however, served for very short periods of time.

SEPTEMBER 12

1857

City of Anaheim Founded

ON THIS DAY IN CALIFORNIA HISTORY the city of Anaheim was officially founded. The original settlement was comprised of 1,165 acres and its first settlers were a "colony" of German vintners who had come here from San Francisco to grow wine grapes.

Starting from this original founding group, Anaheim grew quickly. Within ten years of its founding, forty-seven wineries and scores of vineyards had been established, making it into what was then the state's "wine capital."

Anaheim's farmers initially brought in Yaqui Indians to dig the irrigation ditches they needed to properly water their vines, but later brought in Chinese workers to do this work, and in time, a Chinese community developed in downtown Anaheim.

Things went well until the 1880s when plant viruses attacked the vineyards and killed off most of the vines. Not ones to be easily diverted from their goal of making Anaheim a successful agricultural community, however, the city's farmers turned to cultivating orange trees instead.

For the next seventy years, Anaheim was a fairly sleepy place, comprised, for the most part, of orange orchards and small businesses. Then came Disneyland.

The coming of Disneyland changed everything. Area development took off like a rocket and by the late 1950s orange trees were being plowed under at the rate of one every fifty-five seconds, with motels and subdivisions quickly taking their place.

Home for fewer than 15,000 people in 1950, Anaheim was home for nearly a quarter of a million by 1980. Today the city stretches over forty-six square miles and has a population of over 325,000 people, making it the largest city in Orange County. It is also the wealthiest city in a county that now numbers over 3,000,000 residents.

SEPTEMBER 13

1971

Werner Erhard Announces the Beginning of *est*

ON THIS DAY IN CALIFORNIA HISTORY self-improvement guru Werner Erhard announced at a seminar held in a ballroom of the Mark Hopkins Hotel that he was launching a new self-improvement program called *est* ("Erhard Seminars Training").

Erhard drew on the insights of both Scientology and Esalen to fashion his own unique methodology for "getting in touch with the self." From Scientology he took the idea that people could be transformed by putting them through a process short in duration but high in intensity. From Esalen he took the idea that through encounter-like situations real emotions can be released.

Stripping away the layers of a person's social mask or "façade" was one of *est*'s key goals, in fact, and it was through "the training," a process that was for "esties" what "auditing" was for Scientologists, that this transformation was brought about. *Est* did not present its "faithful" with a full-blown belief system to assimilate the way that Scientology did, however. It provided, in Erhard's words, "a context" in which one could become "sensitive to the dangers and pitfalls of any and all beliefs and belief systems."

The idea that personal transformation is an instantaneous event, not the outcome of some long, drawn-out process, and the idea that to "grow" one must first create the "space" in which growth can occur, are both central to *est*—and both straight out of traditional Zen thinking. As is the idea that in order to live fully, one must live fully "in the present," an idea that Esalen also stressed.

Through two grueling weekend "seminars," sessions that often lasted as long as fifteen hours a day, Erhard and his "trainers" attempted to create "the space" in which a group of people could achieve this Zen sensibility, and master, as he put it, "the philosophical contexts, the ground of being, the presuppositions . . . from which their lives spring."

SEPTEMBER 14

1980

Crystal Cathedral Dedicated in Garden Grove

ON THIS DAY IN CALIFORNIA HISTORY Dr. Robert Schuller's splendid glass church, the "Crystal Cathedral," was dedicated in Garden Grove. It isn't located particularly *near* Hollywood, as it turns out, but it's the perfect example of a church "*gone* Hollywood," routinely featuring celebrity speakers and telecasting its services worldwide using state-of-the-art audio and video technology.

The Crystal Cathedral is made almost entirely of glass and is, in fact, the largest glass building in the world. It is a star-shaped structure, over 400 feet long, 200 feet wide, and 12 stories high. Over 12,000 panes of glass were utilized to cover its exterior and almost 3,000 people can be seated here for services.

Schuller originally came to Southern California from the Midwest, and started his ministry preaching at a local drive-in theater to about 75 people, sitting in their cars. When he finally built a permanent church for his congregation in 1962, he made sure that it, too, included facilities for people to worship from the privacy of their cars and incorporated this same auto-friendly feature into the design of the "Crystal Cathedral."

Schuller first achieved national notoriety as a televangelist with his Sunday morning telecast, *Hour of Power*, and like legendary L. A. evangelist Aimee Semple McPherson before him, left no stone unturned in his efforts to further his ministry.

Each year two major religious pageants are staged at the church, each one organized around a key event in the Christian year: "The Glory of Christmas" in December and "The Glory of Easter" in March. Both feature large casts dressed up in "Biblical" attire, angels that "really fly," and live animals. After all, what could be more "Biblical" than sitting in an all-glass cathedral watching angels attached to wires fly overhead while live camels make their way down the aisles?

SEPTEMBER 15

1921

Jackie Cooper Born in Los Angeles

ON THIS DAY IN CALIFORNIA HISTORY actor, director and producer Jackie Cooper was born in Los Angeles. His name at birth was John Cooperman, Jr., and the year was 1921 (though it is also reported in some accounts as 1922).

Becoming a performer was a natural enough course for Cooper to take. His father was a studio production manager and his mother a performance pianist. But they were busy with their own careers, so it fell to his grandmother to take him to auditions.

The first part to come his way was in a movie called *Skippy* (1931), for which he would receive an Oscar nomination for "Best Actor," and though he wouldn't win, it would mark the beginning of what would turn out to be a long and successful career in TV and movies, including 15 of the *Our Gang* features.

But the 1930s were truly Cooper's heyday as an actor. He played opposite Wallace Beery in *The Champ* (1931), *The Bowery* (1933), *Treasure Island* (1934) and *O'Shaughnessy's Boy* (1935), and played high-profile roles in several other films, too. He was "big" before Shirley Temple was "big" and the first kid to become a headliner in "talkies." His popularity faded as he got older, however, and in 1943 he left Hollywood for the Navy.

After the War Cooper continued to work as an actor, director and producer—this time on TV. He directed some episodes of the hugely popular sitcom *M*A*S*H* and became the executive in charge of TV production at Screen Gems, too. Late in his career he played the character of "Perry White" in the *Superman* films, which is how most people under 40 remember him today.

Cooper's movie days are, of course, long behind him now and he is in his eighties. He's one of those rare few who have succeeded on both sides of the camera, however, and still the youngest actor ever to be nominated for an Oscar in a lead role.

SEPTEMBER 16

1974
"BART" Begins Regular Transbay Service

ON THIS DAY IN CALIFORNIA HISTORY the Bay Area Rapid Transit Service ("BART") began regular transbay service. The idea of building such a system to link the Bay Area together had first surfaced in 1946, primarily in response to the massive influx of newcomers who came here after World War II, causing traffic on Bay Area bridges to become extremely heavy.

It was decided that a comprehsive transportation system linking the Bay's cities together was what was needed, and in 1947, a joint Army-Navy review board recommended that an underwater tube devoted exclusively to high-speed electric train travel was the best way to accomplish this.

In 1951 the California State Legislature created the Bay Area Rapid Transit Commission, a body that was made up of representatives from each of the nine counties which border the Bay, and charged it with creating a Bay-Area-wide development plan. The Commission recommended the creation of a five-county "Bay Area Rapid Transit District," but the project looked so pricey, two counties withdrew from membership.

Nonetheless, in July of 1963 the design of this ambitious system began. Construction began on the Oakland leg of the subway in January of 1966, and in 1967, on the Market Street subway in San Francisco. On January 27, 1971, the final "hole-through" at the Montgomery Street station was completed and on this day in 1974, regular transbay service began.

By the time it turned five in 1977, 120 million people had riden on BART and daily average passenger traffic had climbed to 144,000. Circa 2000 the entire system stretched for 95 miles around the Bay Area, and by the time the system turned 30 in 2002, over 2 billion people had riden it. Getting around the Bay Area this way had, for many Bay Area residents, become a way of life.

SEPTEMBER 17

1959

Groundbreaking Ceremonies for Dodger Stadium

ON THIS DAY IN CALIFORNIA HISTORY groundbreaking ceremonies were held for Dodger Stadium in Los Angeles. The new stadium was located just a few miles from downtown Los Angeles, in an area called Chavez Ravine. It had been home for several generations of Mexican-American families and was named for a late-19th-century County Supervisor, Julian Chavez.

In 1949 a federal bill known as "The Federal Housing Act of 1949" was passed, which granted money to cities to build public housing projects. Civic leaders in Los Angeles decided that they would like to access some of this federal money, and in order to do so, approved the construction of a housing project that was to contain 10,000 living units, many of which were to be located in Chavez Ravine.

The threads that held this community together were of little concern to the powers that be, who viewed Chavez Ravine simply as a place that needed to be tidied up and made new and therefore a prime candidate for "redevelopment."

In July of 1950 all the residents of Chavez Ravine were sent letters from the city telling them that they would have to sell their homes in order to make the land available for the new housing development that the city intended to build. The letter said they would have the first choice from the new homes that would be built, but most of the residents here had no desire to leave their existing homes, or money enough to buy the new ones.

By 1952 most of the residents of Chavez Ravine had been forced from their homes, but political wrangles had kept the promised neighborhood from actually materializing. Ultimately, the city of Los Angeles bought the area back from the federal government and sold it to the Dodgers baseball organization, which was then looking for a place to build a new stadium for its team.

SEPTEMBER 18

1932

Peg Entwhistle Jumps from the Hollywood Sign

ON THIS DAY IN CALIFORNIA HISTORY actress Peg Entwhistle jumped to her death from the letter "H" in the Hollywood sign.

She had come to Hollywood to repeat in films the success she had found on the stage, but things didn't work out that way. Instead, she found no success in Hollywood, and chose to end her life by leaping from the top of the gleaming symbol of everything she had been unable to attain.

The first sign spelled out "H-O-L-L-Y-W-O-O-D-L-A-N-D," the community's original given name, but that was later shortened to "H-O-L-L-Y-W-O-O-D," the name by which the area has been known since the 1940s. Each of the letters in the sign was made of sheet-metal panels painted white and attached to a framework of pipes, wire and scaffolding.

The borders of each of the original letters in the sign were studded with twenty-watt electric lightbulbs, four thousand of them, which could be seen for miles around when less electric light filled the night sky of Los Angeles and the air was not so polluted.

The sign even made appearances in movies and pilots used it as a landmark to navigate by. For many years, whenever a bulb burnt out, it was promptly replaced by a new one; in 1939, however, regular maintenance of the sign stopped. In the years that followed, all four thousand of the bulbs in the sign were stolen and vandals even made off with many of the sheet-metal panels that made up the letters in the sign.

A windstorm blew down the letter "H" in 1949 and some area residents felt that the sign had become such an eyesore and hazard that the time had come to tear it down. Instead, however, its first nine letters were repaired, the last four eliminated, and the sign returned to something like its former glory, reminding everyone who cared to know that *this is Hollywood.*

SEPTEMBER 19

1948

"Pancho" Gonzales Wins U. S. Open

ON THIS DAY IN CALIFORNIA HISTORY Los Angeles native Richard "Pancho" Gonzales won the U. S. Open tennis championships at Forest Hills, New York. It was the fourth and final event in that competition and the win was unexpected.

The years during which Gonzales came of age in L. A. were not good ones for a talented Mexican-American athlete, because tennis was a "white man's game" back then and the people who played it, mostly upper-middle-class. It was not the crowd young Pancho ran in, but no matter. Pancho wanted to play.

He was just twenty years old on this day in 1948 when he won his first U. S. Open tennis championship, a feat he would repeat the very next year. Encouraged by this success, he decided to turn pro, but his first year out he was soundly beaten by superstar Jack Kramer and the experience led him to withdraw from professional competition for a time and work on raising his level of play.

By 1953 he was back and better than ever. He won the U. S. singles championship in 1953, 1954, 1955, 1956, 1957, 1958, 1959 and 1961, and was the singles competition runner-up in 1951, 1952 and 1964. He beat all the great players of his time, including Ken Rosewall, Tony Trabert and Ashley Cooper.

Gonzales was known for his will to win, powerful serve and equally powerful net game. His net play was so good, in fact, that for a brief period during the 1950s the rules of the professional game were changed so that he was not permitted to advance to the net immediately after he had served. It didn't slow him down, though, so the rules were changed back.

Even in his 40s Gonzales was able to beat many of the best players then playing the game, including Rod Laver, Stan Smith, John Newcombe, Roy Emerson and Jimmy Connors, all of them much younger men than he was.

SEPTEMBER 20

1966

Hubert Eaton, Creator of "Forest Lawn," Dies

ON THIS DAY IN CALIFORNIA HISTORY Hubert Eaton, the creator of the Forest Lawn mortuaries and cemeteries in Los Angeles, died. Fittingly, he would be interred within his own creation in a ceremony that included Greer Garson, Ronald Reagan, and Walt Disney, who was an "honorary pallbearer."

The original Forest Lawn was established in Glendale in 1906 by a group of San Francisco businessmen. Hubert Eaton and a partner purchased the property from this group in 1912, and in 1917, Eaton took over its management.

Eaton was almost "cheery" in his approach to death and vowed to create a cemetery as "unlike other cemeteries as sunshine is unlike darkness." What he had in mind was a place filled with majestic trees, wide lawns, fountains and statuary—in a word, a "park"— where the rich and famous could be laid to rest.

Among Forest Lawn Glendale's more memorable features are a re-creation of Leonardo da Vinci's *The Last Supper* in stained glass, full-sized reproductions of Michelangelo's sculptures "David" and "Moses" and three distinctive chapels—"The Little Church of the Flowers," "The Wee Kirk o' the Heather" and "The Church of the Recessional." Eaton even included a funeral home on the grounds, which had not been done before.

Eaton would later establish a similar facility in the Hollywood Hills, but Forest Lawn Glendale is the original, and it is here that many of the nation's legendary entertainment figures are buried, including Humphrey Bogart, Nat King Cole and Chico Marx.

Forest Lawn was long the biggest tourist draw in all of Southern California, until Disneyland finally surpassed it in the 1950s. It nonetheless remains an amazing creation, the final resting place for a quarter of a million people who have passed on and a place visited by over a million of those still living each year.

SEPTEMBER 21

1927

Charles Lindbergh Cheered in San Diego

ON THIS DAY IN CALIFORNIA HISTORY 60,000 San Diegans packed the City Stadium to celebrate Charles Lindbergh's successful nonstop flight from New York to Paris. The whole adventure had really started here, so it was a fitting place to celebrate his success.

In 1925 a man named T. Claude Ryan organized Ryan Airlines in San Diego. That same year his airlines began to make regularly-scheduled passenger flights between San Diego and Los Angeles, becoming the first airlines in the country to do so. By 1929 four other airlines had joined in the competition, making the skies between San Diego and Los Angeles the nation's busiest for passenger air traffic.

In any case, T. Claude Ryan and Ryan Airlines became major players in the early development of California's aerospace industry, and in the spring of 1927, in addition to flying paying passengers back and forth between San Diego and L. A., Ryan Airlines entered into a contract with Charles Lindbergh to build the plane that he would pilot over the Atlantic and into the history books, the *Spirit of St. Louis*.

Just two months after this celebration, San Diego voters passed a $650,000 bond package to develop some of the city's tidal lands into a new metropolitan airport that would be named in Lindbergh's honor and which would be officially dedicated the very next year, on August 16, 1928.

In the years to come, aviation would play an increasingly important role in the San Diego economy, and Lindbergh Field, San Diego's airport, become an increasingly busy place. The aviation industry here would be responsible for establishing more than 42 aviation "firsts," including records for altitude, distance, duration and speed. The first aviation radio would be developed here and the first "night flight" occur here, too.

SEPTEMBER 22

1969 · 1986
A Big Day in Baseball

ON THIS DAY IN CALIFORNIA HISTORY two important events in American baseball occurred involving "Californians." The first one involved Willie Mays, the second, a young man named Fernando Valenzuela. Both were milestones in the game's history.

On September 22, 1969, Willie Mays hit his 600th home run, a feat that only one other player in the game's history up to this point had managed to pull off: Babe Ruth. One sportswriter said that Mays was so good he "should play in handcuffs to even things up," but probably even that wouldn't have helped much.

Mays was signed by the "New York" Giants straight out of high school and during the course of a long major-league career, won the "Gold Glove Award" 12 times, was voted Most Valuable Player in the National League twice (in 1954 and 1965), and finished his career with a .302 batting average and 660 home runs.

On September 22, 1986, a 26-year-old Mexican immigrant by the name of Fernando Valenzuela entered the elite ranks of pitchers in American professional baseball who have won twenty or more games in a single season.

He won the first ten games he pitched as a major-leaguer (for the Dodgers), became the first rookie ever to win the coveted "Cy Young Award," and pitched five shut-outs during his first seven starts. The "magic" behind all of this was a pitch that became known as "Fernando's Fadeaway," a screwball that he could throw at two different speeds.

He was an unlikely superstar athlete. He was built more like the chunky Babe Ruth than such fit-looking modern-day Hispanic superstars as Juan Gonzalez or Alex Rodriguez. But not only could he pitch, he could bat (winning a "Silver Bat" award in 1983), pinch hit when the need arose, and play outfield, too. He was a very capable all-around player.

September 23

1916

Edgar Rice Burroughs Arrives in Los Angeles

ON THIS DAY IN CALIFORNIA HISTORY author Edgar Rice Burroughs arrived in Los Angeles. Like many another immigrant to the area, he had first come as a tourist, seeking relief from the winters of the Midwest. He liked what he saw and soon came to stay.

Burroughs had just recently turned 41 and had made a lot of money writing his Tarzan books. He had been raised in an upper-middle-class home near Chicago, but unlike his three brothers, had no taste for a predictable life in the suburbs

Instead, Burroughs had long been the adventurous sort. He had ridden with the U. S. Cavalry in Arizona, worked as a cowboy and gold prospector in Idaho, and as a railroad policeman in Utah. But he wanted to make money, too, and it was that ambition that brought him to a job at Sears.

But Burroughs was not cut out for life behind a desk, however much he wanted to make money, and so he soon left Sears to pursue a number of get-rich-quick schemes, all of which came to nothing. At 35, he found himself in a job selling pencil sharpeners.

Relief from this dreary fate was not far off, however. For it was about this same time that he got his first story, *A Princess of Mars* (1912), sold, followed, less than a year later, by the book that would be his making: *Tarzan of the Apes* (1912). He had finally found a way to become rich *and* famous, and not stuck behind a desk, a way to shape his future on his own terms.

As he drove into L. A. on this day in 1916, he was already off to a good start, but considerably more success lay just ahead. By 1919 the first two Tarzan movies had hit the nation's movie houses and Burroughs was wealthy enough to buy the 550-acre ranch in the San Fernando Valley that had once been the home of *L. A. Times* publisher Harrison Gray Otis (which he renamed "Tarzana"). He was in the big time to stay.

SEPTEMBER 24

1855

Preserved Heads Sold at Auction

ON THIS DAY IN CALIFORNIA HISTORY the preserved heads of Joaquin Murieta, the "Mexican Robin Hood," and a character known as "Three-Fingered Jack," Murieta's right-hand man, were sold at auction for $36, to satisfy an outstanding judgment.

Murieta was a legendary figure in 1850s California. He formed a band known as "The Five Joaquins," who busied themselves rustling livestock, robbing miners, and killing those who resisted their efforts. "Three-Fingered Jack" (real name Manuel Garcia) was the *sixth* member of the band.

All told, these six banditos are said to have stolen more than $100,000 in gold, over 100 horses, an untold number of cattle, and to have killed 19 people, including 3 lawmen. So it should come as no surprise that they were at the top of every California lawman's "Most Wanted List."

On May 11, 1853, California governor John Bigler signed an act that created the California Rangers, a group whose express purpose was to capture and arrest The Five Joaquins. They were each to be paid $150 per month for their services, but the real money would come from successfully capturing them. Getting that done would bring $5,000 to split up among themselves.

On July 25, 1853, a group of these Rangers came upon a band of young Mexican males in San Benito County who they believed to be The Five Joaquins. In the confrontation that ensued, two members of the band were killed, one believed to be Murieta, the other, Three-Fingered Jack.

The Rangers cut off the head of one and the hand of the other to "prove" that they had, in fact, killed them and the remains were put in a container and circulated throughout the state for viewing (not everyone believed the Rangers had the right men). Some say the legend of Zorro was inspired, in part, by Murieta's life.

SEPTEMBER 25

1890

Legislation to Create Sequoia National Park Passed

ON THIS DAY IN CALIFORNIA HISTORY President Benjamin Harrison signed legislation officially creating Sequoia National Park, the nation's *second* national park. A week later Congress passed legislation setting aside an additional area of giant redwoods that would one day become Kings Canyon National Park.

Sequoia is famous for two kinds of "natural wonders": the world's largest trees (the *Sequoia gigantea*) *and* the highest mountain in the contiguous United States (Mt. Whitney, 14,495 feet). Of the two, it is probably the "Big Trees" that have brought the area the most fame. They are unique to California, unforgettably imposing, and cover some 15,000 acres.

Thirty to sixty million years ago, the Big Trees and their coastal cousins, the "coast redwoods," were plentiful throughout the Northern Hemisphere, but with the coming of the glaciers (during the last Ice Age), most of them were knocked down, and the ones that stand today are the descendants of those that somehow survived.

The sequoias are not the oldest living things in the world (that distinction goes to California's bristlecone pines), but they are certainly one of the hardiest things on earth, and not one of them has ever been found dying of old age.

It is difficult for someone who has never seen these trees to imagine just how big they are. The only way to do *that* is to stand beneath and just look up.

The "General Sherman Tree" is so big it has *limbs* larger than the largest known *trunks* of several other kinds of trees and its own trunk is so wide, a tunnel large enough to place three cars side by side could be cut through it. It is 275 feet high (almost the length of a football field) and 40 feet in diameter. In the late 19th century, when a socialist community called the Kaweah Colony lived in this area, it was known as the "Karl Marx Tree."

September 26

1914

Jack LaLanne Born in San Francisco

ON THIS DAY IN CALIFORNIA HISTORY Jack LaLanne was born in San Francisco. He was destined to grow up to become a bodybuilder and open gyms of his own. By the time he was 19 he had opened ten gyms in Northern California, and by 21, had opened the nation's first weight-training facility for women.

That was in 1936, and though it was not a popular idea at the time, it eventually caught on and put bodybuilding on the road to becoming a mainstream exercise practice for men *and* women.

In 1951 LaLanne began conducting "exercise classes" on TV, and by 1960, was broadcasting his gospel of physical and mental rejuvenation through regular physical exercise into the living rooms of some two-and-a-quarter million Americans every day. He boasted that he was to the body what the Reverend Billy Graham was to the soul, and his own 48-28-35 frame (at 40, no less!) seemed to offer persuasive evidence he was right.

In a few short years LaLanne managed to parlay his personal commitment to exercise and diet into a sizable following and fortune. "Working out with Jack," and using nothing but your body, a nearby chair, and a get-with-it attitude, made LaLanne a big part of daily American life for a time, and an enduring part of American popular culture.

He once swam handcuffed from Alcatraz to the San Francisco shoreline, once swam the width of the icy-watered Golden Gate itself (towing a two-ton boat), and once did 1,033 pushups in twenty-three minutes, a world record at the time.

LaLanne was so committed to getting and staying fit that his name eventually became synonymous with the pursuit of physical fitness all over America. In 2005, at the age of 91, he was still going strong and still putting himself through exercise regimens that men considerably younger couldn't handle.

September 27

1905

Burnham's "City Beautiful" Plan

On this day in California history famed Chicago architect David Burnham, the man responsible for such design wonders as the 1893 World Columbian Exposition in Chicago, presented his plan for transforming San Francisco from the miscellany of frame structures it was into a coherent and beautifully-laid-out metropolis.

This kind of transformational thinking was very much in the air in late-19th- and early 20th-century America. And there was no city more in need of it, perhaps, than San Francisco, a city known before the Great Earthquake and Fire of 1906 laid it to waste for its ugliness, not its beauty.

In 1902 former mayor of San Francisco James D. Phelan approached Burnham with the following proposal: draw up a master plan for remaking San Francisco similar to the one that he had developed for Washington, D. C. Two years later, he and a group of San Francisco heavyweights formed the "Association for the Improvement and Adornment of San Francisco" to promote beautification of the city and bring the best current thinking about the best way to do that to the attention of the city's leaders.

Burnham was in many ways the perfect choice. He and his partner, John Root, had played major roles in setting the urban design course for the city of Chicago, including designing some of its first skyscrapers, and he had already done some major work in San Francisco, too, including designing the *Chronicle* Building, the Mills Building and the Merchants Exchange.

Problems impossible to foresee soon got in the way of realizing the ideas laid out in Burnham's plan—the Great Earthquake and Fire that hit on April 18, 1906, chief among them—and when the city set about the task of rebuilding, it chose to build back along familiar lines, not new ones. But there was a time, a brief time, when everything might have turned out differently.

SEPTEMBER 28

1542
Juan Cabrillo "Discovers" California

ON THIS DAY IN CALIFORNIA HISTORY Portuguese explorer Juan Cabrillo sailed into San Diego Bay and became the first European to lay eyes on California. He had been sent here to find the "Strait of Anian," a waterway shortcut through North America that many 16th-century geographers believed to exist and that many explorers of the time had tried hard to locate.

Cabrillo never found the Strait of Anian (it didn't, as it turned out, exist), but he did manage to explore some 800 miles of the California coastline, discover San Diego Bay and the Santa Barbara Channel Islands in the process, and put ashore at Catalina Island and at points where today stand the cities of San Pedro, Santa Monica and Ventura.

Things didn't end well for Cabrillo, however. He did not impress the viceroy who had sent him here with his accomplishments, and died just three months after a fall he took on San Miguel Island, probably as a result of an infection that developed in the arm he broke when he fell. Nevertheless, he was the first European to explore this coastline and his efforts would inspire later explorers to pick up where he left off.

Cabrillo's men buried him on San Miguel Island, the westernmost member of the four northern Channel Islands, and originally named it in his honor, though Vizcaino renamed it when he sailed through in 1602. As important as he was, however, no one knows to this day just where on the island he is buried.

San Miguel is a rugged place, surrounded by rough seas, and a favorite of area wildlife. In fact, it boasts the most diverse population of fin-footed marine mammals to be found anywhere in the world and is the nesting ground for sixty percent of the seabirds that nest in the Channel Islands. With but a few exceptions, humans have had no luck making the island their home.

September 29

1958

Clark Kerr Becomes Chancellor at U. C.

ON THIS DAY IN CALIFORNIA HISTORY Clark Kerr, one of the nation's higher-education giants, became the twelfth president and first chancellor of the University of California system.

He was the driving force behind California's 1960 Master Plan for Higher Education, which called for a three-tiered structure for postsecondary education in California, with the community college system at the bottom, the California State University system the next rung up, and the University of California on top.

The idea was to provide access to a college education for all talent and budget levels and distribute that access throughout the state, and it was a vision that would profoundly reshape postsecondary educational systems worldwide.

But despite his desire to provide access to a college education for all Californians, Kerr quickly came under attack from the state's then staunchly right-wing leadership, who felt he was far too open-minded about academic freedom, and students who felt he wasn't open-minded enough.

The arrest in 1964 of a student for protesting the ban then in force on political activity on campus provoked hundreds of students to stage a 32-hour sit-in that ultimately precipitated what is known as the "Free Speech Movement," and Kerr suddenly found himself in the middle of a divided house, trying to appease everyone and managing to please no one.

In 1966 governor-elect Ronald Reagan proceeded to "handle the problem at Berkeley." He insisted that Kerr wasn't hard enough on the dissident students at Berkeley, and working with the FBI, got Kerr ousted as president. But whatever Reagan's opinion of him was, Kerr will long be remembered as the man who put the University of California on track to become one of the true academic powerhouses in the world.

SEPTEMBER 30

1955
James Dean Killed in a Car Wreck

ON THIS DAY IN CALIFORNIA HISTORY actor James Dean was killed in a car wreck near a wide spot in the road called Cholame in San Luis Obispo County. He was just 24 at the time and at the very beginning of his career.

The Dean family originally moved to Los Angeles when James was five, but they had lived in the city just three years when his mother passed away. He was sent back to Indiana to be raised by an aunt and uncle and lived there for the next thirteen years. But after high school he returned to L. A., where he attended both Santa Monica College and UCLA.

In L. A. Dean got involved with actor James Whitmore's acting workshop and found some work in television commercials, as well as some roles in films and on the stage. Whitmore told him he should go to New York if he wanted to become a "serious" actor and Dean took the advice.

Dean got himself admitted to the "Actors Studio," which led to a role on Broadway in *The Immoralist* (1954) and that, in turn, led to a screen test at Warner Brothers.

Warner Brothers thought he'd be right for the role of Cal Trask in *East of Eden*, and the rest, as they say, is history. That same year he won the role of Jim Stark in *Rebel without a Cause* (1955), the role that would make him permanently bigger than life, and moved to Hollywood.

He celebrated this success by buying a Porsche and racing it in Palm Springs, Bakersfield and Santa Barbara before departing for Marfa, Texas, to shoot *Giant* (1956). After the shoot, he returned to Hollywood and then immediately headed north to Salinas to race his new car. On that trip, however, he got in a wreck and died. With his passing, he became a legend and one of the most iconic actors in all of American film history.

This Day

in

October

OCTOBER 1

1940

Chandler's *Farewell, My Lovely* Published

ON THIS DAY IN CALIFORNIA HISTORY novelist Raymond Chandler's masterpiece, *Farewell, My Lovely,* was published by Alfred A. Knopf.

In a writing career that took off in the late 1930s and endured until the mid-1950s, Chandler wrote some of the best and most influential American crime fiction ever written. *The Big Sleep* appeared in 1939, *Farewell, My Lovely* in 1940, *The High Window* in 1942, *The Lady in the Lake* in 1943, and *The Long Good-Bye* in 1953, the principal books on which his reputation rests.

He had been born in Chicago, but moved to London with his mother in 1895. He later studied in both France and Germany, but returned to London in 1907 and became a British citizen. In 1912 he returned to the United States, and lived for a time in St. Louis and Omaha, but finally moved to Los Angeles.

In 1913 Chandler took some bookkeeping courses and soon found work as an accountant. In 1917 he joined the Canadian army and in 1918 shipped out to France. In 1919 he returned to the United States, where he briefly toured the Pacific coast before taking a job at a bank in San Francisco.

But Chandler preferred life in the southern end of the state and soon moved back to L. A. By 1922 he was doing the bookkeeping for an oil syndicate and rose to the position of vice president. But in 1932 he was fired for his drinking and absenteeism.

Chandler spent the last forty-five years of his life living all over Southern California. In addition to the time he spent living in Los Angeles in the nineteen tens and twenties, he also lived at various times in Arcadia, Big Bear Lake, Pacific Palisades, Idyllwild and Cathedral City in the mountain and desert areas east of L. A., and in La Jolla, which was where he and his wife lived from 1946 until his death in 1959 at age 70.

OCTOBER 2

1816

The *Rurik* Sails into San Francisco Bay

ON THIS DAY IN CALIFORNIA HISTORY the Russian vessel *Rurik*, with naturalist Adelbert von Chamisso on board, sailed into San Francisco Bay. It had come here to get fresh supplies from the Russian base station at Fort Ross sixty-eight miles to the north.

At this point in its history, the presidio at San Francisco was a largely neglected outpost of New Spain, so a visit from just about anyone was a welcome sight. It provided an opportunity to get news of the outside world and to socialize in a place where opportunities to do either were scarce.

The Russians had recently established themselves on Bodega Bay and at Fort Ross, so that they could hunt sea otter and grow crops to ship north to their settlement at Sitka, Alaska. They also knew that Spain had a very tenuous hold here and no doubt felt confident that their effort to establish a modest presence in the area would not be seriously challenged.

In any case, during their October visit to the San Francisco presidio in 1816, the crew of the *Rurik* met then-governor of California, Pablo Vicente de Sola, and the officers and soldiers then stationed there. The governor expressed his concern about the Russian presence within his borders, hoping, no doubt, that his visitors could somehow persuade those in charge at Port Bodega and Fort Ross to leave.

During the course of the *Rurik*'s stay in San Francisco Bay, Chamisso, the chief naturalist on board, was curious about the kinds of plant life that thrived in the area, including a poppy which Governor Sola brought to his attention personally. That flower would one day be known as the "California poppy," California's "state flower." Chamisso, however, gave it the somewhat more cumbersome name of *Eschscholtzia californica*, to honor of the Rurik's surgeon, Johann Friedrich Eschscholtz.

OCTOBER 3

1942

"Hollywood Canteen" Opens Its Doors

ON THIS DAY IN CALIFORNIA HISTORY the Hollywood Canteen opened its doors. It was the idea of film stars Bette Davis and John Garfield and was modeled after a place called the "Stage Door Canteen" in New York City. The idea was to provide a place where military men and women could have a little fun when they were on leave during World War II.

One thing the Canteen needed was "hostesses" and one good source of these hostesses was the local aircraft factories that built planes for the war. With so many men away fighting, the factories were "manned" by the nation's women, women who came from all around the country to work here—and maybe get a shot at becoming stars themselves.

Women would spend eight hours working in an aircraft factory, ring off at, say, midnight, and dance until 3 a.m. at the Canteen. They were serving their country two ways!

And the plan of using a factory job in L. A. as a springboard to Hollywood stardom worked well enough for some. This was how Marilyn Monroe got her start. An army photographer named David Conover spotted her working at an aircraft plant in Van Nuys and asked her if he could take some pictures of her. She agreed, and the rest, as they say, is history.

Hollywood stars staffed the Canteen, too. Servicemen might find themselves dancing with Hedy Lamarr and getting a sandwich served to them by Marlene Dietrich or Rita Hayworth. Frequently, the stars also performed for their visitors. Rita Hayworth danced and sang. Bing Crosby and big band leader Kay Kyser made music. Roy Rogers brought his horse "Trigger" by for everyone to see.

The Canteen remained open until "V-J Day," August 15, 1945, and it is estimated that some 3,000,000 people benefitted from its services.

303

OCTOBER 4

1970

Singer Janis Joplin Dies

ON THIS DAY IN CALIFORNIA HISTORY singer Janis Joplin died in Los Angeles. Her fame spread quickly once she became the front voice for the band "Big Brother and the Holding Company," but by the end of her life, she was widely-known and -loved in her own right, one of those one-name people, like "Garbo" or "Cher."

Janis was born in Port Arthur, Texas, a "gas and oil" town on the east Texas coast. As a teenager, she developed an interest in the work of the Beat poets and in things like blues and jazz, the music of Bessie Smith and Odetta and "Leadbelly."

While trying to find her way in the music business, Janis played in the coffeehouses of Venice and North Beach in California, Greenwich Village in New York City, and in the many live-music venues around Austin, Texas. When an old Austin friend of hers, Chet Helms of "The Band," called her from San Francisco to invite her to come out and audition for the lead spot in an up-and-coming band there, she went.

That band, Big Brother and the Holding Company, had been playing up and down the California coast, but hadn't quite found its sound yet. Janis's amazing, gravelly and emotion-filled voice was the missing piece they needed, and when they played at the Monterey International Pop Music Festival in the summer of 1967, with Janie our front singing "Ball and Chain," the rest of the world finally knew they'd found that missing piece, too.

It would be a wild ride. Big Brother found fame in the summer of 1967, broke up a year and a half later, and Janis moved on to form a new group, more bluesy in its focus. Along with her increasing fame and fortune, she increasingly indulged her taste for drugs and alcohol, too, and it was drugs that would finally claim her, when, on this October day in 1970, she injected an unusually pure dose of heroin in a Los Angeles motel and died.

OCTOBER 5

1923

Edwin Hubble Takes a History-Making Photo

ON THIS DAY IN CALIFORNIA HISTORY Caltech professor of astronomy Edwin Hubble began making a photographic exposure of the Andromeda Galaxy that would literally revolutionize astronomy. Normally, this is the kind of thing that would only be of interest to other astronomers, but what Hubble did was so significant, it would interest just about everybody.

To make his exposure Hubble used the 100-inch telescope at the Mt. Wilson Observatory in the San Gabriel Mountains near Pasadena. He began on the evening of October 5 and completed it in the early morning hours of October 6.

What the photograph showed was that the group of stars Hubble had been observing was farther away from the earth than the known reaches of the Milky Way. Astonomers had long wondered if there were other galaxies than ours out there and Hubble's photo demonstrated there had to be. Since that fateful day, literally millions of other galaxies have been found.

And Hubble not only demonstrated that the universe was much larger than anyone had previously thought, he demonstrated it was expanding, too, and doing so at an ever-more-rapid rate. Prior to him, astronomers had pictured the universe as a place where things remained pretty much where they had originally been "put." Hubble proved this just wasn't so; instead, the universe was dynamic and on the move.

We naturally think of the earth as the center of "things" in the universe, and of the "things out there" in terms of their distance "from us." But Hubble demonstrated that the universe would look pretty much the way it does no matter where in it you made your observations and that those of us "down here" on earth are just part of one immense, expanding whole. Among other things, this confirmed Einstein's theory of General Relativity.

OCTOBER 6

1875

First Findings from the La Brea Tar Pits Made Public

ON THIS DAY IN CALIFORNIA HISTORY Professor William Denton of the Boston Society of Natural History published the first scentific description of some bones he had found in the La Brea Tar Pits near downtown Los Angeles.

What Denton was digging in, it turned out, was one of best-preserved collections of creatures from the late Pleistocene era (10,000 to 40,000 years ago) that had ever been uncovered. Since his initial finds, the bones of at least 59 different species of Pleistocene-era mammals have been recovered here and those of over 135 species of birds. The remains of shellfish, insects and plants have also been found.

Throughout the animal kingdom animals that eat plants are considerably more common than animals that eat meat, but this is not the case with the animals found in the La Brea Tar Pits. Ninety percent of the animals found here were meat-eaters, including camels, giant bison, dire wolves, ground sloths, mammoths, mastodons and sabre-toothed tigers.

Most of the birds found here were predators, too, and include eagles, condors, vultures, and a giant, stork-like bird, now extinct, called a "teratorn."

Predators chasing their prey would be the most likely candidates for getting trapped in the tar and this was no doubt how many of the ones found here met their end. Once trapped, they drew the attention of scavengers, like condors and vultures, and that is no doubt why many of *them* have been found here, too.

The first intensive scientific examinations of the La Brea Tar Pits site were conducted by Professor John C. Merriam of the University of California, Berkeley, in the early years of the 20th century. Since that time, over a million fossil bones from late Pleistocene Los Angeles have been recovered here.

OCTOBER 7

2003

Schwarzenegger Elected Governor of California

ON THIS DAY IN CALIFORNIA HISTORY Arnold Schwarzenegger was elected governor of the state. It was at once a very predictable and very improbable event. Who was more perfectly suited than a world-class bodybuilder, top-tier movie star and successful businessman to nurse the now economically-troubled capital of glamour and glitz back to health? Well, we were about to find out.

Schwarzenegger had been born in a small village in Austria on July 30, 1947. He saw bodybuilding as his ticket out and it was an opportunity that he seized with a vengeance. Before he was done, he'd be the best-known bodybuilder in the world.

Then came the movies: *Stay Hungry* (1976), *Conan the Barbarian* (1982), *The Terminator* (1984), *Predator* (1987), *Total Recall* (1990), *Terminator 2* (1991), *True Lies* (1994) and *Terminator 3* (2003). And he wasn't just about pumping iron, murder and mayhem, either. He did comedy, too, most notably *Twins* (1988) and *Kindergarten Cop* (1990). In addition to everything else the man had going for him, he also had a sense of humor.

Now, as the result of a uniquely "California" political innovation—the "recall"—he had become the 38th governor of the state. The man he unseated, Gray Davis, was nothing if not unpopular. On his watch California had suffered through the worst energy crisis and developed the largest budget deficit in its history, developments that made him an easy target for a popular challenger.

Schwarzenegger's first brush with American politics came with his appointment to the "President's Council on Fitness and Sports" by George Bush the First, who christened him "Conan the Republican." Whether he might someday make a run for the Presidency is an interesting question, but before anything like that could come about, the long-standing law about being a native-born American would have to be changed.

OCTOBER 8

1933

Coit Tower Dedicated

ON THIS DAY IN CALIFORNIA HISTORY Coit Tower was dedicated in San Francisco. Some say it is designed in the shape of a fire hose nozzle (it is dedicated to the city's firefighters), others disagree, but whatever the verdict on that subject, it remains one of the city's most recognizable landmarks to this day.

The person behind the Tower's creation was Lillie Hitchcock Coit, a fascinating daughter of early San Francisco. She came to the city with her parents in 1851, just four years old. Her father was an army surgeon, her mother a "southern belle."

In the 1850s firefighters were folk heroes here and fire companies were typically staffed by groups of volunteers who assembled whenever fires broke out.

The legend goes that one day on the way home from school, young Lillie came upon one of these volunteer units—Knicker-bocker Engine Company No. 5—trying to pull its engine up Tele-graph Hill. But the company was short of men and struggling mightily to get the job done. It's said that young Lillie threw down her schoolbooks, rallied some bystanders to help, and that together with the men of Knickerbocker Company No. 5, pulled the fire engine up the hill.

Lillie became Company No. 5's "mascot" and was even given an honorary firefighter's uniform to wear. She was also awarded a diamond-studded, gold badge that read "No. 5," a badge she was still wearing sixty-six years later when she died.

Lillie became a rich woman when she grew up and late in life donated a third of her fortune to be spent in a way that would "add to the beauty" of her beloved San Francisco. After her death in 1929, a competition was held to choose an appropriate "addition." It was won by a prominent local architect named Arthur Brown, Jr., and led to the creation of what we know today as "Coit Tower."

308

OCTOBER 9

1776 · 1791

Missions Dolores and Soledad Founded

ON THIS DAY IN CALIFORNIA HISTORY, and exactly fifteen years apart, Mission Dolores and Mission Soledad were founded.

Franciscan missionaries built Mission San Francisco de Asis on the shores of a little inlet on San Francisco Bay that was called Laguna Dolores. As time went by, the nearby village of Yerba Buena changed its name to San Francisco and the mission's name became shortened by locals to "Dolores."

Mission Dolores struggled from the beginning. Built so close to Yerba Buena, it had to compete with the town for land and to deal with the area's foggy climate, hardly an ideal situation for agricultural pursuits. And though they were initially attracted to the Mission, the Indians often succumbed to the pull of the city's bright lights nearby, or a life of freedom across the Bay.

Mission Soledad was the 13th of California's 21 missions. It was named by Portola himself for "Our Lady of Solitude," and it is an apt name, for Mission Soledad was built along a lonely stretch of highway in central California, and of all the missions built in the state, had the toughest go of it.

It was near no major settlement and the soil it sat on was tough to work. The damp winds that blew through in the wintertime were no comfort, either. Summers tended to be too dry or too wet and the mission's adobe buildings to disintegrate quickly under such conditions. The Indian population never grew very large and an epidemic that swept through the mission in 1802 killed off many of those who did live there.

When Father Vicente Francisco de Sarria died here in 1835, what little there was left of Mission Soledad died, too. The mission buildings were left to deteriorate, and though restoration efforts have been undertaken in recent years, the mission remains, for the most part, a ruin.

OCTOBER 10

1911

Recall, Initiative and Referendum Voted In

ON THIS DAY IN CALIFORNIA HISTORY the state's voters voted in some important amendments to its constitution. In 1895 the California Direct Legislation League had been founded, with the stated purpose of making the initiative, referendum and recall realities in California politics. In 1911 they finally succeeded.

The leader of this effort was Dr. John Randolph Haynes, who had come to Los Angeles from Philadelphia in 1887. In 1900 he was elected to a Los Angeles board whose mandate was to draft a new city charter. Haynes worked hard to have initiative, referendum and recall provisions incorporated into its language, but the document was later challenged in the courts and ruled invalid.

In 1902 a new board charged with the duty of drafting a new city charter was elected, but this time Haynes was not among its members.

No matter. Never one to simply sit by and let events unfold as they would, Haynes brought the president of the National Direct Legislation League to Los Angeles to speak before the newly-convened board about the importance of including provisions for the initiative, referendum and recall in its charter and they were persuaded to do so. The very next year, 1903, the voters of Los Angeles ratified the document.

Now that he had succeeded in getting these provisions written into the city charter of Los Angeles, Haynes next turned his efforts to getting them incorporated into the *state* charter.

This was no easy task, however, because the Southern Pacific Railroad had had California's politicians in its pocket for years, and getting things done through bribery was standard operating procedure. To introduce a system in which California's voters would actually have some say in what went on in their state was a thoroughly revolutionary idea.

OCTOBER 11

1984

Inventor of the "Mai Tai" Dies

ON THIS DAY IN CALIFORNIA HISTORY "Trader Vic" Bergeron, the inventor of the "Mai Tai" ("the best") cocktail, died.

He had created the drink that made him famous 50 years before, at the original Trader Vic's in Oakland. It was a "tropical drink," as they say, which means it was colorful and included a powerful clear liquor mixed with fruit juice. The Mai Tai was no exception, a mixture of Jamaican rum, orgeat (an almond-flavored syrup), orange curacao, rock candy syrup and the juice from a fresh lime.

Bergeron had been born in San Francisco and grew up in Oakland. In 1934 he opened a restaurant and bar called "Hinky Dinks" across the street from his parents' grocery store; in 1937 he changed the place's name to "Trader Vic's" and the décor from "rustic" to "tropical island paradise." The menu took on a Polynesian/Chinese cast and a four-page exotic drink menu was introduced.

The second Trader Vic's opened in Seattle in 1949 and throughout the 1950s additional restaurants were opened all along the Pacific coast.

In 1963 Trader Vic's expanded into the European market, opening its first restaurant in London, and in 1971, one in Munich. In 1974 the company opened a restaurant in Tokyo, and in the years that followed, new restaurants popped up all over the place—in Atlanta, Singapore, Osaka, Hamburg and Bangkok. Beginning in 1994, they were brought to the Middle East, when restaurants were opened in Abu Dhabi and Dubai.

The business empire that Bergeron built around his tropical cocktail continued to sophisticate itself through the years. In 1946 he created his own food production company and that same year published *Trader Vic's Book of Food and Drink*. In 1960 California wines were added to the beverage list and in 1972 the Trader Vic's bartender's guidebook appeared.

OCTOBER 12

1885

Fresno Incorporated as a City

ON THIS DAY IN CALIFORNIA HISTORY the city of Fresno was incorporated. Unlike most of California's big cities, Fresno had no Spanish or Mexican roots, but was created by a group of people who decided that their future lay with creating an agricultural empire, not with digging for gold.

In 1860 the population of Fresno County was officially listed as "4,304 whites, 305 Chinese, and 3,294 Indians," 7,903 individuals in all. In 1872 the Southern Pacific Railroad decided to build a train station here, and from that point on, the population grew.

From the beginning Fresno has been the market and shipping center for the San Joaquin Valley. Irrigation was first introduced in 1866, and from that time to this, it has done nothing but grow. Today, some 800 miles of canals and pipelines irrigate over 150,000 acres of farmland here, making it possible to grow crops that would be impossible to grow without them.

In the late 19th century Agoston Haraszthy introduced wine grapes to the Fresno area, a farmer named M. Theo Kearney established the raisin-growing industry here, and the Roeding family introduced the cultivation of Smyrna figs. Wine grapes, raisins and figs all remain major crops in the area, but a wide variety of others have been introduced and flourished here, too.

In more recent times the once predominantly agricultural character of the Fresno area has begun to change, however.

More and more land once dedicated to growing fruit trees and crops has been plowed under so that more homes and commercial buildings can be built. The entire population of the county was just 276,515 as recently as 1950, but by the year 2000 the population of the city of Fresno alone had grown to 427,652 (in a metropolitan area then exceeding 1,000,000) and shows every sign of getting larger in the years ahead.

OCTOBER 13

1958

Phil Spector Makes his Pop Music Debut

ON THIS DAY IN CALIFORNIA HISTORY the pop classic "To Know Him is to Love Him," by a Los Angeles trio who called themselves the "Teddy Bears," made it onto the Billboard "Top 40." One of the members of that trio, Phil Spector, had written and arranged the song, and would soon go on to bigger things.

Spector played a big role in creating recording opportunities in sixties L. A. By 1962 he had established his own record label and big-time performers had begun to seek out his services. More would do so in the years just ahead.

Spector moved quickly from performing to songwriting to production in his music career. His first success as an independent producer came in 1961 with a song called "Pretty Little Angel Eyes" and that same year he also had success with a song called "Every Breath I Take" that Gene Pitney made into a hit.

He wrote, cowrote, or was the producer on such rock classics as "Spanish Harlem," "Corinna Corinna," "He's a Rebel," "Da Doo Ron Ron," "Then He Kissed Me," "Be My Baby," "(Today I Met) The Boy I'm Gonna Marry," "Walking in the Rain," "You've Lost That Lovin' Feelin'," and more.

It was Spector who came up with the idea of the "girl group" and he gave the world such memorable ones as the Crystals and the Ronettes. He also produced the Righteous Brothers, the Ike and Tina Turner of "River Deep—Mountain High," and worked his magic on some Beatles and Rolling Stones records, too.

What Phil Spector will be remembered for most, however, is a production technique known as the "Wall of Sound." To achieve it, he assembled large groups of musicians and then squeezed them into the tight quarters of his studios to play. The result was a dense and dramatic background for each and every song he recorded: "little symphonies for the kids."

OCTOBER 14

1947
Chuck Yeager Breaks the Sound Barrier

ON THIS DAY IN CALIFORNIA HISTORY Capt. Chuck Yeager broke the sound barrier while flying over the test ranges at California's Muroc Field (now Edwards Air Force Base) in his Bell X-1 rocket plane. The Bell X-1 was an experimental aircraft that had been designed in the shape of a .50 caliber bullet, an object known to be capable of moving through the air faster than the speed of sound.

Yeager had joined the United States Army Air Corps straight out of high school. One day after he shot down his first enemy airplane in 1943, he was himself shot out of the skies, but managed to evade capture with the help of French Resistance fighters. He was able to get himself to Spain, and under normal conditions, would have been prohibited from flying combat missions again.

Instead, he personally appealed to General Dwight D. Eisenhower for an exception and "Ike" granted the request. Yeager would fly 64 more combat missions before World War II came to an end, and down 13 more planes, 5 of them in a single day.

Six years later, in 1953, also at Muroc Field, the speed of Mach 2 (twice the speed of sound) was reached in an experimental aircraft. On this occasion the pilot was Scott Crossfield and he did it in a Douglas "Skyrocket," a plane that had already set world records for altitude (83,235 feet) and speed (Mach 1.88), even though it had only been designed to reach Mach 1.6.

What allowed the Douglas Skyrocket to go so fast was something known as "swept-wing technology," a design calling for wings angled back at 35 degrees, creating less "drag" and consequently permitting the plane to move more efficiently through the air. Crossfield achieved this landmark on November 20, 1953, but just three weeks later, on December 12, 1953, Yeager took back the crown when he reached Mach 2.44, also becoming the first pilot ever to reach this speed in "level flight."

314

OCTOBER 15

1969

New Bank of America Headquarters Opens

ON THIS DAY IN CALIFORNIA HISTORY the new Bank of America head-quarters at 555 California Street in San Francisco opened its doors. Bank of America ("B of A") had led America into the modern age of banking, credit, and financial services and its founder, native son Amadeo P. Giannini, had organized the nation's first successful branch bank in 1904, calling it the "Bank of Italy."

Giannini had been born in nearby San Jose in 1870 and had worked in his family's produce business in the heavily Italian North Beach area of San Francisco as a kid. It didn't take long for him to see that his future lay not in providing goods and services himself, however, but in financing those who did. By age 32 he had worked himself into a position as director of a savings-and-loan society that catered to San Francisco's Italian community.

In a state that was itself a "self-contained economic empire," with an economy as diverse as that of the nation itself, branch banking permitted Giannini to create the functional equivalent of a "national bank."

In the years to come he would develop his organization into an *actual* national bank and rename it the "Bank of America." (He obviously thought it had a big future.) By 1940 it had grown into the largest bank in the world.

Over the years, the Bank of America would introduce a number of innovations to American retail banking, including the first electronic check handler and the first successful all-purpose credit card for general use—"BankAmericard"—innovations that would profoundly reshape the way Americans handled the process of buying goods and services. It was joined in these efforts by the Bank of California, which created the first "consumer-sized CDs," simplified checking accounts and "Master Charge," the credit card that was the forerunner of the now ubiquitous "Master*Card*."

OCTOBER 16

1972

Creedence Clearwater Revival Calls it a Career

ON THIS DAY IN CALIFORNIA HISTORY the preeminent American rock band of its day called it a career. They were California boys from El Cerrito, a small town near Berkeley, and under the name of Creedence Clearwater Revival ("CCR"), they recorded some of the most memorable rock and roll music ever made.

The bands members were John and Tom Fogarty, Stu Cook and Doug Clifford. They honed their craft in the Fogartys' garage, and four years later, auditioned for Fantasy Records, where an executive changed their name to the "Golliwogs," to make them "sound more English." The "British Invasion" was underway and no record label wanted to miss out. The Golliwogs recorded seven records, all of which went largely unnoticed.

The last of the seven, "Porterville," was re-released under the name "Creedence Clearwater Revival"—"Creedence" from the name of a friend, "Clearwater" from nothing more exotic than a beer commercial they had seen, "Revival" to convey the idea that under their new name they had been "revived" or brought back to life.

Creedence played a couple of years on the central California club circuit and then things began to happen for them. Their debut album, *Creedence Clearwater Revival*, appeared in 1967, just in time for the "Summer of Love" and the flowering of the San Francisco rock music scene. Five more albums were brought out over the course of the next two years: *Bayou County, Green River, Willie and the Poor Boys, Cosmo's Factory* and *Pendulum*.

By 1970 CCR had made itself into the number one rock band in America, largely due to the writing, producing and singing talents of John Fogarty whose voice *was* the sound of CCR. But his dominance of the group was also the cause of its demise. Brother Tom left in 1971 and the remaining members of the group recorded and released their seventh and last album, *Mardi Gras*, in 1972.

OCTOBER 17

1989
Loma Prieta Earthquake Hits

ON THIS DAY IN CALIFORNIA HISTORY the Loma Prieta earthquake hit the San Francisco Bay area.

It was a big quake, a "7.1," the largest one to hit the Bay Area since the Great Earthquake and Fire of 1906, and it struck during the course of the World Series then being played between the San Francisco Giants and the Oakland Athletics. Game 3 was just about to begin and it was 5:04 p.m.

The damage inflicted was extensive. A section of the San Francisco-Oakland Bay Bridge collapsed and a section of the upper deck of the Chester Nimitz Freeway that runs along the east shore of San Francisco Bay pancaked into the lower deck, crushing dozens of motorists and their cars when it did. The Embarcadero Freeway was so badly damaged, it was later torn down.

At least twenty-seven fires broke out across the city, including one that shut down the city's 911 telephone equipment and one that damaged several apartment buildings in the city's swanky Marina District. As had happened during the earthquake of 1906, citizen "bucket brigades" were formed to assist the city's firefighters.

Scientists from the United States Geological Survey determined that the earthquake's epicenter had been at Mt. Loma Prieta in Santa Cruz County. Fissures hundreds of yards long and as much as twenty inches wide were found along the San Andreas Fault in this area and a huge undersea landslide was triggered in Monterey Bay.

Several important buildings in San Francisco were damaged by the quake, including Candlestick Park, where the series was being played, the city's main library, the War Memorial Opera House, the de Young Museum and the California Palace of the Legion of Honor. When it was over, 62 people had been killed, 3,757 injured and more than 12,000 left homeless. Property damage across the area was estimated at $6 billion.

OCTOBER 18

1955

Antiproton Discovered at Berkeley

ON THIS DAY IN CALIFORNIA HISTORY the "antiproton" was discovered at the University of California at Berkeley. Berkeley had been a major center of scientific research for years, for this was where the first workable cyclotrons or "atom smashers" were built, and it was by smashing atoms that the antiproton was discovered.

What made an antiproton different from a proton, or any "antimatter" different from "matter," was what physicists call its "reverse electrical charge." The two kinds of matter have the same *mass*, but an *opposite electrical charge*, and that property turns out to be important because when matter and antimatter collide at high speeds, a significant amount of energy is released, energy that can potentially be harnessed for human use.

The problem is that the amount of antimatter available at any given time is very small, so even though its *potential* value is high, it's difficult to arrange enough "collisions," in a reliable and controlled way, to create significant amounts of energy. Still, even in the tiny amounts that *can* be created, antimatter has proved itself useful for doing things like diagnosing and treating disease.

Research using Berkeley's cyclotrons was also instrumental in adding new elements to the periodic table. The majority of what are known as the transuranium elements, 93 through 106, were "produced" in these machines, several of them given names that would link them forever to the Golden State, like "berkelium," "californium," "lawrencium," and "seaborgium."

Berkelium and californium were named to honor the university and the state, of course, lawrencium to honor Ernest O. Lawrence, the professor primarily responsible for building Berkeley's first cyclotrons, and seaborgium for Glenn Seaborg, the chemist whose research teams discovered many of the isotopes that made the cyclotrons so famous.

OCTOBER 19

1953

Ray Bradbury's *Fahrenheit 451* Published

ON THIS DAY IN CALIFORNIA HISTORY author Ray Bradbury's landmark novel, *Fahrenheit 451* (the temperature at which paper burns), was published by Ballantine Books.

The novel is set in a future where books have been banned, and its leading character, a "fireman" named Guy Montag, is a professional "book-burner." He meets a girl who tells him about a time when books were legal and begins reading them himself. When he's found out, he must run for his life.

So goes the plotline of *Fahrenheit 451*, just one of many fine books that Bradbury has written over what is now a 60-year writing career. In 1947 his first book of stories, *Dark Carnival*, came out, and in 1950, the book that would be the making of his name and career, *The Martian Chronicles*, appeared. *Fahrenheit 451* was published three years later, in 1953.

Though he initially thought about becoming an actor, two influential teachers of his at Los Angeles High School saw a different future in store for him. They introduced him to literature and taught him how to write short stories, and in time, he joined the "Los Angeles Science Fiction League," a decision that would have a decisive influence on the course of his writing life.

Bradbury began his writing career immediately after graduating from high school. He sold newspapers on a Los Angeles street corner to make money and spent the rest of his time reading and writing. By 1943 he had begun to write full-time.

He has won the "World Fantasy Award for Lifetime Achievement," as well as the "Grand Master Award" from the Science Fiction Writers of America. He has called science fiction "the most important literature in the history of the world, because it's the . . . history of our civilization birthing itself," so "the whole history of mankind is nothing but science fiction." And so it is.

319

OCTOBER 20

1991
Oakland/Berkeley Hills Fire Breaks Out

ON THIS DAY IN CALIFORNIA HISTORY a conflagration known as the "Oakland/Berkeley Hills Fire" broke out in the hills to the north and east of these two cities. A small fire had broken out the day before in this area, but the winds were mild and it appeared that the fire had been brought under control.

Deep within the ground cover of the burn site, however, it smoldered on, and when firefighters returned to the area to finish cleaning it up, it reignited and quickly spread to vegetation nearby. Less than an hour later, it had blown out of the canyon where it had started and was completely out of control.

The strong winds that had come up on this autumn morning blew the fire up one hill and down another, to the east, then to the southwest, and then to the northwest, toward the city of Berkeley. What began as several small fires soon became several big ones, and finally, *one* big one, threatening to send the entire area up in smoke. The fire burned so hot and fast that 790 structures were incinerated in the first hour alone.

By 5 p.m. air temperatures had begun to cool down and the speed of the winds to decrease. This stopped the fire from spreading further, but the areas burning burned on, fueled by the thousands of structures already engulfed in flames.

For thousands of years, fires like this have periodically raged through areas like this. That is not something new. The problem arises when people insist on building their homes in these areas, relatively remote and hard to access, and surrounded by combustible vegetation. That *is* new.

By the time the fire had burnt itself out, 25 people were dead, 150 injured, and nearly 2,500 homes had burnt to the ground. In addition, 437 apartment and condominium units were destroyed and over 1,600 acres charred. The cost? $1.5 billion.

320

OCTOBER 21

1868

San Francisco Hit by Biggest Quake to Date

ON THIS DAY IN CALIFORNIA HISTORY the biggest earthquake to hit San Francisco to date rocked the city. It began at 7:53 in the morning and lasted nearly a full minute. The violent shock waves rolled east to west and brought men, women and children running from their homes in a panic, some no doubt suspecting that the Day of Judgment was at hand.

About a third of the city's citizens were still in bed when the tremor struck, the other two-thirds busy getting ready for the day ahead. Business in the city came to a halt, and many people just whiled away their time in the city's public plazas, too fearful about what might be coming next to return to their homes.

One of the spires of the Jewish Synagogue located between Broadway and Vallejo Streets toppled to the ground and part of its rear wall collapsed. Cracks also appeared in the synagogue's walls and many of its windows were broken out.

Glass bottles in downtown drugstores were thrown to the floor and shattered into a thousand pieces, as was glassware in the homes of city residents. In some buildings, entire walls were separated from one another, making the structures unstable and creating a fear that they might collapse.

Considerable damage was reported in the Chinatown area of the city. The firewall of one brick building just off Dupont Street collapsed on top of a small frame building nearby, crushing it into rubble, and the side of one building was so bowed out by the quake that it had to be shored up with braces to keep it from falling.

There was general damage to structures throughout the city. City Hall was badly damaged, as was the Customs House, the City and County Hospital, and a laundry list of other structures in the city. Some feared that real-estate values would suffer because of what had happened, but that did not turn out to be the case.

OCTOBER 22

1988

Ceremony at City Lights Bookstore

ON THIS DAY IN CALIFORNIA HISTORY a ceremony was held at San Francisco's City Lights Bookstore to celebrate the renaming of twelve city streets (well, "alleys") for ten California writers (most of them associated with San Francisco), the mother of modern dance, Isadora Duncan, and sculptor Beniamino Bufano.

The California writers who were honored this way were Ambrose Bierce, Richard Henry Dana, Jr., Dashiell Hammett, Bob Kaufman, "the Jacks," Kerouac and London, Frank Norris, Kenneth Rexroth, William Saroyan, and the most famous of the state's early writers, Mark Twain.

Bierce worked as a journalist in the city during the late-19th and early-20th centuries and was known for his acid wit. Richard Henry Dana, Jr., wrote his *Two Years before the Mast* after visiting here as a young seaman in the 1830s and Dashiell Hammett's work captures the feel of life here in the 1930s. A lesser-known figure, poet Bob Kaufman, got an alley named in his honor, too.

Jack Kerouac only brushed up against San Francisco for a short period of time, but he did hang out at City Lights Bookstore some and spent six months working on *On the Road* at his friend Neal Cassady's home on Russian Hill. Jack London was born in the city and was the author, among other things, of *The Call of the Wild* (1903). Frank Norris wrote *The Octopus* (1901) here, Kenneth Rexroth led the "San Francisco Renaissance" here, and William Saroyan, originally from Fresno, spent time here, too.

Mark Twain didn't care much for San Francisco, but did work here as a journalist in the 1860s. Mother of modern dance Isadora Duncan was a San Francisco native. Sculptor Benny Bufano lived in San Francisco for some fifty years, creating images that celebrated his love of peace and hatred of war, examples of which can be found in prominent places all over town.

OCTOBER 23

2003
Disney Concert Hall Opens in Los Angeles

ON THIS DAY IN CALIFORNIA HISTORY the first of three galas celebrating the opening of the avant-garde Disney Concert Hall in Los Angeles was held. The hall had been designed by Frank Gehry, long noted for the unique and futuristic directions in which he has taken modern architecture, and it would be, among other things, the new home of the Los Angeles Philharmonic Orchestra.

In 1987 the late Lillian Disney made a gift of $50 million to build this hall. Subsequent gifts from the Disney family—and the accumulated interest on Lillian Disney's initial gift—brought the Disney family's total contribution to this project to over $100 million. Los Angeles County contributed land for a site and some additional funding for construction to begin, and in 1988 Frank Gehry was selected to design the hall.

The Disney Hall is 293,000 square feet, cost $274 million to build, and has superb acoustics. Its memorably wavy steel exterior is designed to look like a ship with its sails unfurled, the idea being, said Gehry, to give the impression of moving over water. The Hall's central auditorium seats 2,265 and continues this theme; it is designed with the look and feel of a ship's hull.

The dramatic curves of the building's exterior are covered with twenty-two million pounds of stainless steel, 12,500 individual plates, some as short as 13 inches and some as long as 110 feet. No two are the same and some weigh as much as 165,000 pounds. Linked end to end, they would stretch for 49 miles.

The interior of the Hall is primarily made of wood, making it as calming as the exterior is, at least for some, unsettling; the carpets and upholstery have an abstract floral motif woven through them, a tribute to Lillian Disney's love of gardens and gardening. The whole facility is a stunning addition to the Bunker Hill Music Center complex.

OCTOBER 24

1871

Massacre of Chinese in L. A.

ON THIS DAY IN CALIFORNIA HISTORY a massacre of Chinese gang members in Los Angeles made national headlines. Two Chinese gangs, "Nin Yung" and "Hong Chow," had been fighting over a woman, and during the course of the hostilities, two white men were inadvertently shot and killed.

The Chinese had successfully integrated themselves into the city's economic life in the 1860s, but nonetheless an uneasy peace between the city's white and Chinese citizens remained. Sometimes the peace was broken, as it was on this day in 1871.

When local authorities arrived to break up the gun battle between the gangs, some gang members barricaded themselves in an adobe structure located on the then-infamous Calle de los Negros. Robert Thompson, one of the citizens assisting the police, was shot during this effort, and a few hours later, died from his wounds. As he lay dying, a mob reported to be about 500 strong (almost nine percent of the city's population at the time) formed at a place called Wollweber's Drug Store on Main Street.

L. A.'s population in 1871 was made up largely of desperadoes and ne'er-do-wells and this group was well represented here this day. They typically spent their days looking for a fight or some excuse to unleash a little mayhem and this shooting of Robert Thompson was just what they needed to get things going.

Part of the mob chopped holes into the roof the Coronel Block adobe and began firing their guns through those holes, none too careful about who they might hit. Those they were unable to shoot, they hung, and some whom they shot and killed, they hung anyway, just to make whatever sick point they were trying to make. One of the victims of this violence, Wong Tuck, was hung twice. The first time the rope broke, but the second time it held. Seventeen others were dispatched with a rope, too.

OCTOBER 25

2003

Wildfire Breaks Out in San Diego

ON THIS DAY IN CALIFORNIA HISTORY, at 5:37 in the afternoon, a wildfire that would come to be known as the "Cedar Fire" was reported burning in Southern California's Cleveland National Forest. Before firefighters could bring it under control, it would burn itself into the second largest wildfire in California history.

The Cedar Fire began in central San Diego County, just south of Ramona, and during its first sixteen-and-a-half hours, it burned some thirty miles to the southwest, incinerating 100,000 acres in the process and killing 13 people living just north of the town of Lakeside. Hundreds of homes in the "Scripps Ranch" area of San Diego were on fire at this point and homes along the San Diego coastline were in jeopardy, too.

The Fire forced authorities to evacuate the main air traffic control station for San Diego and Los Angeles, which shut down all commercial air traffic along this particular flight corridor and disrupted air traffic throughout the United States.

On the evening of October 26, the fire moved deeper into central San Diego County, burning hundreds of homes in the towns of Alpine, Harbison Canyon and Crest. This is an area that had been hit hard thirty-three years earlier during the "Laguna Fire," the *second*-largest wildfire to hit California up to this time. The Cedar Fire was about to surpass it.

By the evening of the 27, as the Santa Ana winds that had been driving the fire died down, it appeared that it was beginning to lose some of its ferocity. But then the westerly winds kicked up, bringing it back to life, and driving it in an eastward direction, consuming another 114,000 acres in the process. By the time the fire was fully contained on November 3, 280,278 acres had been burned, 2,820 buildings destroyed (2,232 of them homes), and 14 people killed, including one firefighter.

OCTOBER 26

1936

First Generator at Hoover Dam Kicks In

ON THIS DAY IN CALIFORNIA HISTORY the first generator at Hoover Dam went into full operation. It was a momentous event, for the dam would make it possible for what was soon to be an enormous population in the far southwestern United States to sustain itself in this dry desert area.

Construction on the dam had begun in September of 1930 and was finished in 1935. Getting this much concrete to set up correctly was no easy task. In fact, special cooling tubes had to be built into the concrete, because without them, it would have taken *more than a century* to get this much concrete to harden.

The physical dimensions of the dam alone were staggering. It stood 726.4 feet high, was 1,244 feet across (at the top), 660 feet thick (at the bottom), and weighed 6.6 million tons. When it was finished, it became the first individual structure to contain more masonry than the Great Pyramid.

It was also the highest dam in the world when it was completed (it now ranks 18th) and was capable of storing up to 9.2 trillion gallons of water in its reservoir. It was capable of generating over 2,000 megawatts of hydroelectric power from its 17 generators, too, providing power to what is today a population of around 25,000,000 in this part of the United States.

Hoover Dam (originally named "Boulder Dam") is named for the thirty-first president of the United States, Herbert Hoover, who played a major role in its creation.

Hoover was himself an engineer and had worked for a long time in that profession before getting involved in politics. His first efforts to get the dam built occurred during his years as Secretary of Commerce during the Harding and Coolidge Administrations and continued during his years as president. It may well be the single most important thing he helped bring about.

OCTOBER 27

1940

Maxine Hong Kingston Born in Stockton

ON THIS DAY IN CALIFORNIA HISTORY novelist Maxine Hong Kingston was born in Stockton. Her parents, Tom Hong and Ying Lan Hong, were Chinese immigrants who made their living running a laundry in Stockton. Maxine, the oldest of six, would become a fresh and important new voice in American writing.

The story goes that Kingston's American name was inspired by a blonde woman the family knew who was lucky at gambling. Her Chinese name, "Ting Ting," actually came from a Chinese poem about self-reliance. She would certainly need to be both self-reliant *and* lucky to survive as a writer.

Kingston struggled mightily with the English language when she first entered school. She had difficulty with both written and spoken English and even flunked kindergarten. But that difficulty would pass and she would eventually win a scholarship to the University of California at Berkeley, from which she would graduate with an A. B. degree in English in 1962.

After graduation Kingston taught English and math in the East Bay city of Hayward for a couple of years, but in 1967 she and her husband decided to leave this country that had then become drenched in antiwar violence and drugs, and move to Japan. On the way they stopped in Hawaii, and ended up staying there for seventeen years.

It was while living in Hawaii that Kingston finished her first novel, *China Men* (1980). She had published a book of memoirs four years before, *The Woman Warrior: Memoirs of a Girlhood Among Ghosts* (1976); *China Men*, of course, in 1980; *Hawaii One Summer* in 1987; *Through the Black Curtain*, also 1987; *Tripmaster Monkey: His Fake Book* in 1989; and most recently, *The Fifth Book of Peace* (2003) and *Veterans of War, Veterans of Peace* (2006). We can only hope that more work in this vein will be forthcoming.

OCTOBER 28

1919

Volstead Act Passed and "Prohibition" Begins

ON THIS DAY IN CALIFORNIA HISTORY the U. S. Congress passed a piece of legislation known as the Volstead Act. The Eighteenth Amendment to the Constitution had been ratified by Congress earlier in the year and prohibited the making, selling or shipping of alcoholic beverages in the United States. The Volstead Act defined what an "alcoholic beverage" was.

By defining an alcoholic beverage as any brewed, fermented or distilled drink that contained more than one half of one percent of alcohol, the Volstead Act made wine, as well as beer and the more traditional distilled spirits, things like whiskey, vodka and gin, off limits for Americans.

Many of California's winemakers went out of business altogether during the fourteen years that Prohibition lasted. There were 713 wineries operating in California prior to Prohibition, but only a handful still in operation in 1933 when it ended. As with most laws, there were loopholes, and it was through those loopholes that the survivors managed to climb.

One "loophole" involved the making of "medicinal" and "sacramental" wines. If a wine was made for medicinal or sacramental purposes, that is, made to be used in the treatment of a patient or as part of a religious ritual in a church, that wine was legal to make, sell and ship. If it contained less than one half of one percent alcohol, that is, which the law required.

Another important loophole was the provision that allowed families to make up to 200 gallons of wine a year for *personal* use. Some California wineries utilized this loophole by making what were called "wine bricks" or "loaves," grape concentrates that people could use to make wine at home. Nonetheless, it would take a long time for the industry to recover. There would not again be 713 wineries operating in the state until 1986.

OCTOBER 29

1877

Denis Kearney's Fieriest Oration Yet

ON THIS DAY IN CALIFORNIA HISTORY labor activist Denis Kearney delivered his fieriest oration yet in defense of the rights of the working man. Kearney had developed quite a reputation for delivering fiery orations and to draw the attention not only of the city's workingmen, but of the rich and powerful as well.

On this day in 1877—the *evening* of this day, to be exact—Kearney had drawn a large crowd to hear him rail against the injustice that railroad baron Charles Crocker was "inflicting" on a Chinese citizen of the city who owned a small lot with a house on it in a city block that Crocker was trying to consolidate, one occupied today by Grace Cathedral.

The lot was owned by a man named Jung and Jung didn't want to sell. In an effort to "encourage" him to change his mind, Crocker had a high wooden fence built on three sides of Jung's lot, so high that it blocked out the sunlight, making it, the crafty Mr. Crocker no doubt hoped, a very unpleasant place to live.

But this high-handed treatment of Jung came to the attention of Denis Kearney, always on the lookout for a social injustice worthy of his attention, and he decided to deliver his rant about it on Nob Hill itself, within shouting distance of the homes of some of the city's wealthiest men—Central Pacific Railroad tycoons Stanford, Hopkins, and Huntington, "Silver King" James Flood, and old Charlie Crocker himself.

Never one to understate his case, Kearney called the railroad barons "thieves" who would soon feel the lash of the Workingmen's Trade and Labor Union of San Francisco that he was then trying to form to right the wrongs of the power elite against the working class. He was so intemperate in his views, even the Workingmen's Party of California would not grant him admission to its ranks. Not surprisingly, Kearney soon found himself in jail.

OCTOBER 30

1966

The "Zodiac Killer" Takes His First Victim

ON THIS DAY IN CALIFORNIA HISTORY a serial killer who would come to be known as the "Zodiac killer" took his first victim, 18-year-old Cheri Jo Bates, near the parking lot of the library annex at Riverside City College. It didn't appear that rape or robbery was the motive, because Cheri Jo's clothes had not been disturbed and nothing had been taken from her purse.

The killer had disabled his victim's car and then offered to help her get it going. Sometime later, he apparently lured her back into a dark area between two empty houses where he stabbed her three times in the chest, once in the back, and slashed her seven times across the throat. She had also been choked, beaten and slashed about the face.

In the months to come the killer would send letters to the Riverside police, the local newspaper and Cheri Jo's father, detailing the particulars of the crime. A correspondence carried on between the killer, local newspapers and the police regarding other murders led some to think that they were all the work of the same person, one who signed his letters, "Zodiac."

Beginning in late 1968 another series of murders of young people began in northern California, first near the towns of Vallejo and Benicia and later at a variety of other locations in that area. On January 30, 1974, a San Francisco newspaper received the first confirmed letter from the killer in nearly three years, which included this notation at its end: "Me-37; SFPD-0."

Though several different theories as to who the Zodiac killer was have been advanced through the years, no one has ever been apprehended and charged with the crimes. One candidate is a Vallejo resident referred to in a book about the case as "Robert Hall Starr," but as this is being written, the case remains open, and just who the killer is for sure remains unknown.

OCTOBER 31

1994

Death Valley Designated a National Park

ON THIS DAY IN CALIFORNIA HISTORY Death Valley was designated a national park. It is a forbidding place, eighty-five miles south and a few mountain ranges east of Kings Canyon and Sequoia National Parks, as empty of vegetation as those places are full, as flat as those places are mountainous, as hot as those places can be cold.

Every year since records have been kept, summer temperatures in Death Valley have reached at least 120° F, but on July 10, 1913, the day the "official" temperature in the Valley got up to 134° F, the Valley became "the hottest place on earth." In fact, it was the hottest temperature ever officially recorded in the Western Hemisphere. No wonder that the Indians called it *Tomesha*, "ground afire."

Mineral wealth, real *and* imagined, has also helped bring fame to the Valley. Gold was the first important mineral mined here, but good-sized silver deposits have been found, too. The *big* money-maker, however, has been *borax*.

Borax was first discovered in 1856 and first commercially exploited here in 1864, and it would turn out to be the *most* precious mineral ever mined in the Valley. Most people have heard of borax in connection with cleansers and detergents, and even if they haven't, they may have heard of the "twenty-mule teams" that once dragged wagons full of it out of the Valley.

Though it's hard to imagine looking at it today, sixty-five thousand years ago Death Valley was covered with water to a depth of 600 feet. But in heat like this, water evaporates quickly, so unless there's plenty more falling behind it, it's not long before it's all gone. Two thousand years ago water still covered the Valley to a depth of thirty feet, but then there was an earthquake and the remaining water disappeared into the ground. It's been gone ever since, though, amazingly, many different kinds of plants and animals somehow manage to survive here.

This Day

in

November

NOVEMBER 1

1776

Mission San Juan Capistrano Founded

ON THIS DAY IN CALIFORNIA HISTORY Mission San Juan Capistrano was founded on the southern coast of present-day Orange County. It was the seventh of California's 21 missions and had originally been established by Fermin Lasuen on October 30, 1775. Hostile Indians drove the missionaries from the site, however, and Junipero Serra came the following fall to *re*establish it.

Construction began on the Great Stone Church of Mission San Juan Capistrano in 1796 and was completed in 1806; it was later destroyed, however, by an earthquake that struck the area on the morning of December 8, 1812.

Forty people, all Native Americans, were killed. They were attending mass when the church walls suddenly fell in and the roof collapsed. The quake was a strong one (estimated magnitude of 7.5), but the fact that the church was not a particularly sound structure in the first place didn't help things, either.

Nonetheless, Mission San Juan Capistrano prospered. During its first 20 years several buildings were erected on the mission grounds, including a little church that is still in use today. This church, the "Serra Chapel," is considered to be the oldest church in California and the only one still standing where Fr. Serra himself is known to have celebrated mass.

Each year, on or about the 19th of March (St. Joseph's Day), flocks of swallows return to the mission to build their mud nests in the ruins of the old church. When it collapsed in 1812, the arches that once gave it its support remained, and it is in these arches that the birds build their nests. They spend the summer months here and then on or about October 23, the "Day of San Juan," they fly 6,000 miles south to Argentina to spend the winter. As the south coast of Orange County continues to develop, however, the size of the flocks descending on the mission each year continues to thin.

335

NOVEMBER 2

1947

Howard Hughes Flies the "Spruce Goose"

ON THIS DAY IN CALIFORNIA HISTORY moviemaker, aerospace genius and internationally famous multimillionaire Howard Hughes got the massive seaplane that he designed for the U. S. military airborne for approximately one mile in Long Beach Harbor.

He had been born into a wealthy family in Houston, and in the 1920s decided to go out West to make his mark in the movies. He did, but ultimately went on to make even bigger marks in the worlds of aerospace and electronics. Hughes correctly foresaw the huge role that advanced technology would play in the post-World-War-II military and created a company to supply that technology.

In 1947 Hughes was accused by a United States Senate investigating committee of not fulfilling his wartime airplane-building contracts and getting paid huge sums of money for planes that had never been built. One such accusation involved Hughes's commitment to build a "seaplane" for the military.

In order to prove that he had built such a plane, Hughes went out to Long Beach Harbor and fired up the engines of a gigantic wooden aircraft that was officially known as the "H4" or "Hercules" seaplane, but popularly known as the "Spruce Goose" (because it was made mostly of wood), and took off.

The plane had been built at Hughes's Westchester assembly plant and was (and still is) the largest aircraft ever built. It had a wingspan of 320 feet, was powered by eight huge engines, and weighed 300,000 pounds. Many people thought the plane was just too big to be flown, but Hughes proved them wrong.

In any case, the Spruce Goose flew—if only for about a mile and only for about a minute—and though it was never flown again, Hughes continued to conduct research on it until 1952 and maintain it in a Southern California hangar, at an annual cost of $1,000,000, for the rest of his life.

NOVEMBER 3

1877

"Black Bart" Pulls His Last Holdup

ON THIS DAY IN CALIFORNIA HISTORY highwayman "Black Bart" pulled his last holdup. He had been robbing area stagecoaches for some time, but on this particular day a passenger unloaded a shotgun in his direction and at least one of the shells hit him. In the confusion that followed, he left behind some of his belongings, and it was those belongings that led lawmen straight to him.

Black Bart's first robbery occurred along a stretch of road that ran along the Russian River between Point Arenas and Duncan's Mills. He was wearing a long white coat and a flour sack with holes in it to see through. He stepped out in front of a stagecoach, leveled his shotgun at the driver, and ordered him to stop. Last, but not least, he ordered the driver to "Throw down the box."

On this first job, Bart escaped with $300 in coins and a $305 check drawn on a San Francisco bank. What was interesting, though, was what he left behind: four lines of verse, which read: "I've labored long and hard for bread—/ For honor and for riches—/ But on my corns too long you've tred—/ You fine-haired sons of bitches." The lines were signed "Black Bart, the Po8."

Bart's next job was in the high Sierras and this time he did a little better: $379 in currency, a diamond ring worth perhaps $200, and a silver watch. He also took a bag of U. S. mail and again left some verse for investigators.

And so Bart proceeded through six years of robbing stagecoaches until this morning in 1877. The Calaveras County sheriff was able to trace the miscellaneous provisions found at the scene of the crime back to the woman who had sold them to Bart, but the key piece of evidence tying him to the crime was the laundry mark on a handkerchief he'd left behind. That mark led investigators to his laundry and, ultimately, to him. He would serve four years at San Quentin and then disappear into history.

NOVEMBER 4

1892

Oil Discovered in L. A.

ON THIS DAY IN CALIFORNIA HISTORY oil was discovered in L. A. Well, to be exact, local Indians had found it long before, but this time its "discoverers" were a couple of white men who understood the commercial possibilities of what they were looking at.

And so it was that on this day in 1892 Edward L. Doheny, an unsuccessful 36-year-old gold and silver prospector from Wisconsin, and Charles A. Canfield, also a prospector and a friend of Doheny's, tapped into a sizable pool about a mile northwest of downtown Los Angeles, in the middle of a residential neighborhood. Their discovery would unleash a variety of extraordinary effects, not the least of which was California's third big population rush.

In no time at all, an "oil boom" was on and wildcatters swarmed over the city; homeowners trampled their gardens, ripped out trees, and even tore down their homes to make room for drilling equipment. By 1897, 2,500 wells were pumping away in a half-mile-wide area stretching south and west from Elysian Park, and between 1897 and 1899, another 500 were brought in. It turned out that there was a lot of oil underneath L. A.

The discovery of oil in L. A. had a lot to do with turning the city, and the rest of Southern California, into a big place. It provided low-price fuel for new industries, thousands of new jobs, and the capital to build new homes and streets. It provided the money to build ports at San Pedro and Long Beach, and to channel water from the Owens River to the residents of Los Angeles.

Working in conjunction with a large supply of available land, year-round sunshine, and the newly-established movie industry, oil helped Los Angeles grow quickly into a *very big* place. A mere 50,395 in 1890, by 1900 the city's population had grown to 102,479, and by 1910, to 319,198. Today, nearly 10,000,000 people live in the greater Los Angeles area, city and county combined.

338

NOVEMBER 5

1913

Los Angeles Aqueduct Opens

ON THIS DAY IN CALIFORNIA HISTORY waters flowing south from the Owens River in the southern Sierras to their intended destination in the San Fernando Valley "arrived." It was a momentous day in the city's history and the making of the San Fernando Valley as a viable place for thousands to make their home.

Public funds for building the aqueduct that brought this water to the city had been approved by the voters of Los Angeles back in September of 1905, and less than two years later, a design for the aqueduct had been worked out. It would be the longest aqueduct in the Western Hemisphere—235 miles—and to build it, 500 miles of roadway and 2,300 buildings would have to be built (many of them to house workers), 240 miles of telephone line laid, and 250 workers kept busy just mixing cement.

Building the aqueduct also required that 50 miles of hard rock be tunneled through. Work crews earned incentive pay for beating their "ten-day targets," and in March of 1910, one crew tunneled through 604 feet of this rock, a record at the time.

On this morning in 1913 a crowd of some 30,000 to 40,000 were on hand to celebrate the official opening of the Aqueduct, many of them holding cups to sample the mountain water that would be released through the Aqueduct's spillway gates this day. City Engineer William Mulholland was on hand too, of course, saying, with his characteristic brevity, "There it is. Take it."

Though the Los Angeles Aqueduct added some 258,000 gallons a day to the city's water supply, no sooner was it completed than the city started looking for *other* supplies of water. By 1941 the Colorado River Aqueduct would be in place, adding enough capacity to provide water for 10,000,000 people, and by the mid-1970s, water from Northern California's Feather River would be flowing through water taps all over Southern California, too.

NOVEMBER 6

1961
Bel Air-Brentwood Fire

ON THIS DAY IN CALIFORNIA HISTORY the worst brush fire in the history of Southern California tore through the Bel Air and Brentwood neighborhoods on L. A.'s west side.

The fire began high up on a slope in the Santa Monica Mountains that divide the San Fernando Valley from Los Angeles proper. It raced to the top of those mountains, leaped over Mulholland Drive, and then charged down into Stone Canyon on the south slope.

The flames were fed by fifty-mile-per-hour Santa Ana winds, which drove the flames west and south from the mountains, and their heat created thermal air currents which lifted countless pieces of flaming debris into the air, causing the already fast-moving fire to move all that much faster. The fact that the area had long been enduring drought conditions before the fire broke out didn't help things, either.

Despite the best efforts of the firemen who were battling the flames, they could not be brought under control. They incinerated 484 homes in Brentwood and Bel Air (as well as 21 other buildings) and scorched 6,090 acres of valuable watershed land in the Santa Monica Mountains. Amazingly, no one was injured or killed.

This area was made to order for a catastrophe of this type. No other area in the world has such a high concentration of expensive homes surrounded by so much flammable brush or situated in places so hard to get to. And many had roofs made of highly flammable and easily detachable wood shakes and shingles, making each one a perfect wick for the raging fire.

Once set afire and detached from roofs by the fierce winds that blew this day, these burning shingles and shakes set off innumerable new fires by landing on the roofs of still other homes and in the dense brush around them. It was a self-perpetuating nightmare of truly epic proportions.

NOVEMBER 7

1939
"Ham and Eggs" Not on the Menu

ON THIS DAY IN CALIFORNIA HISTORY a special referendum election was held in California to vote on what was known at the time as the "Ham and Eggs" pension proposal. Like other Americans, Californians had struggled through the Great Depression, and by the end of the 1930s, were more than ready for some kind of relief.

As the Depression wore on into the mid 1930s, several groups emerged to help Americans weather the hard times and provide them with adequate income to survive. Social Security and unemployment insurance did not appear until 1936, and to fill that void, private groups organized to propose benefit plans of their own, one of which was "Ham and Eggs."

The movement had its roots in an idea that had been advanced by Yale economist Irving Fisher in 1931: to get the American economy moving again, said Fisher, people needed to start spending money. Since most of them had none, the government should issue "warrants" each week and require that people spend them on their immediate needs, like food—like "ham and eggs."

A radio commentator named Robert Noble got wind of the idea and began to discuss it on station KMTR in Los Angeles. Every Monday, said Noble, the state of California should issue warrants valued at $25 to every unemployed resident over the age of fifty and require that they spend them during the course of the week.

It appeared that the "Ham and Eggs" pension proposal had found a broad base of support among California's voters and a petition signed by 789,000 people, a *quarter* of California's registered voters at the time, was presented to the state's Secretary of State that put it on the 1938 election ballot. Nonetheless, it failed to garner enough support in the election to pass, and the following year, on this day, it was again put on the ballot, again voted on, and again went down to defeat.

NOVEMBER 8

1966
Ronald Reagan Elected Governor of California

ON THIS DAY IN CALIFORNIA HISTORY Ronald Reagan was elected governor of California—for the *first* time. He had been performing on one stage or another all of his adult life and he had now made it onto one of the greatest stages in American politics—the governorship of California.

Reagan had been a Californian almost forty years at this point. He had been born in Illinois and became a sports announcer after college. In 1937 he went to California to cover a Chicago Cubs spring training game, and while there, took a screen test, was signed by Warner Brothers, and began to make movies.

For the most part, Reagan played a leading man in B movies, things like George Gipp ("The Gipper") in *Knute Rockne, All American* (1940), and the young man whose legs were amputated in the movie *Kings Row* (1942). After his movie career played itself out in the late 1950s, Reagan moved to television, where he also enjoyed success for several years.

By the time he ran for governor of California in 1966, Reagan had made quite a name for himself as a staunch conservative. He had begun his political career by speaking out against Communism and pro-Communist actors during his first tenure as president of the Screen Actors Guild between 1947 and 1952, and it was a theme he would turn to again and again during his political career.

In the early 1950s Reagan supported Republican candidates Dwight Eisenhower and Richard Nixon, while still affiliated with the Democratic Party, and in 1964, having by that time become a Republican himself, supported Republican Barry Goldwater in that year's presidential election. During the Goldwater campaign Reagan repeatedly delivered a speech entitled "A Time for Choosing," still known as "The Speech," which led to the proposal that he run for governor of California.

NOVEMBER 9

1884

Meeting Held to Establish the Kaweah Colony

ON THIS DAY IN CALIFORNIA HISTORY a meeting was held to discuss establishing a community that would be known as the "Kaweah Colony." Its intended site was in eastern Tulare County, on the banks of the Kaweah River, and it would be one of a number of secular utopian living experiments attempted in the state during the late 19th and early 20th centuries.

The community's founder, Burnette G. Haskell, had been born in Sierra County in 1857 and had studied at the University of California. He was admitted to the California bar in 1879, but became a journalist rather than a lawyer. He edited a radical labor journal called *Truth*, whose motto was "*Truth* is five cents a copy and dynamite is forty cents a pound."

But Haskell and his followers ran into strong outside opposition to their community from the beginning, largely because of its alleged plans to log the nearby redwood forests as a means of economic support. They would spend seven long years trying to puzzle out the practical details of creating their colony, four of them just trying to build a road to the forests they'd planned to log. It would prove to be too much for them and they disbanded in 1892.

"Llano del Rio" was a similar secular utopian experiment based in the high desert northeast of Los Angeles that was founded in 1914 by a man named Job Harriman. Harriman had run, without success, for governor of the state (1898), Vice President of the United States (on the Debs ticket, 1902), and mayor of Los Angeles (on the Socialist Labor Party ticket in 1911).

Harriman's idea was to create a "working" socialist community. Starting out with just five families, the community grew to *nearly 900* members by 1916. Unlike Kaweah, it did manage to produce most of its own food, but never managed to achieve full self-sufficiency or overcome petty internal infighting.

NOVEMBER 10

1901

Pacific Electric Railway Incorporated

ON THIS DAY IN CALIFORNIA HISTORY Henry E. Huntington's Pacific Electric Railway was incorporated in Los Angeles.

Henry E. Huntington was a Southern California transportation tycoon who learned the business from his much-feared and ruthless uncle, Collis, a member of the group of men responsible for building the Southern Pacific Railroad (the "Big Four"). The Huntingtons certainly believed in keeping it all in the family. Henry's first marriage was to the sister of his uncle's adopted daughter, his second to his uncle's widow, Arabella Duval Huntington.

With the fortune that he inherited from his uncle, Henry Huntington did two things. The first thing he did was invest part of it in an L. A. transportation enterprise known as the Pacific Electric Railway. Between 1901 and 1908 he extended its tracks throughout the area that would come to be known as "Greater Los Angeles"—to Long Beach and Santa Monica, to Riverside and San Bernardino, to Santa Ana and Newport Beach.

Every time Huntington's railway added a new city to its route, that city became a feasible new suburb for Angelenos to live in and a hotbed of new construction activity. More so than anything else, it was Huntington's interurban railway that caused L. A. sprawl into the loosely-woven set of suburbs it remains to this day.

The second thing Henry did, beginning in 1903, was to begin collecting rare books and manuscripts, and fine art.

The books he collected were primarily concentrated in 18th- and 19th-century English literature. The art he collected consisted primarily of English, French and American painters from the 18th, 19th and 20th centuries. The best-known paintings in the collection are Gainsborough's *The Blue Boy* and Thomas Lawrence's *Pinkie*, both the work of 18th-century English painters, but Huntington's collections were filled with many other treasures as well.

344

NOVEMBER 11

1885

General George S. Patton, Jr., Born in San Gabriel

ON THIS DAY IN CALIFORNIA HISTORY legendary World War II General George S. Patton, Jr., was born in San Gabriel. The Pattons had money from his mother's side of the family and a long tradition of military service on his father's side. If ever there was an American "born to lead," Patton was the man.

Patton's mother was the granddaughter of Benjamin Davis Wilson, a respected and affluent citizen of early Los Angeles who married into the wealthy Yorba family.

Patton's paternal grandfather was a Confederate brigadier general and his father the first district attorney for the city of Pasadena and first mayor of San Marino. Patton's father introduced him to Homer, Shakespeare and the Bible, and to John Singleton Mosby, a Confederate cavalry officer who served under Jeb Stuart.

Patton aspired to military glory from an early age. He graduated from West Point, worked as an aide to General John J. Pershing in the pursuit of the Mexican bandit, Pancho Villa, and served with distinction during World War I, ultimately being put in charge of the U. S. Army's "Tank Corps." By the end of the war Patton had been promoted to the rank of colonel.

After World War I Patton served under both Eisenhower and MacArthur, and fought hard to make the U. S. Army a mechanized unit. It took him some time to be heard on this subject, but eventually he was, and during World War II he commanded the U. S.'s Second Armored Division.

Patton fought with distinction during World War II and was instrumental in turning the Battle of the Bulge into a victory for the Allied forces. He routinely drew the wrong kind of attention from his senior command, however, who thought him too much of a "cowboy" and loudmouth (which he was) and, in the end, it was those traits that would be his undoing.

NOVEMBER 12

1936
San Francisco-Oakland Bay Bridge Opens

ON THIS DAY IN CALIFORNIA HISTORY the San Francisco-Oakland Bay Bridge officially opened for traffic. The two segments that went into its making came together on Yerba Buena Island in the Bay—one extending to the city of San Francisco, the other to the shores of the East Bay or "Oakland." The segment running to San Francisco was composed of two suspension bridges, the one running to the East Bay of truss bridges and a cantilever bridge.

The idea of bridging San Francisco Bay was a monumentally ambitious task, for it required a bridge *four-and-a-half miles long* (not counting approaches) and piers that sometimes stretched down more than two hundred feet below the Bay's surface. Extraordinary engineering challenges had to be met, and met with no loss of artistic grace in the finished product.

The "Bay Bridge," as it came to be known, made it possible to live in Oakland or Berkeley and drive to work in San Francisco, just as the Golden Gate Bridge made it possible for people to live in Marin and drive across the bridge to work in the city. It created a dramatic change in the way life was lived here, and population and business booms were quick to follow.

The idea of spanning San Francisco Bay by bridge had been discussed since the days of the Gold Rush. Newspaper articles appeared during the early 1870s that discussed the idea and by 1872 a committee charged with drawing plans to construct a "railroad bridge" across the bay was already at work.

Also in 1872, "Emperor Norton I," the delightful San Francisco eccentric, decreed that a bridge be built across the Bay, and though the idea had wide popular appeal, the Bay was thought to be too wide and deep for such a thing to be practical. In the 1920s, however, support for building a trans-bay bridge gained momentum, and by the early 1930s, work had begun.

NOVEMBER 13

1849
Peter Burnett Elected Governor

ON THIS DAY IN CALIFORNIA HISTORY Peter Burnett was elected the first governor of American California. He had been born in Tennessee and had held a variety of different jobs to this point. He had been a storekeeper, a farmer, a lawyer and a judge.

He had played an important part in getting the territorial government in Oregon set up, too, where he proposed that all "free Negroes" be required to leave. Any who failed to do so, said Burnett, should be arrested and whipped at six-month intervals until they complied. Perhaps that might have been a clue to his supporters in California that he might not be an altogether ideal choice for governor in a state that was entering the Union "free."

In 1848 Burnett left Oregon for the California gold fields, but was not there long before he went to work for "Captain" John Sutter's son instead, helping him manage his business affairs. Not long after that, then-military-governor of California Bennet Riley made him a superior court judge, from which position he advocated forming a state government in California and holding a Constitutional Convention.

Under the new state constitution drafted at that Convention, Burnett was elected governor and immediately departed for San Jose, the state capital at that point, to take office. But be quickly tired of the job, and in January 1851 resigned so that he could return to San Francisco to practice law. In 1857 he was appointed to the Supreme Court of California, but resigned in 1858.

From 1863 to 1880 Burnett served as president of the Pacific Bank of San Francisco and would retire from there having made himself a fortune. He published three books—two about religious belief and one a book of memoirs—and lived to the ripe old age of 87, long enough to see San Francisco grow into one of the leading cities in the nation.

NOVEMBER 14

1792

George Vancouver Sails into San Francisco Bay

ON THIS DAY IN CALIFORNIA HISTORY Captain George Vancouver became the first Englishman to sail into San Francisco Bay. In 1789 the attention of the outside world to the Pacific Coast of modern North America was focused, if it was thinking about this area at all, on the fur-trapping opportunities available in the Nootka Sound area of Vancouver Island. That year two British and two Spanish ships came to the area to claim it for their respective countries and build a fort and trading post.

But just which country might prevail in taking possession of the area was a matter of doubt. One of the Spanish captains arrested one of the British captains and took his ships as well. When word of this got back to England, the English threatened to go to war with Spain over the matter, and the upshot of it all was that Britain and Spain signed a treaty in which Spain was forced to relinquish its up-till-then exclusive claim to the lands fronting the Pacific north of present-day California.

In any case, in 1792 Captain George Vancouver was sent to Nootka Sound to work out the details of applying the treaty to British interests here and to repossess any property that had been seized from English traders. His was also directed to map the North American coastline all the way from Nootka Sound to San Diego, which he did as he and his crew made their way down the coast.

Vancouver was amazed at how tenuous Spain's hold on California was. Given the fact that Spain had dominated the western hemisphere for three centuries, he no doubt thought that he would find more sophisticated settlements here than he did. The Presidio of San Francisco consisted of nothing more than a collection of mud huts "protected" by two unusable cannons, however, and once the word got out, it wasn't long before other world powers would arrive to stake their claim, too.

348

NOVEMBER 15

1932

f/64 Group Has a Showing at the de Young Museum

ON THIS DAY IN CALIFORNIA HISTORY an exhibit of the work of a group of photographers calling themselves "Group f/64" (after the lens setting on a traditional camera that renders images with the greatest depth and detail) began at the M. H. de Young Museum in Golden Gate Park.

The "Group" included then up-and-coming California photographers Ansel Adams, John Paul Edwards, Preston Holder, Sonya Noskowiak and Henry Swift, as well as established photographer, Imogen Cunningham, and the Group's leader and best-known member at the time, Edward Weston. Their goal was to get photography recognized as an art form unto itself.

Back in the early 1930s this was an altogether new way to look at photography. What the Group was saying was that the art of photography was not in "making pictures," but rather in testing the limits of the medium itself, the different ways in which a camera could be used to "render images." The important thing to focus on, they said, was what made a photographer *different from* a painter; after all, it was in those things that made one art form different from another that its own possibilities were to be found.

In any case, that was the Group's conceptual point of departure and the reason it thought the whole matter worthy of serious discussion in the first place. Lloyd Rollins, then director of San Francisco's de Young Museum offered to stage an exhibition of their work, which began on this day in 1932 and ran for six weeks. Eighty photographs were shown.

Group f/64 only lasted for about a year as a formal organization, but the idea of photography that brought them together would shape the art of photography profoundly in the years to come. Photography was now officially acknowledged to be an art all its own, and its serious practitioners "artists" in every sense of the word.

NOVEMBER 16

1884

Adolph Spreckels Opens Fire on Michael de Young

ON THIS DAY IN CALIFORNIA HISTORY Adolph Spreckels, son of sugar baron Claus Spreckels, opened fire on Michael de Young, publisher of the *San Francisco Chronicle*, in the *Chronicle*'s offices downtown. The paper had been running a series of articles on the conditions then prevailing at the Spreckels sugar plantations in Hawaii and the articles made the family look bad.

The Spreckels family had become rich and powerful through their involvement in the sugar business and Claus Spreckels was no one to mess with. He had gotten his start in the business by winning a chunk of the island of Maui in a poker game and it was on this land that he built his first sugar cane refining plant. He would later build one on the shores of San Francisco Bay, too.

Michael de Young and his brother Charles had founded what was then called the *Daily Morning Chronicle* in 1865. The paper routinely lampooned San Francisco's high and mighty and it was this habit of taking pot shots at those who could shoot back that provoked the Spreckels attempt on Michael's life.

This kind of journalism sold newspapers, though, and that's of course why the de Youngs practiced it. When local Baptist minister Isaac Kalloch ran for mayor of the city in 1879, the paper tried to derail his campaign by revealing details of his past love life that he no doubt would rather had remained secret. Kalloch railed at the de Youngs from his pulpit and *Charles* de Young tried to shoot him down in front of his own church.

Kalloch was seriously wounded, but not only recovered, he was elected mayor. When the *Chronicle* started in on him again after the election, Kalloch's son resolved the matter once and for all by killing Charles de Young with a gunshot to the neck. The citizens of the city clearly thought the son did the right thing and acquitted him of his crime on the grounds of "reasonable cause."

NOVEMBER 17

1904

Isamu Noguchi Born in Los Angeles

ON THIS DAY IN CALIFORNIA HISTORY 20th-century sculptor, designer, craftsman and landscape architect Isamu Noguchi was born in Los Angeles. He was the child of a Japanese poet, Noguchi Yonejiro, and an American writer, Leonie Gilmour. He had lived in the city less than two years when his parents decided to relocate to Japan, which is where he spent his childhood.

In 1918 Noguchi was sent back to the United States to be educated and graduated from La Porte High School in Indiana. After graduation he enrolled at Columbia University to study medicine, but it wasn't long before he thought better of that decision and chose to pursue a full-time career as a sculptor instead. He became acquainted with contemporary abstract sculpture and surrealism and ultimately went to Paris, where he worked with the great modernist sculptor, Constantin Brancusi.

When he returned to New York, he found no audience for his abstract work, but did find an audience for the portraits he sculpted, so it was with those that he began.

Noguchi did not limit himself to sculpture and landscape architecture, either. He also designed stage sets for dance maven Martha Graham and lamps and furniture, including some very imaginative work he did in collaboration with designer Charles Eames, for the Henry Miller furniture company in 1948.

Noguchi's work can be seen not only at the Isamu Noguchi Garden Museum in New York City, but also in other cities around the world. It includes a bridge he designed for Hiroshima's "Peace Park," a sunken garden for the Beinecke Rare Book and Manuscript Library at Yale University, gardens for IBM's headquarters in Armonk, New York, a children's playground in Tokyo, and a 400-acre park in Sapporo, Japan, that was his final project as a landscape architect.

NOVEMBER 18

2001

COPIA Opens in Napa

ON THIS DAY IN CALIFORNIA HISTORY COPIA, the American Center for Wine, Food & the Arts, opened its doors on the banks of the Napa River. It was named for *Copia*, the Roman goddess of wealth and plenty (she carried a cornucopia or "horn of plenty") and nothing quite like it had ever existed before.

Back in the late 1980s winemaker Robert Mondavi started thinking about building a museum that would display "wine-related art and artifacts from the Napa Valley and other wine-growing regions around the world," and also include, he thought, some "educational exhibits" to show how the history of wine went back to the Egyptians, Greeks and Romans.

Well, that was his initial formulation of the idea, but in time that formulation began to take new directions. He began to think that people might be better served by "interactive displays" that showed them how to make wine, and what the entire process, season by season, really looked like.

This kind of thinking naturally led to the idea of educating people about "tasting wine," which in turn led to thinking about which foods went best with which wines. Mondavi had envisioned this place as a haven of sorts for wine lovers, food lovers and lovers of the arts, and so all of these things found their way into his final formulation of the Center. It would at once be a monument to the good life and a stunning example of it.

"The idea," as Mondavi says in his autobiography, *Harvests of Joy* (1998), "was <to build> a world-class center for the arts in the town of Napa. The center would turn the Napa Valley into an international crossroads not just for wine and food, but for painting, sculpture, music, dance, photography, graphic design, and arts education for children." It would be a work of art, too, just as Mondavi's best wines were.

NOVEMBER 19

1954

Sammy Davis, Jr., Loses Left Eye in Auto Accident

ON THIS DAY IN CALIFORNIA HISTORY legendary song-and-dance man Sammy Davis, Jr., lost his left eye in an auto accident in San Bernardino. He was only 5'4" tall and about 130 pounds soaking wet, but that tiny frame housed an enormous personality and talent. He could, and did, fill a room.

Davis was born in Harlem, New York, on December 8, 1925, to a couple of dancers, his father black, his mother Puerto Rican. In 1933, just seven, he starred in a short musical comedy called *Rufus Jones for President* about a black child who dreams he becomes President of the United States. It was his first big opportunity to show what he could do and show it he did.

In 1941 Davis met singer-actor Frank Sinatra while in Detroit, a friendship that would last the rest of his life. He would later meet Dean Martin, Joey Bishop and Peter Lawford, too, and with them form a "brotherhood" of hardcore party boys who dubbed themselves the "Rat Pack." Together they made Las Vegas the night-club-performance capital of the world.

As a child, Davis toured widely as a vaudeville entertainer, and often appeared in states with strict child-labor laws, states that might have prevented him from working, had they known he *was* a child. Anticipating the problem, his managers billed him as "Silent Sammy, the Dancing Midget," giving the impression that he was really just a very small adult.

On this day in 1954 Davis was involved in a car crash in San Bernardino while en route to record the theme song for a Tony Curtis film called *Six Bridges to Cross* (1955). For a while after the accident, he chose to wear an eye patch, but actor Humphrey Bogart convinced him to remove it, saying that he didn't want to be known as "that actor with the eye patch." Davis did and never lost a beat. His fame would do nothing but grow in the years ahead.

NOVEMBER 20

1855
Josiah Royce Born in Grass Valley

ON THIS DAY IN CALIFORNIA HISTORY Josiah Royce was born in Grass Valley, a small mining town in the western foothills of the Sierra Nevada mountain range. His parents were English immigrants who had married in New York and then settled in Iowa. In April of 1849 they decided to go further west still, a decision which ultimately brought them to Grass Valley.

Royce was home-schooled throughout the first ten years of his life and what other schoolchildren there were in Grass Valley met for classes at his home. Mrs. Royce was a pious woman and liberally laced her lessons with religious instruction, too. Josiah did not find the experience congenial, however, and often sneaked off to spend Sunday mornings with area old-timers instead.

In any case, when he grew up, Royce studied at the University of California at Berkeley and later earned a Ph.D. from Johns Hopkins University. He returned to Berkeley to teach English for a while, but after that joined the faculty of the philosophy department at Harvard, where he had initially gone to substitute teach for the eminent William James, then on sabbatical.

In 1883, one year after he first arrived in Cambridge, the editors at local publisher Houghton Mifflin were casting about for an author to write the "California volume" in their *American Commonwealth* series and decided that Royce, then a junior professor at the local college *and*, they knew, a native of the Golden State, would be just the guy to do it.

The result was *California, From the Conquest in 1846 to the Second Vigilance Committee in San Francisco: A Study of American Character* (the state's first ten years as an *American* place), published in 1886, in which Royce strives to illuminate just what the conquest of Mexican California says about the American character. It is well worth reading to this day.

NOVEMBER 21

1885

Transcontinental Railroad Comes to San Diego

ON THIS DAY IN CALIFORNIA HISTORY the first passenger train from the eastern United States arrived in San Diego. It was an Atchison, Topeka & Santa Fe train and it was an important event in what would come to be known as the "Boom of the Eighties" in Southern California.

That same year Santa Fe locomotives first rolled into Los Angeles, too, and by early 1887, rates for rail travel from the Mississippi Valley to Southern California had plummeted from the $125 they had been to as little as one dollar.

Newcomers praised California's climate, its picturesque landscape, its "easy" way of life, and in countless letters "back home" commented on the area's suitability for new business enterprise. The railroads, the biggest beneficiaries of all this activity, were quick to join this chorus of praise and distributed pamphlets promoting California at railway stations all over the United States.

For the most part, those who came out West in the 1870s, '80s and '90s were well-to-do. Some were looking for a pleasant new place to live after having spent the better part of their lives living in the harsher climate of the American East and it was this group that moved to Santa Barbara, Pasadena, and Redlands.

Some were looking for new places to spend the winter and it was for them that the many fine tourist hotels that were built in Southern California during these years were erected, places like the Arlington in Santa Barbara (1876), the Raymond in Pasadena (1886), and the Hotel del Coronado in San Diego (1888).

These were the years during which names like Chaffey and Lankershim and Van Nuys rose to prominence, marking the end of the time when the first families of Southern California all had Hispanic roots *or* Hispanic surnames, the years when *Anglo* America truly began to make its presence felt.

NOVEMBER 22

1935
Pan Am "Clipper" Makes its First Transpacific Flight

ON THIS DAY IN CALIFORNIA HISTORY the first Pan American Airlines commercial flight took off from an airfield in Alameda County to begin its maiden voyage across the Pacific. It was so heavy with passengers and cargo the captain had to fly his plane *under* the Bay Bridge to get it out over the ocean and on its way.

California has long been home to flying firsts. The first transcontinental flight completed in twenty-four hours flying time took off from here (in 1921), as did the first all-passenger airline (1925), and it was here that the first plane to successfully cross the Atlantic was designed and built (Charles Lindbergh's *Spirit of St. Louis*, by San Diego's Ryan Aviation in 1927).

The first "world flight" by a commercial airliner (1941-1942) originated here, as did the first transcontinental round-trip flight completed in one day (1946), the first transcontinental round-trip solo flight between sunrise and sunset (1955), and the first round-the-world nonstop *jet* flight (1957).

This was where the first "jetways," those metal hallways down which modern-day air travelers typically walk to board their flights, were invented (1959), where the first municipal airport legislation was framed (in 1910), where the first municipal air control board was established (at San Diego, in 1927), and where the first airport hotel was built (the Oakland Airport Inn, 1929). Even the first flight attendant in the nation was hired here (Ellen Church, in 1930).

And so it was the natural place for something like the nation's first scheduled nonstop air service between the continental United States and the Far East to begin, too. Douglas, Lockheed, Northrop and North American were all California companies and ones that would be responsible for building most of the aircraft used in the nation for passenger travel, aerial warfare, and the exploration of outer space. It was a pattern that would continue.

NOVEMBER 23

1876

Thomas More Storke Born in Santa Barbara

ON THIS DAY IN CALIFORNIA HISTORY Thomas More Storke, a man who would come to be known as "Mr. Santa Barbara," was born. Santa Barbara had been an American city just 26 years at this point and the nation itself was just turning 100.

Storke's father, Albert, had come to Santa Barbara after the Civil War to teach at Santa Barbara College. He married into the Ortega family here, which made his son, Thomas, a perfect example of the "new" Californian of the time—a blend of the Yankee immigrants then making their way into this area and the well-to-do Spanish residents who had lived here for a hundred years.

In Storke's case, the "blend" was a distinguished one. His Hispanic roots went all the way back to Lieutenant José Francisco de Ortega, the man who established the presidio at Santa Barbara in 1782; you couldn't get much more "Santa Barbara" than that. He attended the city's public schools, and following that, Stanford University, from which he graduated in 1898.

After college he returned to Santa Barbara, where he worked as a rancher and citrus fruit grower, bought the *Santa Barbara Independent* newspaper and later, the *Santa Barbara Daily News*, which he made into such a success that it drove the *Independent* out of business. He would remain editor and publisher of what would eventually become the *Santa Barbara News-Press* for a long time to come, eventually winning a Pulitzer Prize for his work.

Storke helped put Wilson in the White House in 1912 and in return was made Santa Barbara's Postmaster in 1914. In November of 1938 he was appointed to the U. S. Senate seat then held by William Gibbs McAdoo, who had abruptly resigned. He served just fifty-six days, until January 3, 1939, and afterwards returned to Santa Barbara, where he would spend his remaining 32 years, dying on October 12, 1971.

357

NOVEMBER 24

1947
"Hollywood Ten" Hung Out to Dry

ON THIS DAY IN CALIFORNIA HISTORY a group of men who ran the American movie business convened a meeting at the Waldorf-Astoria Hotel in New York City at the end of which they issued a statement condemning the actions of a group of screenwriters and directors known as the "Hollywood Ten."

The "Ten" were accused of being Communist sympathizers and included Alvah Bessie, a journalist, novelist and screenwriter who wrote a book about the experience called *Inquisition in Eden* (1965); an Ivy-League-educated director and screenwriter named Howard Biberman; Lester Cole, who would later collaborate on screenplays under an assumed name, as well as teach screenwriting at Berkeley; and Edward Dmytryk, who would ultimately become a "friendly" witness who "named names."

Ring Lardner, Jr., was one of the "Ten." Son of famed humorist, Ring Lardner (author of *Gullible's Travels*), he spent a year in prison, as did the others, and was forced to work under pseudonyms or uncredited, though he would eventually make a comeback in 1970 and write the screenplay for *M*A*S*H*.

John Henry Lawson, a cofounder of the Screen Writers Guild, was a member of the Group. As was Albert Maltz, who suffered the same fate as the others; his name would not grace a film credits list again until 1970 when he would get credit for the screenplay of *Two Mules for Sister Sara*. Samuel Ornitz, one of the founders of the Screen Actors Guild, was a member, too.

Adrian Scott was a screenwriter and producer who had been brought to the attention of the Committee by Dmytryk. He was sentenced to a year in prison, and following his release, never worked in films again. The last of the ten was Dalton Trumbo, who under an assumed name wrote *Bridge on the River Kwai* (1957) and under his own, *Spartacus* (1960) and *Exodus* (also 1960).

358

NOVEMBER 25

1914

Joe DiMaggio Born in San Francisco

ON THIS DAY IN CALIFORNIA HISTORY New York Yankees baseball legend Joe DiMaggio was born in the Bay Area town of Martinez. The name his parents gave him wasn't "Joseph" or "Joe"; it was "Giuseppe Paolo." He was the eighth of nine children, and the year after he was born, the family moved to San Francisco.

In San Francisco DiMaggio's father worked as a fisherman and it was his hope that his five sons would all one day become fishermen, too, as DiMaggios had done for generations before him. But the boys found baseball more to their liking and three of them would one day turn pro.

In October of 1932 Joe was playing semipro baseball when his 20-year-old brother, Vince, then playing with the San Francisco Seals, persuaded his manager to let Joe play shortstop in the last three games of the season. Joe wasn't much of a shortstop, as it turned out, but he could definitely *hit* the ball. During the 1933 season alone, he hit in 61 straight games.

On May 3, 1936, DiMaggio made his debut as a New York Yankee. The Yankees hadn't made it to the World Series since 1932, but with the addition of DiMaggio to their batting lineup, they won the Series in 1936, 1937, 1938 and 1939. He would go on to lead the Yankees to nine titles in thirteen years.

On February 7, 1949, DiMaggio became the first player in professional baseball to be signed to a six-figure contract. But he had accumulated a lot of injuries over the course of his career, and just two years later, announced his retirement.

But before he did, he managed to make himself into one of the game's undisputed legends. One-time teammate Jerry Coleman once said that "Joe DiMaggio understood what it meant to be Joe DiMaggio. . . . He had to be perfect every day. He had to be Joe DiMaggio every day."

NOVEMBER 26

1968
New President Takes the Reins at San Francisco State

ON THIS DAY IN CALIFORNIA HISTORY renowned semanticist S. I. Hayakawa was named acting president of San Francisco State College. He had had a distinguished academic career and taken the administrative reins at a particularly turbulent time in the school's history. Not only was it the heart of the sixties, San Francisco State was in the eye of the storm.

When Hayakawa took over, students at the school had recently staged "sit-ins," manned picket lines, and even broken into the school's Administration Building to express their displeasure with the nation's political direction and with the kind of education they were getting. They were upset about racial discrimination, upset about the draft and the war in Vietnam, upset about being subjected to what they saw as an "irrelevant" curriculum.

In the midst of all this turbulence, John Summerskill, then president of San Francisco State, resigned, and Robert Smith, his replacement, soon discovered he couldn't stand the heat, either, and resigned, too. It then fell to Hayakawa to lead the school out of all this chaos and put things back in order.

Hayakawa was strongly opposed to the student strike then disrupting life at San Francisco State and more than willing to take a stand against it.

Just one day after assuming the presidency, he climbed atop a sound truck that had been positioned at the corner of 19th and Holloway Streets (he was 62 at the time) and ripped out the wires running to the public address system that students were using to express their views. He then delivered his own speech to a genuinely dumbfounded audience.

In 1976 Dr. Hayakawa left the academic community when he won a seat in the United States Senate, where he served until 1983. He died in 1992.

NOVEMBER 27

1826

Jedediah Smith Party Reaches Mission San Gabriel

ON THIS DAY IN CALIFORNIA HISTORY Jedediah Smith, mountain man and early explorer of much of what is now the Far Western United States, reached Mission San Gabriel accompanied by seventeen trappers that he had led southwest from the Great Salt Lake and across the Mojave Desert, searching for beaver.

The party was guided by two Mission Indians, runaways, and was the first recorded overland journey of such a party from what was then the nation's far-western border to California.

From Mission San Gabriel the Smith party continued south to San Diego, where Smith secured permission from the Mexican governor to trap wildlife. Afterward, they headed north, and on May 20, 1827, Smith and two members of his party crossed the Sierra mountains, becoming the first white men to do this.

Once on the other side of the mountains, the three men crossed the Great Basin and headed for Utah, and on July 3, 1827, rendezvoused with the rest of their party at Bear Lake. Smith remained here ten days, just long enough to provision a party of eighteen for two years, and then retraced his steps of the year before, trekking southwest from Utah and back across the Mojave Desert.

On this trip, however, Smith's party was ambushed as they crossed the Colorado River, and ten of its eighteen members were killed. The survivors somehow dragged themselves across the Mojave to their base camp on the Stanislaus River.

Late in 1827 Smith led a party of twenty northward from his camp on the Stanislaus, along with 300 horses and mules. They were hoping to find a pass through the Sierras, but were unable to do so, which forced them to go farther and farther north, and finally into present-day Oregon. There, on the morning of July 14, 1828, all but he and two other members of that party were massacred. They had been out scouting at the time.

NOVEMBER 28

1602
Explorer Vizcaino Names Catalina Island

ON THIS DAY IN CALIFORNIA HISTORY explorer Sebastian Vizcaino anchored off an island he named "Santa Catalina." Cabrillo had sailed through these waters sixty years before and named the island "San Salvador," but it was Vizcaino's name that stuck.

Catalina has had an interesting history. It has been the home of an Indian tribe (the Gabrielenos), a colony of Old Mexico and a hideout for smugglers, and Nevada Senator James G. Fair (one of the San Francisco "Silver Kings") once even suggested that it be converted into an Apache reservation.

In 1887 realtor George Shatto laid out the island's first and only city, Avalon, and began the process of transforming Catalina Island into a resort. Big-game sportfishing has long drawn sportsmen to the island; it was here, in fact, that big-game sportfishing got its start (in 1898) and here that the "rules" of sportsmanlike saltwater angling were originally formulated. Tuna, swordfish, marlin and barracuda once teemed in the waters off the Catalina coast and big-game fishermen came from all over the world to fish for them.

The years between 1919 and the beginning of World War II are regarded as Catalina's "golden era." Early Hollywood headliners loved to dock here during these years and a number of Hollywood's early films were shot on the island, too, including *Mutiny on the Bounty*, *Treasure Island* and *McHale's Navy*.

The "Big White Steamer" started making its daily runs between San Pedro and Avalon in 1924, the Casino overlooking Avalon Bay was completed in 1929, and some of the city's most distinctive residences, places like the Wrigley and Zane Grey homes, were built during these years, too. The island's glass-bottom boats were also popular with tourists (as they remain to this day) and gave visitors to the island a memorable look into those waters in which Vizcaino dropped anchor long ago.

362

NOVEMBER 29

1895
Choreographer Busby Berkeley Born in L. A.

ON THIS DAY IN CALIFORNIA HISTORY choreographer Busby Berkeley was born in Los Angeles. By the time he was a teenager, the movie business was emerging here and that is where he would, in time, stake his claim to fame.

In 1918 Berkeley joined the army as a lieutenant, but instead of drawing duty directing artillery fire, he found himself directing parades. When the war ended, he was "ordered" to stage shows for the soldiers and this is how he got his first training as a choreographer.

After returning to the States, Berkeley became a stage actor and assistant director for some small acting troops. Forced to take over the direction for a musical named *Holka Polka*, he found he had talent for this kind of thing and, in time, he became one of the top dance directors on Broadway.

When he came to Hollywood, Berkeley found that the way dance directors worked left a lot to be desired. They staged the dances, but the director controlled camera placement and the editor decided which takes made their way into the film.

Berkeley wanted full control of the process. He wanted to train the dancers and stage the dances, film the routines and do close-ups, too. He persuaded producer Sam Goldwyn to let him take full control of this part of the films he worked on and the result was some of the finest and most memorable dance routines ever worked out in the movies.

But in the less exuberant times of the early 1930s, musicals fell out of fashion and Berkeley considered returning to Broadway. Before that happened, however, producer Darryl F. Zanuck asked him to direct the dance and musical numbers in his latest project, *42nd Street* (1933). Berkeley accepted and went on to become the presiding genius behind virtually all of the great Warner Brothers musicals made between 1933 and 1937.

NOVEMBER 30

1943

Nat "King" Cole Trio Makes its First Recording

ON THIS DAY IN CALIFORNIA HISTORY Nat "King" Cole and his trio recorded "Straighten Up and Fly Right" for Capitol Records. It was their first recording and Nat was only in his mid-20s.

He had been born in Alabama, his father a butcher and a deacon in the local Baptist church. The family moved to Chicago when he was still a child and it was there that he got his education in music, sneaking out of the house to listen to musicians like Louis Armstrong, "Fatha" Hines and Jimmie Noone.

The work of "Fatha" Hines would prove to be a major influence on Cole's musical development, and in the mid-1930s, still just a teenager, Nat took the name "Nat Cole" (his given surname was "Coles") and formed a band of his own. In 1936, when he was not yet quite 20, his band made its first recording; the band had also begun to find regular engagements in Chicago's clubs.

In addition to the work he was doing with his own band, Cole also played piano in a ragtime musical review that had been put together by Broadway great, Eubie Blake. The group was performing in Long Beach when the whole thing fell apart and Nat decided to form his own group, the "King Cole Swingers."

When the trio recorded "Straighten Up and Fly Right" for Capitol in 1943, it was still a very new label, but it would turn out to be a great choice. The records the trio would make for Capitol would make mountains of money for the label and "Nat King Cole" a household word throughout the land.

Cole was the first bandleader to introduce the "drummerless" trio and his band's technical virtuosity was admired by prominent musicians like Count Basie. Ballads like "Mona Lisa" (1950) and "Unforgettable" (1951) became his signature songs, but other tunes became big hits, too, including "Ramblin' Rose" (1962) and "Those Lazy-Hazy-Crazy Days of Summer" (1963).

This Day
in
December

DECEMBER 1

1986
World's First Five-Figure Hotel Suite Debuts

ON THIS DAY IN CALIFORNIA HISTORY the world's first five-figure hotel suite debuted. The eight-room accommodations included four fireplaces, three bedrooms and a library with a secret passage. It was offered by San Francisco's Fairmont Hotel, and all for the princely sum of $10,000 a night.

James G. Fair, the man for whom the Fairmont Hotel was named, had hit it big—very big—when western Nevada's Comstock Silver Lode came in in the 1860s, and his daughters, Tessie and Virginia, wanted to honor his memory in some very public way after his death. The Fairmont Hotel was what they came up with.

Construction began in 1902, but by 1906, the costs of continuing to build had become too much of a burden for the sisters and so they sold the project to two brothers named Herbert and Hartland Law. As it turned out, the Great Earthquake and Fire of 1906 was just days away, but of course no one knew that at the time. It was, if nothing else, great timing for the Fair sisters.

Remarkably, the Fairmont withstood the violent shaking of the earthquake that rolled through the city of San Francisco on April 18, 1906, but was no match for the ensuing fires that broke out in its wake. By the early morning hours of April 19 the fires had climbed to the top of Nob Hill, knocking out mansion after mansion, and finally consuming the Fairmont itself.

Exactly one year after their hotel had gone up in smoke, the Law brothers held a banquet celebrating its reopening, featuring 600 pounds of turtle, thousands of oysters, plenty of wine to wash it all down with, and a fireworks display which put architect Julia Morgan's fine design work in the spotlight for all to see. The Fairmont, like the rest of downtown San Francisco, had come back from the brink and now, almost 80 years later, the best room in the house cost $10,000 a night.

December 2

1938

Lethal Gas Replaces Hanging at San Quentin

ON THIS DAY IN CALIFORNIA HISTORY the first execution by lethal gas in California was conducted at San Quentin Prison.

The execution of those who had been convicted of committing capital crimes was first authorized in California in 1851. On February 4, 1872, specific instructions as to where such an execution must take place were incorporated into the Penal Code: "A judgment of death must be executed within the walls or yard of a jail, or some convenient private place in the county."

In 1891 these instructions were made even more specific, restricting executions to the grounds of state prisons—"A judgment of death must be executed within the walls of one of the State Prisons designated by the Court by which judgment is rendered"—and that is how they have been handled ever since.

There were only two state prisons in California in 1891, San Quentin and Folsom. There were apparently no official rules that judges followed when deciding whether to send a given offender to one place or the other, but it does appear that repeat offenders were typically sent to Folsom.

The first execution conducted by the state was conducted at San Quentin, on March 3, 1893. The first state-conducted execution at Folsom occurred on December 13, 1895. In 1937 the state legislature voted to replace hanging with lethal gas and on this day in 1938 the first such execution was carried out.

The names of California's principal prisons have become part of the American language—"Alcatraz," "Folsom," "San Quentin"—words synonymous with big-time American crime. These are places where many of the nation's best-known criminals have been locked up—Al Capone and "Machine Gun" Kelly at Alcatraz, Johnny Cash at Folsom, "Black Bart" at San Quentin—making them the best-known prisons in the nation.

DECEMBER 3

1981

Walter Knott Dies in Buena Park

ON THIS DAY IN CALIFORNIA HISTORY amusement-park and berry entrepreneur Walter Knott died at his home in Buena Park. He had been born a little over fifty miles east in San Bernardino almost 92 years before. He created an enduring Southern California icon— "Knott's Berry Farm"—and popularized the Boysenberry.

Knott's Berry Farm, at first just that, eventually evolved into a theme park, too (America's first one, as it turns out), and continues to evolve to this day. Knott's original idea was to build a replica western ghost town from the remains of some real ones to honor California's pioneer past—including that of his own grandparents who were themselves a part of it—and at the same time evoke some sense of what it was like for the state's first American immigrants to live here.

Over time, this idea was expanded and combined with a wide variety of rides and attractions, to create the nation's third largest theme park (only Disneyland and Disney World are larger).

In the more than eighty years since Walter and Cordelia Knott first sold the berries they grew on their Buena Park farm from a wooden stand on California Highway 39, "Knott's" has grown into an amusement, dining and retail enterprise that includes some 135 rides and attractions, 20 restaurants, and shops handling everything from souvenirs and clothes to candies and jams.

Knott's grandparents came to California in a covered wagon in 1868 and he built the "Ghost Town" that was his farm's first "attraction" both as a tribute to them and as a place to entertain the thousands who patiently waited in line each year to eat at his wife's "Chicken Dinner Restaurant." Many of the buildings in Ghost Town date back to the mid 19th century when Knott's grandparents first arrived and were once part of thriving desert mining communities that faded away when the ore they mined ran out.

December 4

1964

"Free Speech Movement" Begins at Berkeley

ON THIS DAY IN CALIFORNIA HISTORY the "Free Speech Movement" began on the campus of the University of California at Berkeley. It started out as a demand by a group of students that the university permit political activity on campus and acknowledge the students' right to "free speech" and "academic freedom."

The group was informally led by a student named Mario Savio and the concessions they ultimately secured from university administrators are often cited as the official starting point for the student protests that swept across American university campuses during the 1960s and early 1970s.

Some of the activists who participated in the protests at Berkeley had worked closely the previous summer with a group of political activists known as "Freedom Riders," who were trying to get black Americans in the Deep South registered to vote. They had now set up tables on campus to solicit donations to support their civil-rights efforts, but the university had a strict policy prohibiting political activity on campus and so these efforts quickly met with opposition.

On October 1 there had been a sizable "sit-in" of Berkeley students to protest the arrest of a former student on campus, and at one point, some estimates say, as many as 3,000 students were involved. The upshot was that the police were not able to move their car and prisoner for some thirty-six hours.

The charges against the arrested former student were ultimately dropped, but the fact that the students had held local police hostage this way provoked the university to file charges against the organizers of the sit-in, which in turn provoked a student protest that almost shut the university down. Sproul Hall, the campus administration building, was "taken over," and, on December 3, 800 students were arrested.

370

DECEMBER 5

1934

Author Joan Didion Born in Sacramento

ON THIS DAY IN CALIFORNIA HISTORY renowned American author Joan Didion was born in Sacramento. She was a fifth-generation Californian whose family had long inhabited the Sacramento Valley, which made her somewhat different from most of the Valley's inhabitants, in and of itself.

The books that Didion writes, fiction and nonfiction, are powerful examples of modern American writing at its best. Whether it is the "early Didion" of *Slouching Towards Bethlehem* (1968), or the more recent Didion of *The Year of Magical Thinking* (2005), her writing is clear, spare, and unforgettable.

After high school Didion went to the University of California at Berkeley, where her first opportunities to do some serious writing arose and from which she graduated with a degree in English in 1956. She got a job writing for *Vogue* magazine after graduation and has lived a bicoastal life ever since.

It was at *Vogue* that Didion began to come into her own as a writer, publishing the novel *Run River* in 1963, *Slouching Towards Bethlehem* (a collection of essays) in 1968, *Play It As It Lays* (a novel) in 1970, and in 1977, *The Book of Common Prayer*. In 1979 she published *The White Album* (more essays).

She has also engaged political themes in her writing—in *Salvador* (1983), *Democracy: A Novel* (1984) and *Miami* (1987), and in more recent times, her engaging account of growing up in Sacramento, *Where I Was From* (2003), has appeared.

In 2003 and 2005, Didion lost both her husband, author John Gregory Dunne (late 2003), and her daughter, Quintana (in 2005, just 39 years old). Her book *The Year of Magical Thinking*, written after her husband's death but before her daughter's passing, is a powerful account of what it means to love a husband and a child and how fragile, at bottom, all lives are.

December 6

1969
Altamont Rock Festival in Livermore

ON THIS DAY IN CALIFORNIA HISTORY a free rock concert known as the "Altamont Rock Festival" began at the Altamont Speedway in Livermore. The Rolling Stones were the headliners and some 300,000 people were in attendance. It got ugly fast and it's an event often cited as the "official" end of the 1960s.

Altamont had all the makings of a great rock-music day. The greatest rock-and-roll band in the world was headlining and Santana, the Grateful Dead, Jefferson Airplane, Crosby, Stills, Nash and Young, and the Flying Burrito Brothers were scheduled to play, too. There was reason to believe this would be another of rock music's finest hours, another one for the ages.

But for a variety of reasons, things didn't work out that way. Simply deciding where to hold the concert was a major challenge. The concert was originally supposed to have been staged in San Francisco, like so many free concerts before it, but it became clear early on that too many people would be coming to make that workable, so an alternative site would have to be found.

Moving a big rock concert on short notice is no small thing, of course. Staging and sound equipment can't quickly be spirited from one place to another, so it was important to settle on a place to hold the event. But the biggest problem of all would prove to be the group that was chosen to provide "security" for the event: a northern California chapter of the Hells Angels.

Unfortunately, the Angels acted as one might expect. They drank rivers of alcohol, smoked their body weight in grass, and chased it all down with plenty of acid (LSD). A predictably unfortunate outcome was the result: a young black man was beaten to death with pool cues. Just four months earlier, Woodstock had suggested that the Age of Aquarius was at hand, but at Altamont, that hope dissolved into "Satanic Majesty's Request."

DECEMBER 7

1941

Japanese Attack Pearl Harbor

ON THIS DAY IN CALIFORNIA HISTORY a squadron of Japanese suicide bombers attacked American forces stationed at Pearl Harbor in Hawaii. It was an event that would have an immediate effect on the American war effort, triggering what came to be known as the "War in the Pacific," but it would also have an immediate and profound effect on California's future development, too.

The California coast was the natural point of departure for troops en route to the war in the Pacific, and so it was also the natural place to build and base the many ships and planes needed to take them there. The war workers who came out West needed homes, too, of course, and those then available were hardly sufficient to provide for that need. Completely new communities had to be built to house them.

In his 1949 classic, *California: The Great Exception*, author Carey McWilliams provides a vivid description of one of these "instant cities," the Los Angeles suburb of Westchester. It seemed to have risen out of nowhere, says McWilliams, "real" yes, but at the same time, "unreal," too, swelling from a population of virtually nothing to 30,000 in just nine years.

Most of the servicemen who came out West in the early 1940s had as little intention of making the West Coast their home as the Gold Rushers had had of making it theirs, but many did stay on after the war, a third of a million in California alone.

Between 1940 and 1947 California gained three million new residents, in fact—about as many people as lived in the entire state at the end of the First World War, 30 times as many as came during first 10 years of the Gold Rush. By 1948 newcomers were coming in at the rate of 20,000 a month, and by 1960, that figure had doubled to 40,000 a month. By 1962 the state's population was growing by 1,600 new people a day.

373

DECEMBER 8

1863
Park for New State Capitol Building

ON THIS DAY IN CALIFORNIA HISTORY Governor Leland Stanford noted in his annual address to the state legislature that the government would create a park to surround the new state capitol building then under construction in Sacramento. Construction had been underway for two years when Stanford spoke.

San Jose had been selected as the site of California's first state capital, a choice made by the Constitutional Convention that met at Monterey in 1849. In June of 1851 it was moved to Vallejo, then to the East Bay city of Benicia, and finally, in 1854, to Sacramento, where it has remained ever since.

Sacramento was a good north-central choice for the capital's permanent home, made at a time when over 95% of the state's population lived in the northern end of the state, and located just 90 miles northeast of San Francisco, then the state's principal city. The building that architects M. F. Butler and Reuben Clark designed is a beautiful one, too, Roman Corinthian in style and reminiscent of the nation's capitol building in Washington, D. C.

The capitol building is surrounded by 40 acres of meticulously-manicured gardens, the gardens that Leland Stanford had talked about planting back in 1863. They include trees from around the world, as well as a life-size statue of Father Junipero Serra, the cleric who established the first of the state's missions.

There is a Civil War Memorial Grove in the midst of these gardens, too, that was planted in 1897 with saplings from famous Civil War battlefields. It contains memorials to the Californians who fought in the War with Mexico (which brought California into the United States), the Civil War, the Spanish-American War, World Wars I and II, the Korean War, the Vietnam War, and the Persian Gulf War, and is one of the most beautifully-laid-out capitol grounds in the land.

DECEMBER 9

1968
Computer Mouse Introduced to the Public

ON THIS DAY IN CALIFORNIA HISTORY the computer mouse was first demonstrated publicly in San Francisco.

The occasion was an event called the "Fall Joint Computer Conference," at which a Stanford Research Institute (SRI) scientist named Douglas C. Engelbart demonstrated something he called the "X-Y Position Indicator for a Display System." That doesn't sound like something the average American would have a need for, but, in time, it would turn out that it was.

Before the creation of the "mouse," doing things with a computer required the user to remember a large number of "codes" and that was not something either easy or fun to do—except, perhaps, for a few technical types who liked that kind of thing.

With a "mouse" all that was required of a computer user to do things with their computer was to move their indicator device around on its "pad" until the cursor arrow on their monitor pointed to some icon they wanted to activate. By simply clicking the cursor on the icon, the computer automatically kicked in and did the rest. Now here was something everyone could do.

On this day in 1968 the "mouse" Engelbart and his SRI associates were demonstrating was not the sleek little job every computer user today is so familiar with. It was a metal box with a couple of wheels attached to it to make it easy to move around that had been built by an SRI staff member named Bill English.

During Engelbart's 90-minute presentation at San Francisco's Civic Auditorium, a variety of now commonplace computer functions were shown for the first time, including e-mail, word processing and a demonstration of how someone using a mouse could configure and program their computer for their own purposes, something that wasn't possible on a mass scale before. The computer was on its way to being useful for everyone.

December 10

1950

Ralph Bunche Awarded Nobel Peace Prize

ON THIS DAY IN CALIFORNIA HISTORY black Angeleno Ralph Bunche was awarded the Nobel Peace Prize. He had actually been born in Detroit, but his parents moved to New Mexico for health reasons, and after they died, his grandmother brought him and his sister to Los Angeles to live. He was just 12 at the time.

Bunche thrived in Los Angeles. He graduated valedictorian of his class at Jefferson High School and went on from Jefferson to the University of California at Los Angeles where he studied international relations, and graduated *summa cum laude*, as well as valedictorian of his class there, too.

Funded by $1,000 raised by the black community of Los Angeles and a scholarship from Harvard University, Bunche went on from UCLA to do graduate work at Harvard. He finished his master's in political science in 1928, and for the next six years, alternated between a teaching assignment at Howard University in Washington, D. C., and completing his doctoral work at Harvard.

Bunche was long active in the American civil rights movement. He authored *A World View of Race* in 1936, participated in a Carnegie Foundation survey about black life in America that resulted in the publication of Gunnar Myrdal's classic book about the subject, *An American Dilemma* (1944), helped Dr. Martin Luther King, Jr., lead his famous march in Montgomery, Alabama, in 1965, and supported both the NAACP and the Urban League in their work to improve the lot of black people in America.

On this day in 1950 Bunche was awarded the Nobel Peace Prize. What had brought him to the attention of the Nobel Committee was his effort to negotiate a peace agreement between the Arabs and Jews in Palestine, an effort which brought hostilities to a close, for a time, in 1949. Israel had proclaimed itself an independent nation just the year before.

DECEMBER 11

1964

Singer Sam Cooke Shot and Killed

ON THIS DAY IN CALIFORNIA HISTORY legendary soul singer Sam Cooke was shot and killed at the Hacienda Motel in Los Angeles.

He had been born in Mississippi, but grew up in Chicago, where he sang in church as a kid and teenager and was part of a then nationally-famous singing group called the "Highway QC's." As the leading gospel groups of the 1940s came through town, Cooke had the opportunity to sing with all of them.

In December 1950 Robert Harris, lead singer of a group called the "Soul Stirrers," quit the group. Cooke became the group's new lead singer and would spend the next six years recording and touring with them. They were one of the biggest acts in gospel music at the time, so it was a big step up for Cooke.

He quickly became a gospel superstar, but soon found himself wanting to sing more "popular" material. At the time, however, it was taboo for a gospel singer to sing "secular songs," so he actually had to *leave* the Soul Stirrers to sing pop, and though it was a big loss for gospel music, it was a huge gain for pop music. Now all music lovers could hear what Sam Cooke could do.

In 1957 Keen Records released Cooke's first big pop hit, "You Send Me." It sold 1.7 million copies, became a number one hit and made him a star. It was followed by several others, including "Only Sixteen" (1959), "Chain Gang" (1960), "Another Saturday Night" (1963), and "Shake" (1965).

But it would all come to a screeching halt on this night in 1964 when Cooke checked into the Hacienda Motel in South Central Los Angeles with a female companion named Lisa Boyer. Some kind of disagreement developed and Lisa left the room. Cooke followed to find her, and at one point broke into the motel's management office, thinking she had hidden in there. No doubt fearing for his own safety, however, the motel manager shot him dead.

December 12

1925

Milestone Motel Opens for Business

ON THIS DAY IN CALIFORNIA HISTORY the "Milestone Mo-Tel" in San Luis Obispo first opened its doors for business.

It was the brainchild of a California hotel man named James Vail who had watched the development of "autocamps" in the 1910s and "municipal campgrounds" in the 1920s, and saw a ready market for quick, easy and affordable roadside accommodations for people who wanted to travel using their own cars, and who needed places to stay along the way.

The idea was also inspired, at least in part, by a concept as old as Spanish California itself: the state's missions. The missions were spread out along the California coast the way they were to create periodic resting points, spaced about a day's horseback ride apart. By providing a comfortable place to rest during the course of a multiday journey, the motel served a similar purpose.

Vail's original intention was to create a chain of eighteen motels running from San Diego to Seattle, each one a day's drive from another and each done in Mission Revival style design, making them architectural echoes of the missions themselves. This first one in San Luis Obispo had a red-tile roof and a bell tower (modeled after the bell tower at Mission Santa Barbara), fifty-five rooms and cost $2.50 for an overnight stay.

But not long after Vail had gotten his first motel off the ground, dark clouds began to gather on the horizon.

Less than four years after opening day the stock market crashed, and not long after that, the Great Depression was in full swing. That sense of well-being and security that so often seems to lead people to the open road in the first place evaporated, and instead of becoming one in a chain, the Milestone became one of a kind. But Vail had hit on an idea whose time had come and others would one day eagerly pick up where he had left off.

DECEMBER 13

1934

Producer Richard D. Zanuck Born in Los Angeles

ON THIS DAY IN CALIFORNIA HISTORY film producer Richard D. Zanuck, son of the legendary head of 20th Century-Fox, Darryl F. Zanuck, was born in Los Angeles. It was the heart of the Great Depression and the movie business was doing well.

Zanuck became one of the most successful independent producers in Hollywood, making such blockbuster hits as *The Sugarland Express* (1974), *Jaws* (1975), *The Verdict* (1982), *Cocoon* (1985), *Driving Miss Daisy* (1989), *Deep Impact* (1998) and *Road to Perdition* (2002).

In 1990 Zanuck won an Oscar for his production work on the Best Picture of 1989, *Driving Miss Daisy*. His work on this film also won him a Golden Globe Award, a National Board of Review Award and "Producer of the Year" honors from the Producers Guild of America. And by winning "Best Picture" honors for *Driving Miss Daisy* he became part of the only father-son team in motion-picture history to both win "Best Picture" Oscars.

After graduating from Stanford and serving a stretch in the military, Zanuck joined his father at 20th Century-Fox as a story and production assistant. At the age of 24 he produced his first feature-length film on his own, a film that would go on to win the "Best Actor" award at the Cannes Film Festival.

At the age of 28, Zanuck was made president of 20th Century-Fox, becoming in the process the youngest head of a major studio in Hollywood history. Under his stewardship Fox made such enduring hits as *The Sound of Music* (1965), *Butch Cassidy and the Sundance Kid* (1969), *Patton* (1970), *M*A*S*H* (1970) and *The French Connection* (1971), as well as *The Planet of the Apes* series of movies. He later moved over to Warner Brothers where he oversaw the production of such big-time box office hits as *The Exorcist* (1973) and *Blazing Saddles* (1974).

DECEMBER 14

1963

Baldwin Hills Dam Breaks Loose

ON THIS DAY IN CALIFORNIA HISTORY the Baldwin Hills Dam in Los Angeles broke. The water that was eventually released—292 million gallons in an hour and a half—destroyed 65 homes and left 5 people dead. The dam had been completed in 1951 and provided water to the city's west-side residents.

Eleven days before Christmas in 1963 the Baldwin Hills Reservoir, in an area now occupied by what is known as the "Kenneth Hahn State Recreation Area," began to crack. Within just a few short hours, the leak from what was initially a relatively small crack became a torrent rushing through a gaping and growing hole and cascading down the canyon along Cloverdale Avenue. Many expensive homes were washed away and destroyed.

The crack in the dam was attributed to earth movement caused by pumping too much oil out of the nearby Inglewood oil field. In places where "too much" oil has been pumped out of the ground, it's not uncommon for subsurface pressures in the earth to change to such a degree that the ground itself becomes unstable and collapses into sinkholes, clearly a recipe for disaster if that ground is holding up something like a dam.

This was not the first time that Los Angeles had experienced a major dam collapse. In March of 1928 the St. Francis Dam in the northeastern area of the city had collapsed, sending twelve billion gallons of water racing down San Francisquito Canyon and completely demolishing everything in its path. Between 400 and 500 people were killed.

The collapse of the Baldwin Hills Reservoir resulted in the phasing out of some small local reservoirs in the Los Angeles basin and to the decision to store city water in groundwater basins instead, and behind places like Hansen Dam in the Lake View Terrace area of the city.

DECEMBER 15

1849

California's First State Legislature Convenes

ON THIS DAY IN CALIFORNIA HISTORY the state's first legislature convened in San Jose, then the new state capital, to elect its first two U. S. senators and finish organizing its government.

This gathering of elected representatives came to be known as the "Legislature of a Thousand Drinks." It got this name because one of the delegates, Thomas Jefferson Green, liked to end each session by saying to his fellow delegates, "Well, boys, let's go and take a thousand drinks."

That may not sound like a particularly promising start, but this first gathering of elected representatives nevertheless did a very credible job of organizing their new government, introducing a level of legal, administrative and judicial coherence to the running of the state it had not previously had.

On December 13, 1849, a Thursday, Peter Burnett, a 42-year-old native of Tennessee, was elected California's first American governor, and John McDougal elected lieutenant governor. Two San Francisco residents, George Wright and Edward Gilbert, were chosen to represent California in the House, but the decision about who the state's Senators would be had to wait until the 15th.

The first of the two, John C. Fremont, was well-known throughout the length and breadth of California, and was elected unanimously. The second one, William Gwin, required a little more time to be chosen—three ballots, to be exact.

Gwin had played a prominent role at the constitutional convention and had left Washington, D. C., for California less than a year before, just so that he could make a bid to become one of the state's first two U. S. Senators. Gwin was a Southerner and would play a major role in courting Southern support for California's admission as a "free state," the first big issue California's new Senators would be charged with handling.

DECEMBER 16

1997
Getty Center Opens in Los Angeles

ON THIS DAY IN CALIFORNIA HISTORY the $1 billion Getty Center opened atop the Santa Monica Mountains in Los Angeles. The first "Getty" had opened in Malibu in 1974 and now an even more spectacular facility had been created to house the institution's vast art collections.

The new "Center" included six buildings laid out across a 110-acre "campus": an auditorium, a "North" and "East" building, the museum proper, a "café," and a "research institute." It was an imposing structure on this hillside overlooking the Los Angeles basin to the south and the Pacific Ocean to the west and has even been referred to as a modern version of the famous Acropolis overlooking Athens.

Because of height restrictions on buildings in the Santa Monica Mountains, much of the Center is built underground, and all six of its buildings are linked together by underground tunnels. This new and "improved" Getty Museum offers espresso bars, outdoor patios, and a first-class restaurant, and presents its exhibits in "digestible chunks," allowing adequate time and resting places in between each one to rest the mind and feet.

Most museums offer their collections as one gigantic whole, leaving it to the visitor to organize the experience for themselves. The Getty instead organizes the "visiting experience" for you, the way, say, Disneyland or an elegant shopping mall does. There is nothing unplanned about the way things unfold here.

It collects and exhibits classical art and sculpture, European paintings, drawings, sculpture, decorative arts, manuscripts, and photography. It does not collect artwork from the 20th or 21st centuries (with the exception of photography), which is a restriction mandated by Mr. Getty himself in his original bequest to create the museum.

DECEMBER 17

1935

DC-3 Airplane Takes Off

ON THIS DAY IN CALIFORNIA HISTORY the first DC-3 airplane took flight. (The "DC" stood for "Douglas Commercial.") It was a plane that would quite literally revolutionize commercial air travel in the United States and put it on the road to becoming an enormously successful business.

During the first two years following its introduction, Douglas Aircraft sold just over 800 DC-3s, and by the end of that period, they were carrying 95% of the civilian air traffic in the United States. Able to accommodate 21 passengers, it was "roomy" by the standards of the time, and by using powerful 1,000-horsepower engines, could traverse the continental United States in less than twenty-four hours flying time. It did have to make stops to refuel, however.

The DC-3 is widely considered to be the most successful civilian aircraft ever built. Not only was it durable, it introduced a host of aeronautical innovations that would become commonplace on the commercial aircraft that came after it, including the retractable landing gear, wing flaps, variable-pitch propellers, a stressed-skin fuselage and flush riveting.

The DC-3 was also known to be an almost incredibly "safe" airplane. All of the nation's commercial aircraft companies used them (as did the airlines of most other nations, too) and the military used them during all of the major operations it conducted from the 1940s through the 1960s: World War II, the Berlin airlift in 1948, the Korean War and the war in Vietnam.

By the end of 1944 nearly 11,000 DC-3 aircraft had been built (they accounted for nearly 90% of the world's commercial air fleet at the time), and though they would be replaced in the 1950s by jets in a number of areas where they had once been the airplane of choice, at the beginning of the 21st century, there were still some 2,000 of them in service.

DECEMBER 18

1992 · 1996
Landmarks in Television History

ON THIS DAY IN CALIFORNIA HISTORY two events of note occurred in the American television industry, both of them in California.

The first was the death of TV producer Mark Goodson in 1992. There was a time when most of the "game shows" running on American television were "Mark Goodson-Bill Todman productions." Their shows literally owned that time of day.

Goodson was born in Sacramento in 1915, and in 1939, created his first "game show," *Pop the Question*, for San Francisco radio station KFRC. In 1941 he left the West Coast for New York where he met Bill Todman, and the two developed a "quiz show" called *Winner Take All*, which became one of the first shows to run on CBS television when it debuted on July 8, 1948.

In the years to come Goodson and Todman created some of the most popular game shows in television history, including *What's My Line?*, *To Tell the Truth*, *I've Got a Secret*, *Beat the Clock*, *The Price is Right*, *Password*, *Concentration*, and *Family Feud*.

The other event of note on this day in California history was the television industry's decision to adopt a ratings system for television programs. There had long been a desire among the nation's viewers that TV programs be graded somehow so that people had some idea what kind of programming they were letting into their homes. The challenge was finding the best way to do it.

In December of 1996 this conversation came to a head when the major American television networks agreed to adopt a system that would give viewers this head's up. The Telecommunications Act of 1996 had given them just one year to create such a system, and said that if it didn't, the federal government would. The industry wisely decided to take action on its own and a system that rated shows "G," "Y" (okay for kids), "PG," "Y-7," "PG-14" or "MA" (mature) was the result.

DECEMBER 19

1841

"Captain" Sutter Buys Fort Ross

ON THIS DAY IN CALIFORNIA HISTORY "Captain" John Sutter, the pioneer settler whose Sacramento Valley fort would one day grow into the city of Sacramento, signed the paperwork to buy the Russian settlement at Fort Ross. Baron Rotcheff, who oversaw the settlement, met Sutter at his New Helvetia fort, and from there they proceeded to San Rafael, and then, by horse, to Bodega Bay.

Once at the Bay the men boarded the Russian ship *Helena* on which the "official" sales offer was made. The price was $30,000, with $2,000 down. The Russians wanted their first three payments in *produce*, mostly wheat, and the last one in cash. Sutter made his payments in wheat for the first two years and mortgaged his property at New Helvetia to guarantee the balance.

Sutter and his Russian hosts enjoyed a champagne dinner on the *Helena* and then set off in a small boat for Yerba Buena (modern-day San Francisco) to have the sales documents witnessed and recorded.

Just why Sutter wanted to buy Fort Ross is not altogether clear. For one thing, it was not a very good deal. No land was being sold, just the buildings, equipment and livestock. The Mexican government refused to recognize any conveyance of the land because, they said, the Russians didn't own it in the first place.

It may be that Sutter just hoped to pull a fast one on the Mexican government. Not only did he get the deed he originally signed in Yerba Buena, but also a "duplicate" that said Fort Ross and Bodega were his, *as well as* the land on which they sat.

Maybe he thought he could get the deeds switched before the original was filed and recorded and end up with the land anyway. Whatever his motivation, buying Russia's California holdings did not turn out to be a good financial move for him and he would spend the rest of his life trying recover from it.

DECEMBER 20

ON THIS DAY IN CALIFORNIA HISTORY two very important events in the history of the Mt. Wilson Observatory near Pasadena occurred.

The first one was in 1904. That year astronomer George Ellery Hale received word from the Carnegie Institution in Washington, D. C., that they would be funding his project to build an observatory atop Mt. Wilson. Also on this day, exactly four years later, the 60-inch "Hale Telescope" was ready for use.

Hale got his first taste of what it might be like to pursue his interest in astronomy on the West Coast when he honeymooned there in 1890. He had been interested in astronomy since the age of fourteen and had studied the subject at MIT. After visiting the Lick Observatory on Mt. Hamilton, it occurred to him that the West Coast might be a good place for him to work.

In any case, after his honeymoon Hale returned to Chicago to pursue his career in astronomy and became a faculty member at the University of Chicago in 1893, rising to the rank of full professor in 1897, and remaining there until 1905.

He quickly became one of the leading astronomers of his day. He founded the *Astrophysical Journal* (and invented the word "astrophysics"), established the Yerkes Observatory at the University of Chicago (then the home of the world's largest working telescope), and got himself appointed as a fellow of the Royal Astronomical Society, too. Then he went out West.

Under his leadership, the Mt. Wilson Observatory became the leading site of astronomical research in the first half of the 20th century. Astrophysicists working there confirmed *what* galaxies were (clumps of stars)—and that there were an enormous number of them—verified the fact that the universe was not static but expanding, and unearthed many key facts about the workings of the sun, work begun by Hale himself.

DECEMBER 21

ON THIS DAY IN CALIFORNIA HISTORY Gaylord Wilshire, a socialist who had made a fortune selling a "magnetic belt" that he said would improve the wearer's health, filed a subdivision development plan with the Los Angeles County Recorder's Office. It included a broad new thoroughfare that would run from downtown Los Angeles to the Pacific Ocean called "Wilshire Boulevard."

The new road was a "natural pathway" from the city of Los Angeles to the sea. In prehistoric times animals and Indians used it on their travels between the "interior" and the coast. Spanish explorers used it when they trekked through this area in 1769, and so did local residents in the many years since.

In 1921 a man named A. W. Ross was trying to figure out how best to take advantage of the explosive population growth then going on in Los Angeles. He knew that the city was growing west from its center and it was obvious to him that Angelenos, in greater and greater numbers, were choosing to get around this big city of theirs by car.

Putting these two ideas together, Ross decided that what he needed to do to take advantage of this situation was develop some land along Wilshire Boulevard by building a retail shopping complex there, and with a view to doing that, bought 18 acres along the south side of the street between Fairfax and La Brea Avenues.

It was here that Ross built his "Wilshire Boulevard Center," a retail shopping complex specifically designed with the idea that customers would be coming by car. The idea worked like a charm, and because it did, Wilshire Boulevard was put on the path to becoming one of the most important surface streets in all of modern-day Los Angeles. In fact, the portion that runs between Fairfax and LaBrea, the part originally developed by Ross, became known as the "Miracle Mile."

DECEMBER 22

1940
Novelist Nathanael West Dies in a Car Crash

ON THIS DAY IN CALIFORNIA HISTORY novelist Nathanael West died in a car crash near El Centro. He was only 37.

West's name at birth was "Nathan Weinstein" and he was born in New York City, the son of Lithuanian immigrants. He did his university work at Brown, which was also where he wrote a series of sketches that were later collected together into a volume entitled *The Dream Life of Balso Snell* (1931).

A few years after graduation he changed his name to "Nathanael West," and like most of the other talented young American writers of his generation, including Hemingway and Fitzgerald, went off to Paris to write his first book.

Finding a good way to make a living when you're a writer is typically a dicey proposition and writers resolve this problem in a variety of different ways. In West's case, the solution was managing small hotels in New York City.

West's experience of life at the hotels he managed naturally gave him material to use in his writing and it is out of this experience—and time—that his second novel, *Miss Lonelyhearts* came (1933). *A Cool Million* appeared in 1934 and the novel widely regarded as his masterpiece, *The Day of the Locust*, in 1939.

The hotels that West managed were places where other young American writers then trying to make their way lived, too, and it was in them that he befriended such later giants of American letters as Dashiell Hammett, James T. Farrell, Edmund Wilson and Erskine Caldwell, often giving them free room and board.

On the way back from a trip to Mexico with his new wife, Eileen McKenney, West heard that his good friend and fellow writer F. Scott Fitzgerald had died. Greatly upset by the news, he distractedly ran a stop sign, crashing his car, and killing both himself and his new wife.

DECEMBER 23

1930

Bette Davis Arrives in Hollywood

ON THIS DAY IN CALIFORNIA HISTORY a then-unknown actress named Bette Davis arrived in Hollywood. Five years later she won a Best Actress Oscar for her work in the film *Dangerous* (1935), and three years after that, another for her work in the film *Jezebel*.

Bette Davis was born in Lowell, Massachusetts, on April 5, 1908. Her father left the family when she was not quite ten, leaving her mother to figure out how to support the family. Bette and her sister attended a good boarding school, and after that, Bette enrolled herself in the John Murray Anderson Dramatic School.

In 1929, just 21, Bette made her Broadway debut in the hit play *Broken Dishes* and also landed a role as a southern belle in the play *Solid South*. In 1930 she decided to go to Hollywood and make her way in the movie business. She screen-tested for Universal Pictures, and they liked what they saw.

In 1932 Davis's contract with Universal was not renewed and she briefly considered returning to the Broadway stage, but a call from Warner Brothers changed her mind. She signed a seven-year contract with Warners and it was while working for them that the roles that would make her a silver-screen legend came her way, beginning with *The Man Who Played God* (1932).

Davis was a liberated woman on the screen, and off, and her battles with studio executives were legendary. But she was equal to the challenge, and not only won the battles, won the war, and made a very big name for herself in the process.

Davis was known as an actress who could play a variety of difficult roles and set a new standard for what women could do in movies. She pursued a successful film career for six decades, and came to be known as "The First Lady of the American Screen." On October 6, 1989, after a long battle, she succumbed to cancer. She was 81.

DECEMBER 24

1958

Madonna Inn Opens in San Luis Obispo

ON THIS DAY IN CALIFORNIA HISTORY Alex and Phyllis Madonna opened their now world-famous "Madonna Inn" in San Luis Obispo on the Central California coast.

The Inn had just 12 rooms on opening day, but through the years that followed, many more were added, and today the Inn has some 109 rooms and suites. The Inn is truly one of a kind and people from all over the world have stayed there.

Each room at the Madonna Inn has its own "theme." The floors, walls and ceiling of the "Caveman Room," for example, are all made of rock and the room's shower is a rock waterfall. The bedspreads have a leopard-skin design and the stained-glass window in the bathroom even features the image of a caveman.

There is a "Jungle Rock Room" and an "Old World Suite," a "Buffalo Room," an "Antique Cars Room," a "California Floral Room," a "Desert Sands Room," an "Espana Room," an "Indian Room," a "Pony Room," a "Rocky Mountain Room," a "Showboat Room," a "Sweepstakes Room," and a "Tall and Short Room," which has a bed that's six-and-a-half feet long and one that's five-and-a-half feet long.

The bathroom areas that the Madonnas designed for their Inn are part of the show, too. One of the men's urinals has been designed in the shape of a rock waterfall, the other is a copper trough urinal fitted out with a waterwheel. In both cases, when a stream of urine trips a light sensor, the "waterworks" begin.

In the ladies bathroom, the toilets and sinks have been made out of pink Italian marble, the walls covered with red, flocked wallpaper, and the doors of each individual stall fitted with tufted, red-leather panels. The sinks and toilets for children have been scaled down to fit them, too. These are "working" bathrooms, of course, but they are famous local tourist attractions as well.

December 25

1934

Santa Anita Racetrack Opens in Arcadia

ON THIS DAY IN CALIFORNIA HISTORY Santa Anita Racetrack opened to the public in Arcadia. The land had originally been used by mover and shaker "Lucky" Baldwin to race the many thoroughbred horses he owned, but in the early 1930s his daughter Anita, and a group of backers, built the facility that stands here today.

Santa Anita was developed by an organization known as the Los Angeles Turf Club. The actual buildings here were designed by Gordon Kaufmann and are a marvelous blend of design styles old and new: Art Deco and Streamline Moderne, as well as American Colonial and Spanish Revival.

On opening day in 1934, 30,777 people came to the track and it was a hit with the Hollywood crowd from the start. Clark Gable, Bing Crosby, Spencer Tracy, Errol Flynn, Cary Grant, and Charlie Chaplin all became regulars here and many of the horses that have run here have been headliners, too, including Seabiscuit, Silky Sullivan, and Triple Crown Winner, Affirmed.

During World War II thousands of California's Japanese residents were removed from their homes and relocated to various "camps" throughout California and the Far West; the Santa Anita Racetrack was one of the places these people were held prior to being shipped to the "camps."

At the entrance to the track stands a bronze statue of jockey George Woolf (as does one of his favorite mount, the legendary Seabiscuit).

Woolf was regarded as one of the class acts of the sport and the statue was erected to honor him and the standards he stood for. Each year since 1950 the "George Woolf Memorial Jockey Award" has been awarded to the jockey judged to best exemplify those standards. Past recipients have included Willie Shoemaker (1951), Johnny Longden (1952), and Eddie Arcaro (1953).

DECEMBER 26

1966

Celebration of "Kwanzaa" Begins in Long Beach

ON THIS DAY IN CALIFORNIA HISTORY the week-long celebration known as "Kwanzaa" began in Long Beach. It was the creation of Dr. Ron Karenga, then chairman of the Black Studies Department at California State University, Long Beach.

Karenga had been born in Maryland in 1941 and was the fourteenth child of a Baptist minister. He moved to L. A. in the late 1950s to study at Los Angeles City College and went on from there to study at UCLA. He would later get two Ph.D.'s, one from what was then known as the United States International University (now Alliant International University) and one from USC.

In the early 1960s Karenga met legendary black activist Malcolm X and began to embrace the political and social philosophy of "black nationalism." Following the Watts Riots of 1965 he dropped out of the doctoral program in which he was then enrolled to join the "Black Power" movement then on the rise in the U. S.

Karenga first reduced the principles underlying "Kwanzaa" to writing in 1977. The idea originally sprang from his disillusionment with Western religion which, as he says in his book, *Kawaida Theory* (1980), "denies and diminishes human worth, capacity, potential and achievement" by teaching that "humans are born in sin <and> cursed with mythical ancestors who've sinned and brought the wrath of an angry God on every generation's head."

Instead of the "Jonathan Edwards" or "Sinners in the Hands of an Angry God" outlook, Karenga proposed instead that black people work together and focus their efforts on making life better for themselves "down here on earth" through cooperative political, social and economic initiatives. The central idea behind Kwanzaa is the creation of a holiday during which black people can celebrate their own history as a people and not the history of the nation's mainstream white culture.

December 27

1846 · 1902
John C. & Jessie Benton Fremont

ON THIS DAY IN CALIFORNIA HISTORY John C. Fremont, one of the most colorful and controversial figures in the early history of American California, led his troops over the Santa Ynez Mountains in order to launch a surprise attack on the city and presidio at Santa Barbara, then still a key Mexican stronghold.

On the night of December 27, 1846, under orders from Commodore Robert F. Stockton, American California's second military governor, Fremont led his men into Santa Barbara, capturing the city without bloodshed. Three weeks later, on January 16, 1847, Stockton made him California's *third* military governor.

Fremont would go on to become one of California's first two United States Senators, the Republican Party's first candidate for president of the United States and, from 1878 to 1881, governor of the Arizona Territory.

In 1841, the same year he began leading surveying expeditions into the American West, Fremont married Jessie Benton, daughter of powerful Missouri congressman Thomas Hart Benton, who was a major proponent of the nation's westward expansion. Jessie met Fremont through her father and proved to be as adventurous and daring a soul as he was.

Jessie was a writer and played a major role in shaping her husband's *Report of the Exploring Expedition to Oregon and North California*, which appeared in 1845.

When the couple fell on hard times later on in life, it was Jessie's writing that would help sustain them: *A Year of American Travel* (1878), *Souvenirs of My Time* (1887), *Far West Sketches* (1890), and *The Will and the Way Stories* (1891). Having lived a long and busy life, Jessie died at her home on West 28th Street in Los Angeles in 1902, the same day that her husband had, so long ago, captured Mexican Santa Barbara.

DECEMBER 28

1894

James G. Fair Dies in San Francisco

ON THIS DAY IN CALIFORNIA HISTORY "Silver King" James G. Fair died in San Francisco. He had made a fortune from the famous Comstock Silver Lode in western Nevada and another one investing that wealth in San Francisco real estate. He became one of the leading figures of the late-19th-century Far West.

Fair had been born near Belfast, Ireland, but his parents moved to the Midwest when he was just a child. In 1849, only 17 years old, he moved to California in the hope of making a fortune mining gold. That didn't pan out for him, but in 1860 he settled in Nevada, and it was there that he went into partnership with three men who, with him, would become known as the "Silver Kings"—James C. Flood, William S. O'Brien, and John W. Mackay.

With their collective capital and expertise—coupled with a healthy measure of deviousness and the timely failure of some key competitors—the Silver Kings became spectacular examples of a type that would surface again and again in the wide-open frontier economy of late-19th-century San Francisco—the "sudden millionaire," men who became wildly wealthy "overnight."

Money talks, as they say, and Fair's money was no different. He persuaded the Nevada legislature to elect him to the United States Senate, where he served as one of that state's senators from 1881-1887. When his reelection campaign proved unsuccessful, however, he returned to San Francisco.

Fair's daughters were, quite naturally, the beneficiaries of all this wealth, an asset that no doubt helped them make the "big marriages" they made into other wealthy American families. One daughter married William K. Vanderbilt the II ("Willie K."), a member of one of the nation's leading families. The other daughter also married well, and with her sister, planned the construction of the Fairmont Hotel, a memorial to their famous father.

394

DECEMBER 29

1961

Dick Dale Plays the Rendezvous Ballroom

ON THIS DAY IN CALIFORNIA HISTORY the band widely credited with *inventing* "surf music," Dick Dale and the Del-Tones, headlined a concert at the old Rendezvous Ballroom in Balboa Beach. Two other surf-music bands, the Surfaris and the Challengers, played that night, too, as did a new group calling itself the "Beach Boys," who played two songs during intermission.

Stan Kenton and his "Balboa Beach Band" had played the Rendezvous during the early years of World War II. Now the stage was taken by a guy playing electric guitar and sending the sounds of "Let's Go Trippin'" (1961) and "Misirlou" (1962) rolling through the hall. For those who never had the opportunity to hear Dale in his heyday, the soundtrack of Quentin Tarantino's film *Pulp Fiction* (1994) provides a potent taste of Dale's guitar magic.

At the height of his popularity, Dale was attracting audiences of as many as 4,000 or more to his performances and doing it by playing his guitar in a way that had not been heard before. It's said that Jimi Hendrix went down to listen to Dale when he was stationed in the service in San Pedro and that his own legendary guitar-playing was influenced heavily by what he saw Dale do.

It's also said that rock guitarist Eddie Van Halen's guitar-playing was influenced by Dale and the kind of riffs he plays bear the stamp of Dale's lightning-fast style.

"Surf music," as it would turn out, wouldn't have all that long a run in America's pop music spotlight. No sooner had it found its legs than the "British Invasion" was underway and pop music headed in another direction altogether. But some of the work done in its name —the instrumentals of Dick Dale and the Del-Tones and the work of the Beach Boys, that group that played during intermission this night at the Rendezvous Ballroom in Balboa—would live on and find new fans for years to come.

DECEMBER 30

1940
Arroyo Seco Parkway Opens in Pasadena

ON THIS DAY IN CALIFORNIA HISTORY the Arroyo Seco Parkway (the Pasadena Freeway) opened in Pasadena.

In 1897 a nine-mile dedicated pathway for bicycles was built to connect Pasadena to Los Angeles. It followed the stream bed of the Arroyo Seco and required 1,250,000 board feet of pinewood to build. It cost 15 cents to make a roundtrip, and the pathway was lit with electric lights along its entire length. It never really caught on, but it did trace the best way to get from Pasadena to L. A. It was the pathway the first freeway builders would use when they built the Arroyo Seco Parkway.

When it opened, the Arroyo Seco Parkway had a speed limit of 45 miles an hour. Originally, there were two lanes in each direction and a wide shoulder area on either side to allow for emergency stops. Though its onramps and offramps would be considered way too short by today's standards, it was the first modern freeway ever built in the United States and was considered an engineering marvel at the time. It was, in a word, revolutionary.

Once those first few miles of L. A. freeway were in place, more and more miles of freeway kept coming. The idea of building an integrated system of highways to tie the city's far-flung borders together had been around since the mid-1920s and the city had gotten very large in a relatively short period of time. The time had come to make all areas of the city equally accessible from all the others. And, in time, all areas of the state, too.

As the years rolled on, more and more miles of freeway were built across the Southern California area. By 1960 almost two hundred miles of freeway had been built across Ventura, Los Angeles and Orange Counties, and by 1980, five hundred more miles had been added to that. From the very beginning, this system served as a model for freeway systems all over the world.

DECEMBER 31

1961

The Beach Boys Make their First Public Appearance

ON THIS DAY IN CALIFORNIA HISTORY the Beach Boys made their first public appearance as a group, in a New Years' Eve concert held at the Long Beach Municipal Auditorium. It would be up, up, and away from there, in a musical career that would produce some of the finest American popular music ever written.

The group's original lineup included the three Wilson brothers—Brian, Dennis, and Carl—their cousin, Mike Love, and their friend, Al Jardine. They tried a variety of different names on for size during their early years, but it was as the "Beach Boys" that they would ultimately stake their claim to fame.

The Beach Boys found recording success by taking Brian's genius for arranging choral harmonies and applying that skill to the key themes of teenage life in 1960s Southern California—surfing, dating, and driving hot cars. On December 8, 1961, the Boys were signed to a recording contract with Era Records and shortly thereafter their name was changed to "the Beach Boys." On February 17, 1962, "Surfin'" went to #75 on the national pop music charts, and from that point on, the hits just kept on coming.

Capitol Records signed the Beach Boys in June of 1962 and it was Capitol that released "Surfin' Safari." On August 11, 1962, the song got to #14 on the pop charts and its "B" side, "409" found its way to #76. It was filled with the harmonies and rhythms that would be their permanent trademark.

Almost forty more years of musical "hits" awaited the Beach Boys at this point. Their songs began to make frequent appearances at the top end of the pop music charts, and in June 1964, their song, "I Get Around," made it to "#1." Later in 1964, their "Beach Boys Concert Album" became the first *live* album to top the charts; in the spring of 1965 they topped the charts again with their song, "Help Me, Rhonda."

A NOTE ON SOURCES

A VARIETY OF DIFFERENT SOURCES was drawn upon to flesh out the details on the various people, places and events profiled here.

The Internet can be a useful tool in this regard, but one that must be used with considerable caution. The information found there is not always accurate and must constantly be checked against other, "more authoritative," sources, typically books and articles, to be sure that dates, spellings and any number of other details are, in fact, correct.

What I would like to do here is explain my research methodology for the first five days of January. This will give as clear a view as anything can of how the information on the preceding pages was uncovered, evaluated, accepted or rejected.

"January 1" profiles the advent and history of the Rose Bowl in California. This event happens to be covered in a lot of different places, both on the Internet and off, but a more than adequate supply of data was found in just two articles on the Internet, and so those two articles were my exclusive source for the write-up that appears here.

The first one is entitled "Rose Bowl Game History—Tournament of Roses," the second one, "Tournament of Roses." Simply googling "History of the Rose Bowl" readily gets you to both.

SOURCES

"January 2" takes a look at how the first junior high school *system* came about and traces its roots to the Berkeley area of the state. This is a somewhat more obscure piece of information than the origins and history of such a nationally prominent event as the Rose Bowl and, as it turns out, takes a bit more digging to unearth all the details needed for my "January 2" write-up.

You could simply try googling with a search descriptor like "origins of the nation's first junior high school" or "first junior high school system" and you might get lucky with an authoritative Internet article or two, but then again, you might not.

In this case, you kick up quite a miscellany of articles about one aspect or another of the subject "junior high school," but not a thing about the *historical* origins of the institution.

This kind of outcome typically sends me from cyber sources to written ones, and one of the better written ones for tying down the date of an event like the advent of the first junior high school *system* in the United States is Joseph Nathan Kane's *Famous First Facts: A Record of First Happenings, Discoveries, and Inventions in American History* (New York: H. W. Wilson, 1981). And, sure enough, there it is on page 299.

It's hard to fill up an entire page with a fact like that, however, and so in order to flesh out the remainder of the page—as well as show that California has been no one-hit-wonder in the area of educational reform—I turned to my first book, *The Great California Story: Real-Life Roots of an American Legend* (Austin: Northcross, 2004), for much of the additional information that fills up the rest of this page.

"January 3" is all about the advent of the Apple Computer Company. Here we have a more recent-vintage bit of history and one that can be checked against a variety of Internet, historical, and company-derived sources. We consequently have a high degree of confidence that January 3, 1977, is the date the company was incorporated and little need to look beyond information available on the Internet for highlights of the company's founding.

"January 4" uses the date that Leo Fender, founder of the Fender Electric Instrument Company, spent his last day in his office at

Fender as its jumping off point for a look at how that company has contributed to California history. In this case, the Internet is not nearly as useful a resource for information about Fender and his company as it was for turning up detail about the Rose Bowl and Apple Computer.

Consequently, my key source on Leo Fender and his company was a book called *Fender: The Inside Story*, by Forrest White (San Francisco: Backbeat Books, 1994).

For "January 5" the Internet again proved to be a key resource (as it is generally for information about high-profile Hollywood figures). Simply google in "Robert Duvall" and out pours a page full of Internet articles from which to pull dates and details about the star's life and work.

There are topics about which the Internet is noticeably silent and authoritative written studies are the only adequate resource. The profiles of "Captain" John Sutter and Agoston Haraszthy, the founder of the California wine industry, come readily to mind, but there are many others, too. Whenever possible, all information turned up on the Internet has been checked against authoritative written sources as well.

INDEX

CBS Records, 6
Cedar Fire (San Diego County), 325
Central Pacific Railroad, 38, 144, 182, 329
Central Valley Project, 255
Central Valley, Great, 57, 125, 210, 215, 223, 255
Chabot College (Hayward), 209
Chaffey, George, 355
Challenger space shuttle, 186
Challengers, the (band), 395
Chamberlain, Wilt, 88
Chamisso, Adelbert von, 302
Champ, The (film), 283
Chandler family (Los Angeles), 57
Chandler, Harry, 229
Chandler, Raymond, 212, 301
Change Your Brain (Leary), 165
Chaos Crags (Lassen Volcanic National Park), 243
Chaplin, Charlie, 55, 76, 96, 391
Chateau Montelena, 158
Chavez Ravine (Los Angeles), 285
Chavez, Cesar, 125, 247
Chavez, Julian, 285
Cher, 114, 304
Chestnut Street (Pasadena), 113
Chevrolet, Louis, 110
Chico, California, 143
China Men (Kingston), 327
China Syndrome, The (film), 195
Chinatown (Los Angeles), 141
Chinatown (San Francisco), 53, 321
Chinese Exclusion Act of 1882,

208
Chinese in California, 38, 53, 141, 208, 280, 324, 329
Chinese Telephone Exchange (San Francisco), 53
Cholame, California, 298
Chowchilla kidnapping, 215
Chrétien, Henri, 31
Chronicle Building (San Francisco), 295
church in California, first, 216
Church, Ellen, 356
Churchill, Winston, 194
Cinder Cone volcano (Lassen Volcanic National Park), 243
Circus Boy (TV show), 258
City Lights Bookstore (San Francisco), 322
City Slickers, the (band), 135
Civil Action, A (film), 7
Civil War Memorial Grove (Sacramento), 374
Civilian Exclusion Order No. 346, 137
Clansman, The (film), 44
Clapton, Eric, 6
Clarence Darrow for the Defense (Stone), 214
Clark, Eli, 113
Clark, Reuben, 374
Claxton, William, 123
Clay Street (San Francisco), 235
Cleveland National Forest, 325
Clifford, Doug, 316
Clinton, Bill, 40
Cloverdale Avenue (Los Angeles), 380
Clune's Auditorium (Los

410

417

INDEX

J

Jack Paar Show, The (TV show), 206
Jackson Street (San Francisco), 139, 235
Jackson, Helen Hunt, 246
Jackson, Horatio Nelson, 157
Jackson, Michael, 49
Jacobs, Adolph, 183
James, Henry, 55
James, William, 354
Japanese Tea Garden (Golden Gate Park), 136
Jarvis, Howard, 174
Jaws (film), 379
Jazz Singer, The (film), 22
Jeffers, Robinson, 171
Jefferson Airplane (band), 16, 109, 184, 372
Jefferson High School (Los Angeles), 376
"Jenny," Curtiss (airplane), 28
Jeopardy (TV show), 206
Jezebel (film), 389
JFK (film), 195
Jimi Hendrix Experience, the (band), 184
Jobs, Steve, 5
John Barleycorn (London), 256
Johnny Got His Gun (Trumbo), 278
Johnson, Al, 252
Johnson, Grove, 270
Johnson, Hiram, 247, 270
Jones, "Spike," 135
Jones, Dubb, 183
Joplin, Janis, 304

Jordan, David Starr, 90
Jordan, Michael, 88
Judah, Theodore, 144
Jungle, The (Sinclair), 73, 269
junior high school system, first, 4
Junipero Serra High School (San Mateo), 224

K

Kaiser Foundation, 165
Kalloch, Isaac, 350
Kandinsky, Wassily, 248
Karenga, Ron, 392
"Karl Marx Tree," 293
Kaufman, Bob, 322
Kaufmann, Gordon, 391
Kawaida Theory (Karenga), 392
Kaweah Colony, 293, 343
Kaweah River, 343
Kearney, Denis, 329
Kearney, M. Theo, 312
Kearny Street (San Francisco), 235
Keaton, Buster, 76, 191
Keen Records (Los Angeles), 39, 377
Kelly, "Machine Gun," 89, 368
Kennedy, John F., 94
Kennedy, Robert F., 89, 175
Kenneth Hahn State Recreation Area (Los Angeles), 380
Kenton, Stan, 395
Kern City, California, 87
Kern County, 79, 221
Kern County earthquake (1952), 45
Kerouac, Jack, 322

Kerr, Clark, 297
Kesey, Ken, 115
Kezar Stadium (San Francisco),
106, 136
Kezar, Mary, 136
KFI (Los Angeles), 99
KFRC (San Francisco), 384
KFSG ("Kall Four Square
Gospel"), 129
Kicking and Screaming (film), 7
Kid Brother, The (film), 76
Kidnapped (film), 22
Kidnapped (Stevenson), 153
Kilby, Jack, 127
Kindergarten Cop (film), 307
kindergartens, first free public, 4
King City, 18
King Features Syndicate, 41
King of Kings, The (film), 152
King, Billie Jean, 202, 227
King, Dr. Martin Luther, Jr., 376
King, Rodney, 83, 131
Kings Canyon National Park,
177, 293, 331
Kings County, 175
Kings Row (film), 342
Kingston, Maxine Hong, 223,
327
Kinney, Abbot, 204
Kipp, William, 227
Klee, Paul, 248
klystron tube, first, 253; *see also*
technological firsts
KMPX (San Francisco), 109
KMTR (Los Angeles), 341
Knickerbocker Engine Company
No. 5, 308
Knott, Cordelia, 369

Knott, Walter, 369
Knott's Berry Farm, 369
Knowland, Joseph R., 57
Knowland, William F., 57
Knute Rockne, All American
(film), 342
Koon, Stacey, 83
Kraft Music Hall (radio
program), 135
Kramer vs. Kramer (film), 242
Kramer, Jack, 287
Krenwinkel, Patricia, 244
Kroc, Ray, 149
KSAN (San Francisco), 109
Kung Fu (TV show), 156
Kwanzaa, 392
Kyser, Kay, 303

L

L'Echo du Pacifique (San
Francisco), 249
La Brea Avenue (Los Angeles),
387
La Brea Tar Pits (Los Angeles),
306
La Cienega Park (Los Angeles),
145
La Jolla, 237, 301
La Mirada, 99
La Quinta, California, 271
LaBianca, Leno, 244
LaBianca, Rosemary, 244
Ladd, Alan, 130
Lady for a Day (film), 271
Lady in the Lake, The
(Chandler), 301
Lafayette Hook and Ladder Club

oranges, first trainload shipped East, 50
Origin, The (Stone), 214
Ornitz, Samuel, 358
Oroville, California, 263
Ortega family (Santa Barbara), 357
Ortega, José Francisco de, 357
Osbourne, Fanny, 153
Otay Mesa, 262
Otis, Harrison Gray, 229, 291
Our Gang (film series), 271, 283
Out to Sea (film), 195
Overland Monthly, 259, 265
Owens Lake, 180, 221, 229
Owens River, 338, 339
Owens Valley, 180, 229
Owens, Buck, 108
Owens, Gary, 99
Owens, Jesse, 228

P

Pacific Bank (San Francisco), 347
Pacific Coast League (baseball), 58
Pacific Electric Railway, 113, 116, 229, 344
Pacific News, 249
Pacific Palisades, 301
Pacoima, 39
Pageant of Youth (Stone), 214
Palace Hotel (San Francisco), 120, 274
Palace of Fine Arts (San Francisco), 43
Palm Springs, 103, 114, 298

Palm Springs Hotel, 103
Palmer, Arnold, 227
Palomar, Mt. *See* Mount Palomar
Panama-California Exposition (1915-1916), 56
Panama-Pacific International Exposition (1915), 43, 56, 257
Pantages Theater (Hollywood), 172
Pantomime Quiz Time (TV show), 27
Papillon (film), 278
Paramount Pictures, 31, 142, 251
Paris Olympics (1924), 202
Park Boulevard (San Diego), 81
Parkinson, Donald, 141
Parkinson, John, 141
Parmelee, Philip O., 9
Pasadena, 3, 59, 113, 116, 124, 248, 305, 345, 355, 386, 396
Pasadena & Los Angeles Electric Railway, 113
Pasadena Art Institute, 248
Pasadena Freeway, 396
Pasadena Museum of Art, 248
Pasadena Playhouse, 124, 242
Passaro, Alan, 85
Passions of the Mind, The (Stone), 214
Password (TV show), 384
Patchy Groundfog (racehorse), 122
Patton (film), 379
Patton, General George S., Jr., 345
Paul Butterfield Blues Band, 184
Pauley Pavilion (UCLA), 21
Pearl Harbor, 373

435

INDEX

Treasure Island (Stevenson), 153
Treaty of Guadalupe-Hidalgo
(1848), 277
Triangle Pictures, 59
Tripmaster Monkey (Kingston),
327
Tropic of Cancer (Miller), 190
True Lies (film), 307
Truman, Harry, 87
Trumbo, Dalton, 278, 358
Tulare County, 210, 343
Tuleberg (original name of
Stockton), 223
Tuolumne River, 126, 162
Turner, Ike and Tina (singing
duo), 313
TV ratings system, 384; *see also*
television firsts
Twain, Mark, 153, 176, 257,
259, 322
Tweety Bird, 164, 254
Twentieth Century-Fox, 31, 130,
239, 379
Twins (film), 307
Two Mules for Sister Sara (film),
358
Two Years before the Mast
(Dana), 322

U

U. S. Grant Hotel (San Diego),
95
U. S. Mint (San Francisco), 259
Uncle Tom's Cabin (Stowe), 246
Unforgiven (film), 11
Union Pacific Railroad, 141, 144
Union Square (San Francisco),
241

Union Station (Los Angeles),
141
Union-Tribune Publishing
Company (San Diego), 250
United Artists, 96, 254
United Farm Workers, 125, 247
United Nations, founding of, 194
United Railroads (San
Francisco), 222
Universal Pictures, 31, 389
University of California system,
297
University of California,
Berkeley, 8, 16, 43, 51, 61,
70, 73, 87, 91, 107, 139, 155,
165, 214, 256, 261, 263, 270,
297, 306, 318, 327, 343, 354,
358, 370, 371
University of California, Davis,
196
University of California, Los
Angeles, 17, 21, 88, 163, 230,
278, 298, 376, 392
University of California, San
Diego, 186
University of San Francisco, 136
University of Southern
California, 14, 61, 214, 278,
392
University of the Pacific, 155,
223
Urban League, 376

V

Vail, James, 378
Valencia, California, 45
Valens, Ritchie, 39